OptaJoe's Football Yearbook 2016

That thing you thought? Think the opposite.

OptaJoe's Football Yearbook 2016

That thing you thought? Think the opposite.

DUNCAN ALEXANDER

CENTURY

1 3 5 7 9 10 8 6 4 2

Century
20 Vauxhall Bridge Road
London SW1V 2SA

Century is part of the Penguin Random House group of companies
whose addresses can be found at global.penguinrandomhouse.com.

Copyright © Perform Media Channels Limited 2016

Duncan Alexander has asserted his right to be identified as the author of this
Work in accordance with the Copyright, Designs and Patents Act 1988.

First published by Century in 2016

www.penguin.co.uk

A CIP catalogue record for this book is available from the British Library.

ISBN 9781780895543

Typeset in 12/14.75 pt Dante MT Std by Jouve (UK), Milton Keynes
Printed and bound in Great Britain by Clays Ltd, St Ives Plc

Penguin Random House is committed to a sustainable
future for our business, our readers and our planet. This book is
made from Forest Stewardship Council® certified paper.

To Arthur & Edie

Contents

OptaJoe's Football Yearbook 2016

That thing you thought? Think the opposite.

Introduction

Football is a game of opinions. That's a cliché, of course, and football is also a game of clichés. But opinions are, in some ways, the lifeblood of the game, the self-perpetuating essence that has allowed 90 minutes of action on the weekend to dominate the news cycle seven days a week. More importantly, football has a hierarchy of opinions, where the views of people 'in the game' carry far more weight than those who are, by definition, 'outside the game'. Being in the game means you are a proper football fan, someone whose knowledge of the sport is absolute, simply by being part of that sport. It's a world where received wisdom and the law of the hunch reigns supreme. Gut feelings rule and often (but not always) any alternative approach is dismissed as being unsound and hare-brained.

But nothing ever stays the same. Just as football 25 years ago is in many ways unrecognisable from the game in 2016, so the number of people with opinions has multiplied exponentially. A democratisation of viewpoints has given fans (arguably the group of people who are most 'outside the game' despite many of them being 'in the stadium' every other week) the opportunity to offer their views to clubs, players, journalists and each other.

Data is another element of football that has grown

significantly in the last two decades. That's not to say it didn't exist in 1889 (even the industrious Victorians couldn't proclaim Preston North End as the Invincibles without actually recording and publishing their league record), but the compilation of data became more systematic in the mid-1990s when Opta was founded. Initially, the event data was collected merely as fuel for a player-ranking system, before people realised that the raw numbers held more potential than any ultimately arbitrary scoring system. Just as text messaging eventually outshone phone calls, data was here to stay.

In the 1990s, Opta painstakingly collected data by manually collating VHS footage. But by the mid-2000s, data collection had advanced to custom-built software that allowed a real-time data stream (with x and y coordinates) of every ball event in a game to be produced and sent around the world. That collection system has remained roughly the same for the past ten years, with pertinent additions each season. Match data is collected by a team of club specialists who log more than 2000 entries per match. This information is then sent directly to professional clubs and media alike, giving them instant access to a wealth of relevant material.

Thus the concept of pass completion and assists entered the football world in the mid-nineties (aided by the rise of fantasy football management games, one of which spawned a television show which featured a stats man, clothed, of course, in a dressing gown because if you like numbers you hate the outdoors), a time when proper football men ruled the game absolutely. The initial reaction from that sector was less than enthusiastic (Manchester United manager Alex Ferguson was asked about Opta data in the late 1990s and responded 'it's of benefit', a phrase so universally useful it can be applied to almost any question to which you want to give vague and weak backing).

As the 2000s progressed, the accumulation of data meant that for the first time in football history there was an archive of material that could be used to look for trends and offer insight to questions and theories that had, up until this point, only been the preserve of those 'in the game'. Meanwhile, the general public were becoming more comfortable with football numbers that went beyond goals and results, especially once social media took off at the end of the decade and the primeval urge to know more about something than your peers went public. The final element (so far), came in the 2010s when people took the raw data and applied mathematical models to it, hoping to further explain how a chaotic sport has reason at its heart and looking for the sporting holy grail as pursued by their counterparts in baseball, basketball and others in the years before.

That being said, this isn't a book on analytics, although there are elements of that in certain sections. The professional and amateur football analytics community is thriving, with clubs regularly hiring clever and thoughtful people based on nothing more than the quality of their work. They are parachuted into organisations that may have numerous people or factions in opposition to their very existence at the club, yet they have played key roles at recent success stories. Think Leicester City. But this isn't a book about their work either, impressive as it may be. Rather, it's an attempt to bridge the gap between the traditionalists and the boffins, to use data to shine a light on the accepted wisdom of football and see if it holds true, but at the same time not to forget the very essence of the game, the relentless march of opinion.

What follows is my version of the 2015–16 season (and more besides). Data will be paramount in everything you read but the aim is for it to offer shards of insight to the stories and intrigues you've been discussing all season. Like all good football stats, the ideas that follow should leave you with the feeling 'yes, that's what I was thinking all along'.

August–September

Pre-season

Pre-season opinion saw many pundits and thinkers plump for Chelsea to retain their title under José Mourinho or to go close. Finish above Chelsea, went the thinking, and you'll have a great shout. We'll see later how that went, but even without knowing the autumnal fall that the Pensioners suffered, it is fairly clear that we are in the middle of a turbulent decade when it comes to English footballing dynasties. The 2000s, a ten-year period where English clubs even managed to briefly dominate the Champions League, saw the Premier League title retained on five occasions, with Manchester United clocking up three wins in a row in both 2001 and 2009, with a pair of Chelsea titles under Mourinho VI in the middle of the decade.

But the 2010s has seen the quality of teams in the division decline just as the unpredictability of the league has increased (and the two are almost certainly connected). 2010 saw Chelsea end United's Cristiano Ronaldo-inspired three in a row with an attacking performance most unlike the Blues, who ended the campaign with a bumper 103 goals. A year later, in 2011, United regained the title in a largely unremarkable season notable for Manchester City breaking into the top three. Twelve months on and City seized the title from their neighbours in extraordinary fashion, Sergio Agüero's last-minute goal against QPR ending a two-month seesaw at the top of the division. 2013 saw United wrest the crown back under Alex Ferguson for the final time, while 2014 was an unpredicted battle between Man City, Arsenal and Liverpool as the reigning champions ended in seventh under their new manager. (More on that later.) City then failed to follow up a title win for the second time as Chelsea's supersonic start in 2014–15 was enough for them to jog over the line in May. 2016 saw Leicester crowned as the first new winners of the English top division since Nottingham Forest in 1978 and we are still on course, as the table below shows, to see the first decade since the 1960s without a single successful title defence in England.

The honours have been shared throughout the 2010s, with big hitters like Manchester United, Chelsea and Manchester City striking the right formula one season and then failing to refresh their squads or refine their approach adequately a year on. With Leicester shocking the world in 2016 and the likes of Liverpool or Tottenham possible contenders in 2016–17, the current decade could end up like the 1960s, which saw eight different teams win the title in ten years (Liverpool x2, Man Utd x2, Burnley, Tottenham, Ipswich, Everton, Man City and Leeds). Even the 1970s, the decade where Liverpool's domination began to show, saw six different title winners (Liverpool x4, Derby x2, Everton, Arsenal, Leeds and Nottingham Forest). It was looking increasingly likely that such an anarchic make-up was becoming anachronistic in the modern era but the 2010s, helped along by ever-increasing television deals that filter vast amounts of money to the Premier League's middle class.

Decade	Title retained
1890	3
1900	2
1910	0
1920	3
1930	3
1940	0
1950	3

Decade	Title retained
1960	0
1970	1
1980	3
1990	2
2000	5
2010	0

August

> The only team to win their opening two games of a Premier League season and then get relegated were Wolves in 2011–12. Before that it was Chelsea back in the First Division in 1987–88, and that took a play-off. It may be a marathon and not a sprint, but start off sprinting and you'll do OK in the marathon. (NB: don't use this advice in an actual marathon.)

Chelsea's sluggish start to the 2015–16 season was brought to you by the number nine and the letter 'P'. A total of nine goals conceded in their opening four games was the worst defensive performance the club had posted at this stage of a season since letting in ten in 1971–72. While a home defeat to Crystal Palace at the end of August, notable for Falcao's only Premier League goal for Chelsea (honestly, he did score, check the records), was José Mourinho's seventh successive Premier League defeat to a manager whose name began with 'P' (Pulis, Poyet, Pardew, Pochettino, Pulis, Pellegrini, Pardew). Poor.

Fans were even treated to the sight of John Terry being hauled off at half-time in Chelsea's defeat at the Etihad, the first time Mourinho had ever removed his captain from a Premier League game, and coming just a few months after Terry had played every minute of every game for the club in 2014–15.

Manchester City, in contrast, began like a team destined to win the title, keeping clean sheets in their first five Premier League games of the season and, combined with the end of the previous campaign, recording nine consecutive top-flight wins for the first time since 1912. It was the falsest of dawns, however, with City subsequently failing to record consecutive wins between mid-October and the start of April.

It wasn't just Chelsea who opened the new season in an unusual manner. All across the division home teams were buckling and allowing the visitors to take three points. After three matchdays there had been only six home wins, the lowest figure ever recorded at that stage of a Premier League campaign (replacing 2014–15 as the previous low). Aston Villa's win at Bournemouth on the opening day was their only victory in the league until January. Their next game, a home defeat to Manchester United in a rare-now-but-soon-not-to-be-rare Friday-night match, was a dismal display from both teams. The performances of the away teams weren't necessarily impressive, either.

PL season	Home wins after three matchdays
2015–16	6
2014–15	9
1998–99	10
2011–12	10
1997–98	11
1996–97	12
2001–02	12
2002–03	12
2003–04	12
1993–94	13
1999–2000	13
2005–06	13
2012–13	13

Clearly there were some unusual trends making themselves known early on in the season. The subsequent months would show just what this would mean for the campaign as a whole.

> Swansea's Bafétimbi Gomis scored in his side's opening four games of the season, his panther celebration a frequent sight as summer drew to a close. He then managed just one more goal in the Swans' next 32 games as the Welsh side turned from big cats into frightened mice.

★

Michel Vorm's appearance for Tottenham on the opening weekend was fairly unremarkable, the Dutch reserve standing in for Hugo Lloris at Old Trafford after the Frenchman suffered what newspapers reported as 'a freak wrist injury'. But Vorm's solitary game at Old Trafford turned out to be the only time all season that Tottenham featured a player over the age of 30, coming close to matching Middlesbrough's record in 2008–09 when they didn't play a single person in their thirties. Mauricio Pochettino's commitment to youth is well known, but this showed just how young his young lads were.

PL season	Appearances by players in their thirties
Middlesbrough 2008–09	0
Tottenham Hotspur 2015–16	1
Aston Villa 2012–13	2
Aston Villa 1997–98	3
Tottenham Hotspur 2008–09	6
Liverpool 2002–03	9
Tottenham Hotspur 2006–07	9
Aston Villa 2013–14	10
Tottenham Hotspur 2014–15	17
Tottenham Hotspur 2009–10	18

By the end of the season every single person on the planet knew that Leicester had begun the season as 5000-1 shots for the Premier League title. We get it, they weren't expected champions. Less well known, perhaps, is that they were the first eventual champions to start their season with a Saturday 3 p.m. kick-off (surely the very definition of unfancied in the modern game) since Arsenal did in the 2003–04 season. It also meant an end to five seasons of the eventual Premier League champions starting their season on Monday night.

September

September is characterised, some say lessened, by the arrival of the international break. Momentum gathered in August and possibly augmented by a thrilling spree before the transfer window closes is lost as the best players depart for their national sides and the rest are left taking part in slightly bleak training drills with their depleted clubs. This fallow time is invariably accompanied by a spot of navel-gazing about the decline of the Englishman in the Premier League.

The facts are pretty clear. The numbers have fallen steadily throughout the 24-year history of the competition. The first two years of the Premier League (when, other than some adjusted kick-off times and inflatable sumo wrestlers for live games, it was little different from the First Division) saw English players make up more than 70% of the total. Five years later, it had dipped under 50% and has been lower than 40% in each season since 2002–03 with 2013–14 seeing the lowest proportion so far (31.3%).

The highlighted seasons are the ones when new domestic TV deals came into being. It is noticeable that in 1997–98, 2007–08 and 2013–14 (all seasons where the new deal brought in a significantly higher amount of revenue) the proportion of English players to feature in the Premier League fell significantly. Interestingly, the only time in the league's history that a rights package has raised less money than the previous deal (2004) saw the proportion of English players increase, albeit only slightly. It's far from the only reason behind the shifting nationality make-up of the Premier League but it does seem that when clubs are handed significantly increased revenues they'll splash out on foreign talent, which for many reasons is usually cheaper than equivalent English players. With the 2016–19 rights deal bringing in a monster £5.1 billion, and mid-table Premier League clubs already able to outbid continental giants*, it's likely that the next few seasons will see no real rise in English representation and all the introspection that brings with it, although the new rules around home grown players in squads should see the decline arrested.

PL season	Total players	English	% English	TV deal (£)
1992–93	**544**	**387**	71.10	**191m**
1993–94	540	379	70.20	
1994–95	526	360	68.40	
1995–96	502	321	63.90	
1996–97	515	295	57.30	
1997–98	**534**	**271**	50.70	**670m**
1998–99	539	260	48.20	
1999–2000	542	256	47.20	
2000–01	544	239	43.90	
2001–02	**528**	**218**	41.30	**1.2bn**
2002–03	530	209	39.40	

(continued)

* In January 2016, a TalkSPORT article linking Leicester with Sampdoria striker Eder contained the line '*Inter Milan are also keen on snapping the Italy international up, but they are likely to be outbid by Leicester*'. A baffling scenario for anyone who can remember the early 1990s when football fans had the choice on Sundays of watching glamorous Inter on Channel 4 or the more prosaic second-tier Foxes on ITV.

PL season	Total players	English	% English	TV deal (£)
2003–04	517	192	37.10	
2004–05	515	199	38.60	1.0bn
2005–06	536	196	36.60	
2006–07	534	193	36.10	
2007–08	532	175	32.90	1.7bn
2008–09	530	191	36.00	
2009–10	545	183	33.60	
2010–11	544	194	35.70	1.8bn
2011–12	538	201	37.40	
2012–13	523	183	35.00	
2013–14	544	170	31.30	3.0bn
2014–15	531	185	34.80	
2015–16	550	185	33.63	

So intense is the coverage of the Premier League now that there is an urge to apply hyperbole to almost every single event. Take Anthony Martial's goalscoring debut for Manchester United against Liverpool in September. The youngster went from abhorrently overpriced to world class in the space of 12 days. After writing him off, people wondered, nay demanded, that his subsequent debut goal be the best goalscoring debut by a teenager. Not so; Martial was the 154th youngest player to score a Premier League goal and the 27th youngest player to score on his debut.

Arsenal's commitment to reliving the same season every single year is as impressive as it must be infuriating for Gunners supporters. If the summer equals a disappointing venture into the transfer market and the spring sees a Round of 16 exit in the Champions League to one of Bayern Munich or Barcelona, then autumn must mean a concerted struggle to even make it out of the CL group stage, even though they are often placed into what is invariably called a 'comfortable looking' quartet. Even so, 2015–16 saw Arsène Wenger's men push their own boundaries to new extremes.

Drawn in a group alongside Bayern, Arsenal proceeded to lose away at Dinamo Zagreb (forgivable) and then at home to Olympiakos (oops). The Gunners then faced a double-header against the German giants, with a strong possibility of failing to qualify from the initial group stage for the first time since 2000. As it turned out, a surprising home win against Bayern and victories against the other two teams in the reverse fixtures saw the Gunners inch their way through the next stage by the slimmest of margins (a superior head-to-head record against Olympiakos). In 2011–12, ten points was only good enough for Manchester City to finish third in their group but nine did the job for a relieved Arsène Wenger. The London side's pairing with Barcelona in the Last 16 was almost inevitable.

The table below shows the ten teams to progress from a Champions League group stage despite losing their opening two games with Arsenal the second English/British team to do it after Sir Bobby Robson's Newcastle team in 2002–03. As you might expect, none of the ten teams has come close to winning the tournament itself after such a poor start, although special mention to Panathinaikos in 2008–09 who not only lost their opening two matches but then topped the group.

Teams to lose their opening two CL group games and still qualify for the next stage

Club	Season	Group position	Did they win CL?
Arsenal	2015–16	2	No
Galatasaray	2012–13	2	No
Marseille	2010–11	2	No
Panathinaikos	2008–09	1	No

Teams to lose their opening two CL group games and still qualify for the next stage – *continued*

Club	Season	Group position	Did they win CL?
Lyon	2007–08	2	No
Internazionale	2006–07	2	No
Werder Bremen	2005–06	2	No
Bayer 04 Leverkusen	2002–03 1st group stage	2	No
Newcastle United	2002–03 1st group stage	2	No
Dynamo Kyiv	1999–2000 1st group stage	2	No

Group B 2008–09	Pld	W	D	L	GF	GA	GD	Pts
Panathinaikos	6	3	1	2	8	7	1	10
Internazionale	6	2	2	2	8	7	1	8
Werder Bremen	6	1	4	1	7	9	-2	7
Anorthosis	6	1	3	2	8	8	0	6

In terms of Champions League group stage oddities, standings purists will always look fondly at the 2000–01 season where two teams (Sturm Graz and Anderlecht) topped groups with a goal difference of minus three. Graz's group was particularly odd as both they and second-placed Galatasaray had a GD of minus 3 while third- and fourth-placed Rangers and Monaco ended on plus 3. It's a funny old etc.

It wasn't just Arsenal who were finding the Champions League difficult in September. Of the four representatives from the Premier League, only one avoided defeat (Chelsea, and they were playing Maccabi Tel Aviv). As the table below shows, between 2005 and 2011 Premier League sides did not suffer a single defeat in their opening group game, but that since 2012 it has steadily increased.

Defeats by PL teams in opening CL group game	
2005–11	0
2012	1
2013	1
2014	2
2015	3

No one quite grasped the significance at the time, but in September Leicester became the first team since Everton in 2012 to come from behind to claim at least a point in four successive Premier League games. 'This will stand them in good stead for their fight against relegation', people commented, as a single shaft of sunlight illuminated Richard III's tomb.

Manchester United spent much of 2015–16 passing the ball back and forth with no apparent endgame, but occasionally this philosophy did work out for them. Against Southampton on 20 September, a 45-pass move was finished off by Juan Mata to give the team a relatively exciting 3-2 win. Forty-five passes sounds like quite a lot, and it is. In fact, it was 20 passes more than the next longest pass sequence before a goal in the Premier League in 2015–16. The average? 3.01. Perhaps Charles Hughes needs a hipster resurrection.

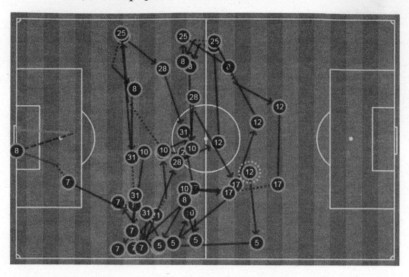

★

Your favourite day of the Premier League season? September 26th would be a good choice, given that only seven single days in the competition's history have seen more goals: 35 in only eight games, including arguably the game of the season (Leicester v Arsenal) was a bumper crop.

Home	Goals	Away	Goals
Tottenham Hotspur	4	Manchester City	1
Leicester City	2	Arsenal	5
Liverpool	3	Aston Villa	2
Manchester United	3	Sunderland	0
Southampton	3	Swansea City	1
Stoke City	2	Bournemouth	1
West Ham United	2	Norwich City	2
Newcastle United	2	Chelsea	2

Highest scoring PL days	Goals	Games played
08/05/93	47	9
05/02/11	41	8
03/10/92	40	10
22/08/92	38	10
27/11/10	36	8
12/04/93	36	9
19/05/13	36	10
26/09/15	**35**	**8**
29/12/12	35	8
26/12/99	35	10

The record for goals on a single day in the Premier League era remains the 47 scored on the last full day of the 1992–93 season. Liverpool thumped Tottenham 6-2, a 4-3 at Oldham, and two 3-3 draws. In top-fight history, it's unlikely that the 66 goals scored on Boxing Day 1963 will be topped anytime soon. It included a 10-1 win for Fulham at home to an Ipswich team that had won the league title just 18 months earlier. No top-flight team has reached double figures since.

Date	Home	Goals	Away	Goals
26/12/63	Blackpool	1	Chelsea	5
26/12/63	Burnley	6	Manchester United	1
26/12/63	Fulham	10	Ipswich Town	1
26/12/63	Leicester City	2	Everton	0
26/12/63	Liverpool	6	Stoke City	1
26/12/63	Nottingham Forest	3	Sheffield United	3
26/12/63	Sheffield Wednesday	3	Bolton Wanderers	0
26/12/63	West Bromwich Albion	4	Tottenham Hotspur	4
26/12/63	West Ham United	2	Blackburn Rovers	8
26/12/63	Wolverhampton Wanderers	3	Aston Villa	3

I

Don't Buy Strikers: The Invaluable Guide to Avoiding Relegation

'We are not going to be able to invent ten games where we can go on an unbeaten run because there are not enough games left'

Steve Kean

Relegation. The R word. The drop. Demotion. Falling through the trapdoor. Sinking without trace. If you're a football fan of any but the biggest clubs in the world, relegation is an ever-present danger. Even in high summer, when your optimism levels are as elevated as those for pollen, your team is only a bad start, a mid-season slump or a late-season collapse from the ignominy of demotion. Bolton Wanderers experienced their fourteenth relegation at the end of the 2015–16 season; only Grimsby Town and Notts County (16 each) have ever had more in the top four tiers of the English football pyramid. Happily for Grimsby, the same season saw them promoted back to the Football League after a six-year absence, although only the most cocksure of Mariners will be convinced that they are back for good. The gods of the drop are easily angered.

What follows in this section, then, is a handy guide to avoiding relegation, or at least trying to. In a world where the bottom team in the Premier League in 2016–17 will receive around £100 million of TV money alone, dropping out of the division is more disastrous than ever. The January transfer window in 2017 promises to be a maelstrom of emergency as clubs in danger of exiting the top flight roll the dice.

Don't Win the Play-offs

Curmudgeons have disliked the play-offs since they were introduced in the late 1980s. They do dilute the purity of a league campaign (itself a completely arbitrary structure) but at the same time they keep dreams alive that little bit longer, and can even end in glory at a large stadium of the Football League's choosing. But the fireworks and pageantry of the Spring Bank Holiday weekend can soon fade when the subsequent season in the Premier League unfolds. Of all the ways to enter England's top division, winning the play-offs is the least sustainable, with just ten of the 24 teams to do it in the Premier League era managing to avoid immediate demotion 12 months later. That said, in the last eight years four teams have gone up via the play-offs and then survived, including Hull in 2008. The Tigers, of course, are the latest winners of the Championship play-offs and, having spent the first 92 seasons of their league history outside the top flight, have been promoted into it three times in eight years. Should they avoid the drop in May 2017, Hull will join West Ham as the only teams to win the play-offs and then avoid relegation the next season on two occasions (the Hammers doing it in both 2005–06 and 2012–13).

Don't Worry About Getting 40 Points

Relegation is as damaging to the health as the bubonic plague and there are almost as many old wives' tales surrounding it. The longest lasting of these is the 40-point safety target, the ancient safety net that managers cling to dearly. 'We've passed the 40-point mark,' they announce proudly sometime in March or April, oblivious to the fact that they had probably been safe for a week or two already.

As is often the way, the element of truth was set early on,

and then received wisdom did its sly work, with people unwilling actually to check and see if what they were saying was still based in reality. Ignoring the first three Premier League seasons, as they contained 22 teams and will obviously inflate the required number of points, we can see in the table below that in both 1996–97 and 1997–98 teams went down with exactly 40 points. 1996–97 is an interesting case as it is the season with the smallest gap between top and bottom in the Premier League era (41 points – the average since the turn of the century has been a massive 62 points), which naturally increased the number of points won by teams lower in the table. Additionally, Middlesbrough, who went down in 19th place, had three points deducted after failing to turn up to their fixture against Blackburn in December due to an apparent flu epidemic in the squad. Those points condemned Boro to the drop: had they not been punished for their cavalier approach to the scheduling, Coventry on 41 points would have gone down in their place.

Season	Points total of final relegated team
1992–93*	49
1993–94*	42
1994–95*	45
1995–96	38
1996–97	40
1997–98	40
1998–99	36
1999–2000	33
2000–01	34
2001–02	36
2002–03	42
2003–04	33
2004–05	33
2005–06	34

(continued)

Season	Points total of final relegated team
2006–07	38
2007–08	36
2008–09	34
2009–10	30
2010–11	39
2011–12	36
2012–-13	36
2013–14	33
2014–15	35
2015–-16	37

*22-team seasons.

Only once since 1997–98 has a team gone down with 40-plus points, and that was the unfortunate West Ham team containing such talent as Jermain Defoe, Joe Cole, Michael Carrick, Paolo Di Canio and 2002 World Cup star Gary Breen. The Hammers dropped into the second tier with 42 points, which in 2013–14 was enough to give Swansea a 12th-place finish. The best team to go down from the Premier League? That's debatable, but almost certainly the unluckiest.

Don't Have an English Manager

As detailed later in this book, the 2015–16 season saw not a single English manager in charge of a team in the final top ten of the Premier League. The competition is still waiting for its first ever title-winning English manager. Put simply, English managers have now become the value option for clubs at the highest level. To taste the difference, you need to go foreign. Here's the evidence, anyway: a massive 71% of teams which have gone down from the Premier League have been led there by an English manager. There's an extremely select bunch of overseas managers who have technically been in charge of a Premier League club relegated in their final game of the season, namely Avram Grant, Felix Magath, Ole Gunnar Solskjær, and, most recently, Rafa Benítez. Grant was in charge of Portsmouth when they went down in 2010 and narrowly escaped being in charge of West Ham in their final game 12 months later, due to the fact that he was sacked the week before. A fine effort.

Managers when team is relegated from PL	%
English	71.2
Rest of UK/Ireland	23.3
Actually foreign	5.5
PL title wins from English managers	0
Last time an English manager finished in the top four	2012

It's worth noting that the last time an English manager led a team to a top-four finish in the Premier League was Harry Redknapp with Tottenham in 2012. (Technically Brian Kidd was in charge of second-placed Manchester City as the 2012–13 season came to a close but it was Roberto Mancini's team.) With the top clubs in 2016–17 all managed by overseas managers, it seems that Redknapp's terrific fourth-place finish will remain the most recent one for at least one more year. In a cruel twist of fate (seemingly reserved for English managers), Tottenham didn't even qualify for the Champions League in that campaign. Chelsea's unlikely victory against Bayern in Munich (the Germans reaching the final in their own stadium, rather than a Teutonic destination in the Cotswolds) under, you guessed it, overseas tactician Roberto Di Matteo, meant that Tottenham were dumped into the Europa League, a competition loathed by English managers almost without exception. Why? No one really knows.

Avoid George Boyd and Benito Carbone

If you make your own luck in the modern game, then certain players have a manufacturing defect. 2016–17 should see the return of George Boyd with Burnley, hoping to make amends for his spell with the club in 2014–15, a campaign in which he became only the fourth player in Premier League history to play for two relegated teams in the same season, after beginning the campaign with Hull. The others, if you want to make a note, are Mark Robins, Steve Kabba and David Nugent. To contribute to one relegation is unfortunate, to contribute to two starts to look downright cursed. But these men pale into insignificance when contrasted with turn-of-the-century Italian Benito Carbone who managed to garner a significant income despite playing for relegated teams in 1999–2000 (Sheffield Wednesday), 2000–01 (Bradford City) and 2001–02 (Derby County). In this period he also featured for Aston Villa and Middlesbrough as clubs shared out the responsibility for his high wages and propensity for spectacular goals. It's not all doom for Carbone, though, as he remains the only player in Premier League history to score on Valentine's Day more than once (in 1998 and 2000). Heartbreaker.

Don't Be Wolves

'*Fool me once, shame on . . . shame on you. Fool me — you can't get fooled again.*' George Bush may have co-owned the Texas Rangers baseball team at one point, but he has never been involved in Wolverhampton Wanderers, if his quote above is any guide. Wolves remain the masters of dropping through the divisions. Not only are they one of two teams to drop from the top tier to the fourth in successive seasons (1984–87, along with Bristol City, 1980–83: truly the 1980s was the decade of the self-inflicted implosion), but, after doing so between

2012 and 2014 they are the only team in English history to drop from the top tier to the third in consecutive campaigns more than once. That anguished howl you make when your team goes down? No one does it better than wolves. Sorry, Wolves.

Don't Buy Strikers

Life was good for Ricky van Wolfswinkel on the evening of 17 August 2013. The temperature in Norwich was a pleasant 19 degrees and the Dutch striker had just scored on his debut for the Canaries in a creditable 2-2 draw with Everton. The newly promoted Norfolk team had spent a club record fee of £8.5 million on a player who came highly recommended, and a debut goal was an immediate repayment of the faith the club had shown. But 17 August was as good as it got for Ricky. In his next 18 Premier League appearances for the club he managed just three more shots on target and ended the campaign with 25 appearances and just that single goal against Everton on the opening day. Norwich were relegated and van Wolfswinkel was exiled to Ligue 1 in 2014–15 and La Liga in 2015–16, his presence at the club too painful a reminder of the broken dreams of 2013.

The point of this sad tale is that Norwich in 2013 were typical of a promoted team. On arriving in the Premier League, with its dramatically increased revenues, they bolstered their squad, and they bolstered it with forward players. After all, goals win you games, right? And winning games keeps you in the Premier League, correct? No.

Let's clarify: winning games will indeed keep you in the Premier League, but relying on newly purchased strikers to do so is a less than reliable method.

The list of top-scoring players for relegated Premier League teams is shown below and contains just one player with 20-plus goals, Andrew Johnson for Crystal Palace in 2004–05, although it should be noted that a hefty 11 of these came from the penalty spot. Charlie Austin's 18 for QPR in 2014–15 is a recent example, but he had already been at the club as they came up from the Championship, so wasn't a new arrival. The exception that proves the rule, really, is Fabrizio Ravanelli at Middlesbrough in 1996–97. The silver-haired Italian scored 16 goals for the big-spending, flu-susceptible North East side. That said, three of his goals came on the opening day and six of his seasonal total (38%) had come by the first week of September.

Season	Team	Player	Goals
2004–05	Crystal Palace	Johnson, Andrew	21
2014–15	Queens Park Rangers	Austin, Charlie	18
2011–12	Blackburn Rovers	Yakubu	17
1996–97	Middlesbrough	Ravanelli, Fabrizio	16
1992–93	Crystal Palace	Armstrong, Chris	15
2006–07	Charlton Athletic	Bent, Darren	13
1992–93	Middlesbrough	Wilkinson, Paul	13
2010–11	Blackpool	Campbell, DJ	13

Let's forget about individual players anyway and look at goals and goals conceded on a wider scale. Listed below are the lowest scoring teams in each Premier League season, with nine of them still managing to avoid the drop, despite troubling the opposition defence less often than any other team in the division that season. Special mention should go to defensive grumbler George Graham who managed Arsenal to a tenth-place finish in 1992–93 with a mere 40 goals and then took Leeds to 11th four years later despite scoring just 28 goals in 38 games, a delightful campaign that included nine goalless draws. One small caveat to the 'who actually needs goals' campaign is Aston Villa's relegation in 2015–16. This was the fourth successive season that the lowest scoring team had gone down, the first time it had happened for this many campaigns in a row.

Lowest scorers in PL season by season

Team	Season	Goals	Position	Relegated
Arsenal	1992–93	40	10	No
Ipswich Town	1993–94	35	19	No
Crystal Palace	1994–95	34	19	Yes
Manchester City	1995–96	33	18	Yes
Leeds United	1996–97	28	11	No
Wimbledon	1997–98	34	15	No
Nottingham Forest	1998–99	35	20	Yes
Watford	1999–2000	35	20	Yes
Bradford City	2000–01	30	20	Yes
Sunderland	2001–02	29	17	No
Sunderland	2002–03	21	20	Yes
Wolverhampton Wanderers	2003–04	38	20	Yes
Blackburn Rovers	2004–05	32	15	No
Sunderland	2005–06	26	20	Yes
Manchester City	2006–07	29	14	No
Watford	2006–07	29	20	Yes
Derby County	2007–08	20	20	Yes
Middlesbrough	2008–09	28	19	Yes
Wolverhampton Wanderers	2009–10	32	15	No
Birmingham City	2010–11	37	18	Yes
Stoke City	2011–12	36	14	No
Queens Park Rangers	2012–13	30	20	Yes
Norwich City	2013–14	28	18	Yes
Burnley	2014–15	28	19	Yes
Aston Villa	2015–16	27	20	Yes

Contrast the lowest scoring teams with the fortunes of the teams with the worst defences in each Premier League season and you can see why teams which think they will be battling the drop should focus on defence. Only once in Premier League history has a team with the worst (or joint-worst in this case) defence avoided the drop and that was Fulham in 2006–07. Their survival was slightly dubious, given that they did so thanks to a 1-0 win against a weakened Liverpool team who were resting players ahead of the Champions League final, a result which confirmed that Lawrie Sanchez's dreary spell at the London club was extended for a few additional months.

Other than Fulham, it's a sorry list of teams that struggled on a titanic scale, from Swindon's 100 goals conceded campaign of 1993–94 (congratulations to Shaun Taylor who was the only Robins player to be on the pitch as all 100 goals went in) to the abject Derby team of 2007–08. And let us not forget the Fulham team of 2013–14 which went through three managers (one of whom, Felix Magath, tried to treat injuries with blocks of cheese) and 39 players. A litany of dismay and disappointment that could all have been avoided with a stronger defence. The message could not be any clearer: don't buy strikers.

Worst defences in PL season by season

Team	Season	Goals conceded	Position	Relegated
Middlesbrough	1992–93	75	21	Yes
Swindon Town	1993–94	100	22	Yes
Ipswich Town	1994–95	93	22	Yes
Bolton Wanderers	1995–96	71	20	Yes
Middlesbrough	1996–97	60	19	Yes
Barnsley	1997–98	82	19	Yes
Nottingham Forest	1998–99	69	20	Yes
Watford	1999–2000	77	20	Yes
Bradford City	2000–01	70	20	Yes

Worst defences in PL season by season – *continued*

Team	Season	Goals conceded	Position	Relegated
Ipswich Town	2001–02	64	18	Yes
Leicester City	2001–02	64	20	Yes
West Bromwich Albion	2002–03	65	19	Yes
Sunderland	2002–03	65	20	Yes
Leeds United	2003–04	79	19	Yes
Norwich City	2004–05	77	19	Yes
Sunderland	2005–06	69	20	Yes
Fulham	**2006–07**	**60**	**16**	**No**
Charlton Athletic	2006–07	60	19	Yes
Derby County	2007–08	89	20	Yes
West Bromwich Albion	2008–09	67	20	Yes
Burnley	2009–10	82	18	Yes
Blackpool	2010–11	78	19	Yes
Wolverhampton Wanderers	2011–12	82	20	Yes
Wigan Athletic	2012–13	73	18	Yes
Reading	2012–13	73	19	Yes
Fulham	2013–14	85	19	Yes
Queens Park Rangers	2014–15	73	20	Yes
Aston Villa	2015–16	76	20	Yes

For the record, Norwich equalled their club record fee for van Wolfswinkel two seasons later when they signed striker Steven Naismith from Everton. The Scot scored once (also on his debut) in 13 appearances for the Canaries and was relegated. Sometimes you just have to learn.

Don't Think It Can't Happen to You

There are still a lot of Arsenal fans who labour under the belief that their team has never been relegated, and I'm sure this particularly long-lasting piece of misinformation is still a staple of pub quizzes the country over. For the record, Arsenal were relegated in 1913 and, contrary to what many people think, did not immediately schmooze their way back into the top flight and leapfrog Tottenham in the process (this did happen, but in March 1919), but instead played two full seasons in the second tier, before the escalating conflict a hundred or so miles away curtailed senior football for four years.

The longest a team has ever gone in the English league system without experiencing relegation for the first time is 43 seasons, with Aston Villa starting as founder members in 1888 before finally succumbing to relegation for the first time in 1936. The Villans have since gone down from the top flight on four other occasions (and once from the second tier) which isn't ideal, but is a better record than their arch-rivals Birmingham who have gone down 12 times from the top flight, more than any other side. It seems that the Second City can't escape the pull of the second division. Ultimately, though, despite the events of the 1910s, Arsenal probably actually are the masters of avoiding the drop. One relegation in 112 seasons of action is pretty good, working out at 0.9%, just ahead of Everton (two relegations in 117 seasons) and Liverpool (three in 112). Manchester United, if you were wondering, have been relegated five times (1894, 1922, 1931, 1937 and 1974), which is as many as the likes of Coventry and Bournemouth. The Cherries, meanwhile, remain the only team to have played in the English top flight and never been relegated from it, with a massive haul of one season at the elite level.

Record After Ten Games

'It's a marathon not a sprint,' people still say, especially if they support a team tipped for relegation and that team has just lost its first game of the season. 'Judge me after ten games,' plead managers as the chairman sharpens his axe ahead of the international break in early September. OK then, let's do that, and, at the risk of angering the 'football didn't start midway through 1981' crowd, let's go back to 1981–82 when the three points for a win rule was introduced to make the comparison nice and neat

---

**Record after ten games of relegated teams
in top flight, 1981–2015**

Average points	8.66
Most points	19 – Chelsea, 1987–88
Fewest Points	1 – WBA, 1985–86
Most wins	6 – Chelsea, 1987–88
Most defeats	9 – WBA, 1985–86
Most Goals	20 – Chelsea, 1987–88
Fewest Goals	2 – Sheffield Wednesday, 1989–90
Most goals conceded	31 – WBA, 1985–86
Fewest goals conceded	8 – Norwich City, 1994–95

The first thing that jumps out is the sheer terribleness of the 1985–86 West Bromwich Albion team. After ten games the Baggies had just one point and had let in a monstrous 31 goals, including 5-1 defeats to Watford and Manchester United. Notable for their shirts, which featured a large no smoking sign on the front, for the fans it was more a case of no hope. At the other end of the scale, Chelsea's 1987–88 outfit were one of the unluckiest teams to go down, having already gobbled up 19 points from their opening ten matches, scoring at a rate of two goals per game. Their eventual demotion as the first play-off losers came after the Blues lost only two regular league games at Stamford Bridge all season, as many as Nottingham Forest, who came third. A mention, too, to Norwich City in 1994–95 who conceded only eight times in their first ten games and enjoy the dubious honour of being one of only three teams to be as high as seventh at Christmas and still go down (along with Notts County in 1892–93 and Tottenham in 1927–28). When you're doomed, you're doomed.

Be the Lucky Promoted Team

Like three shipwrecked sailors stranded on a desert island with just a single knife and fork between them, promoted teams to the Premier League know that, statistically, at least one of them will survive in the coming season. Only once in the Premier League era have all three promoted teams suffered relegation the following season (in 1997–98 when Barnsley, Bolton and Crystal Palace all made their sorry way back to the second tier), while as recently as 2011–12 all three new arrivals survived (Swansea, Norwich and QPR). It's pretty likely, therefore, that at least one of Middlesbrough, Burnley and Hull will be lining up in the top flight in 2017–18; just make sure you're the one left holding the fork when the lights go out.

If All Else Fails, Open Your Parachute

Parachute payments to relegated Premier League sides have been part of the fabric of the competition since the very beginning, hence the unlikely fact that both Notts County and Luton Town (as relegated top-flight teams in 1992) have been beneficiaries of payments, but they have become more known in recent seasons as club debts have swelled and teams sink into the Football League with a sense of panic and urgency. Generally there are two real approaches to the drop and the parachute payments that accompany it. Restructure sensibly (the theory behind the instalments) or use them to maintain a Premier League-quality squad and hope that a swift return to the top flight is forthcoming (otherwise the wage bill can be a rapidly tightening noose). In recent seasons the likes of Wolves, Blackpool, Wigan and Bolton have all gone from top flight to third tier in a short space of time, while other clubs seem to specialise in bouncing back. As the table below shows, Burnley and Hull's swift return to the Premier League is the first time since 2009 that two sides have climbed back at the first attempt, with Burnley in particular seeming to follow the approach that West Brom took in the 2000s of using multiple promotions to the Premier League to slowly expand and improve the club until they reach a point where they can realistically compete and maintain their spot at the highest level.

Teams to bounce straight back to PL	
Season relegated	**Team**
1992–93	Nottingham Forest
1992–93	Crystal Palace
1994–95	Leicester City
1995–96	Bolton Wanderers
1996–97	Nottingham Forest
1996–97	Middlesbrough
1998–99	Charlton Athletic
2000–01	Manchester City
2001–02	Leicester City
2002–03	West Bromwich Albion
2005–06	Sunderland
2005–06	Birmingham City
2007–08	Birmingham City
2008–09	West Bromwich Albion
2008–09	Newcastle United
2010–11	West Ham United
2012–13	Queens Park Rangers
2013–14	Norwich City
2014–15	Burnley
2014–15	Hull City

Even so, it takes only one poor season for such carefully laid plans to unravel, hence the eternal popularity of managers such as Sam Allardyce and Tony Pulis, who, so far, have guaranteed survival at every club they've managed. Some fans may baulk at the style of football proffered, but in the boardroom these men are hailed as giants and magicians (and giant magicians).

Home Truths

Despite the eternal hegemony of Allardyce and Pulis, there is, of course, no foolproof way of avoiding relegation. An increase in the numbers of American owners of English football clubs in the twenty-first century has seen increased chatter about the abolition of the concept of demotion, what with US sport being a closed-shop system where teams are guaranteed their place in the competition (even if there is no guarantee of the franchise staying in their city). As anathema a concept as that is to most Britons (see the continued antipathy towards MK Dons), there is a thread of egalitarianism in American sport that is in stark contrast to the cut-throat dog-eat-dog mayhem of the Premier League, Football League and most competitions further down the pyramid.

But fans will accept the vile shadow of relegation as long as it is accompanied by its glorious brother promotion. The variety and breadth of professional clubs in England across at least five divisions is unrivalled by any other country in the world, testament to the triumph of hope over adversity (at least sometimes). It's not surprising, though, that elevation to a higher league can often lead to poor decision-making, club officials dazzled by the need to make a good go of it and maintain the excitement that the promotion brought to the team in the first place. As we have seen, pragmatism is often the first thing to be discarded, even though a careful, ostensibly 'dull' approach to promotion is probably the most sensible way to deal with it. Concentrate on defending against teams which are, by and large, better than those you faced the previous campaign. Don't panic at the bad results but instead work out the games you can realistically win, and, evidently: Don't. Buy. Strikers.

2

Pep Talk: A Conversation On Guardiola

Summer 2016. Two friends, Joseph Backer and John Convinced, are arguing about the appointment of Pep Guardiola as the coach of Manchester City. Backer is a huge fan of the former Barcelona and Bayern Munich manager and thinks he'll usher in a new era of dominance for two-time Premier League champions City. Convinced, meanwhile, is, well, unconvinced . . .

Joseph: What a coup it is for Manchester City to get Pep. They've virtually guaranteed the title next season.

John: Come on. Pep, or Pep Guardiola as I like to call him as I'm not his friend, has had it easy for his whole career. He took over a Barcelona team with a young Messi and the greatest crop of talent in the club's history, then moved on to a team which had just won the treble, and failed to match his predecessor. Now he's heading to a team with an ageing squad and which could barely scrape fourth in one of the lowest quality Premier League campaigns in living memory. They should have walked it.

Joseph: You've contradicted yourself there a bit, John. If City 'should have walked the league' then surely Guardiola is taking over a team in fine fettle? Or at least one a man of his ability can reshape fairly easily?

John: True, but then that's all he's ever done, like I said. Inherited a great team at Barcelona, inherited a great team at Bayern. Won a load of trophies. Great. Try it at Leeds United, pal.

Joseph: Right, you need some convincing, and I'm the man to do it. Let's go back to the beginning, back to 2008, and specifically this idea that Pep took over a team ready and waiting for glory. In 2007–08 Barcelona finished third. That may sound OK, but they were 18 points *behind* title winners Real Madrid and they let in 43 goals, one fewer than 17th place Osasuna. They were regularly being outclassed in Europe, too – especially by teams from the once all-powerful Premier League. In 2006–07 they had failed to beat Chelsea in the group stage then lost to John Arne Riise and Craig Bellamy's Liverpool in the 'golf swing' game at the Camp Nou.

John: Ah, yes, the era when Steve Finnan used to get further in the Champions League than Lionel Messi. A special time.

Joseph: Exactly. And then in 2007–08, OK, Barcelona got to the semis but lost out to Manchester United. This after only getting past Celtic on away goals earlier in the competition. Celtic! On away goals!

John: OK, I take your point, but this is a club that had won the Champions League in 2006, this isn't Brian Clough taking over Nottingham Forest in the Second Division . . .

Joseph: No, but, like Clough, Guardiola has achieved managerial success at a young age and is not afraid to ditch big names. Look at what he did when he took over at Barcelona, getting rid of Ronaldinho, Deco and Zambrotta, who had made 64 league appearances between them the previous campaign. Comes in, looks about, gets rid.

John: I'm sure Guardiola had input but this is a European super-club, transfers in and out will have been rubber-stamped by committees rather than a parliamentary bill. You didn't need to be a genius to see that Ronaldinho was on the wane, and Deco wasn't exactly great at Chelsea, was he?

Joseph: Deco? You mean the Deco who won the league and cup double in his second season at Stamford Bridge? The last

Portuguese player to win player of the month in the Premier League? That Deco?

John: All right, but here's the thing: Guardiola had spent 2007–08 in charge of Barcelona B in the fourth tier. It's the same club the same philosophy, the same tactics. It's like being promoted from manager of Currys to the *regional* manager of Currys. More responsibility, yes, but essentially the same.

Joseph: I think there's more to managing Barcelona than restocking vacuum cleaners and juicers but . . .

John: Oh, and while we're on it, this whole 'B team' thing sits uncomfortably with me. What happens if you like working at the B team? Or if you get them all the way to the top flight? Yes, I know. It can't happen and that's weird. I don't like it.

Joseph: Remind me to tell you about the 1980 Copa del Rey final some time, then. Back to Guardiola, I think that this idea that he just needed to slot into place at Barcelona is nonsense. He came in and gave the club, any club, one of the greatest seasons in the sport's history. He won six trophies in 2009. Six!

John: True. So what was so good about the 2008–09 season? I mean, I know the headlines: treble winners, ooh Messi's playing as a false nine, passes, passes and passes. So many passes.

Joseph: Actually, the relentless passing came a bit later. Barca had 66% possession on average in the 2008–09 season, which, if you're West Brom, is massive but two years later it had gone up to a staggering 73%. The goals? Well, they scored a measly 76 in the league in 2007–08 (which, if you're West Brom, is massive). In Guardiola's first season, they scored a massive 105. Since then, the club have only ended the season with fewer than 100 goals in two of seven campaigns.

John: Who was the manager for those two seasons?

Joseph: Well, Guardiola, but you get my point. He, along with his ex-muse Lionel Messi, has redefined attacking output in the modern game. Eight hundred and forty-nine goals in eight league seasons for Barcelona. That's more than Southampton have scored in 17 seasons in the Premier League. Where they won it in that first season, though, was in their clashes against the rest of the top six. Thirty-five goals in ten games was 16 more than any of the other five teams managed. It was more than twice as many as Real Madrid, culminating, of course, with that 6-2 win at the Bernabéu in May 2009. Two points from their last four games and they still won the title by nine points. Total annihilation.

John: And yet Manchester United were still favourites ahead of the 2009 Champions League final?

Joseph: *Slight* favourites. Remember, United were the reigning European Champions, had just won the league for a third successive year and had Cristiano Ronaldo in their side. Not that it helped them. No one remembers now, but they actually played well for the first ten minutes of the final but history is written by the victors and after Barcelona took the lead it never looked likely United would come back.

John: They had a better chance than they did two years later, I guess.

Joseph: Yeah, 2011 was the rematch that wasn't even a contest. In 2009, United had only two shots fewer than Barcelona but in 2011 they had three all game, while Pep's boys had 16, as well as making twice as many passes. It was a destruction.

John: That was the peak, wasn't it? That was the moment Guardiola should have packed up and walked off into the sunset. If he doesn't like staying at a club for more than three years he's never going to build a true legacy. Barcelona was *his* club and he took them on that night to a new level and one which he's been chasing ever since. I mean, he hasn't even got to a Champions League final since then, right?

Joseph: That's true. He lost in the semis in 2012, and then again in all three of his years with Bayern, but look at that record: **winners, semis, winners, semis, semis, semis, semis**. Pep guarantees semis more than a zone four travelcard; no wonder he could have named his club once he'd announced he was leaving Bayern.

John: I think that's what I'm struggling with to be honest; Bayern. I can hold my hands up and accept that he transformed Barcelona but his spell in Germany reminds me of, say, Kevin Spacey at the Old Vic: a big-name artistic director who will attract more media attention to a grand institution . . . but won't necessarily do anything that anyone else could not have done'. Now he's going to City to do the same thing.

Joseph: Well, that went in an unexpected direction. But in any case you're wrong, because it's arguable that Guardiola changed Bayern even more than he did Barcelona, especially given he was there for barely 1000 days.

John: Seriously?

Joseph: Yeah, firstly what other manager has had the confidence, or the CV, that early in his career to take a year's sabbatical. Chelsea defeating Barcelona in the Champions League semi-final in 2012 was even more of a travesty than the 2010 reversal to Mourinho's Inter. Most managers would have hunkered down and plotted a way back, probably sacrificing a few principles along the way. Pep went and hung out in New York so his kids could learn English.

John: True, can't remember Brian Horton ever doing that. Although presumably his children can speak English.

Joseph: And when he returned to Europe in summer 2013, like a medieval king from the Holy Land, he was more committed than ever before to his beliefs and philosophy. And then he managed to instil it in one of the most structured and dominant clubs in world football.

John: Go on . . .

Joseph: I know you're sceptical so let's get the Champions League out of the way because that's the albatross around his Bavarian neck. So he exited at the semi-final stage in all three years, firstly to Real Madrid in 2014, then to Barcelona in 2015 and finally to Atlético in 2016. Three Spanish teams, three failures, but three different reasons. 2014 was acknowledged by Guardiola himself to be a tactical error in the second leg, chasing a 1-0 deficit and ending 5-0 down on aggregate by the tie's end. That's not good. 2015 against Barcelona was over after the first leg in Spain but Bayern dominated possession in both games and had more shots over the two matches . . .

John: They failed to hit a single effort on target in the Camp Nou, though. Some homecoming.

Joseph: OK, that's true, and Barca were motivated to beat Guardiola for obvious reasons, but if 2014 and 2015 were fair results over 180 minutes then 2016 was not. Bayern had 53 shots over the two legs to Atlético's 18, yet they went out on away goals after laying siege to Atlético's goal in the closing stages of the second leg. You could replay that exact tie 100 times and Bayern would get through at least 90 times. Look, the Champions League is a tombola when you get to the last four. You've usually got at least two of Real, Barca, Bayern and a guest appearance from Atlético, or Manchester City or Juventus, or maybe even PSG one day. Maybe Leicester are going to Leicester the Champions League next season but we know they won't. In the closing few games it's close to a lottery, so judge a man on the journey, not the pistol fight at the end. Pep's taken a team into the Champions League seven times and reached the semi-final every time. That's blockbuster.

John: Blockbusters. And yet when I hear stories about great achievements in the past I hear about Bob Paisley and Miguel Muñoz, I don't hear about Bob Shankly taking Dundee to a semi-final in 1963.

Joseph: Wait, is he related to Bill Shankly?

John: Yeah, Bill was his younger brother.

Joseph: I didn't know that. Pep has a younger brother, Pere, he's an agent. He's probably never been to Dundee. Bob and Bill, Pep and Pere.

John: Do you want to take a minute?

Joseph: No, no. Let's get back to Pep at Bayern. OK, we've covered the Champions League, let's move on to the Bundesliga.

John: The most competitive league in Europe, oh, no, wait, Bayern have won it for the last four years and in 12 of the last 18 seasons. But season tickets are ten euros everywhere so that's all fine.

Joseph: Spiky, I sense some anger in you. Either way, you need to acknowledge the scale of what Pep did in the Bundesliga. He didn't just win three in a row, he obliterated the challenge from other sides. In his first season he guided Bayern to 19 successive wins in the league. Nineteen! They'd won the title by the 27th game.

John: Yeah, that is quite good.

Joseph: Second season, sets a new Bundesliga record for clean sheets, 22. Lets in just 18 goals. Can only win the title by a meagre ten points, though.

John: Crisis . . .

Joseph: Then the final season, and unlike Alexander weeping because there were no more worlds to conquer, Pep finds some. Bayern win their first ten games of the season, the first time that's ever happened in the BuLi, as annoying people call it, and let in just 17 goals all season, a new German top-flight record. He ends his spell at the club with the best points per game, goals per game and goals conceded per game rates in the competition's history. But it wasn't just the results, it was the method. Read this, John.

John: This quote from Philipp Lahm?

Joseph: Yes, please.

John: *'We can play a back three or a back four, we can play with one or two support strikers, whatever, I don't know how many systems we have.'*

Joseph: That's Philipp Lahm the full-back, who became Phillip Lahm 'The Brain' under Guardiola.

John: A bit like Krang, I guess, but with more mobility.

Joseph: In 102 league games, Pep made 337 changes to the starting XI, so more than three per game. This is someone who adapts and adjusts relentlessly. All these 'does Pep know what he's let himself in for coming to the Premier League?' pieces, come on. He'll have done his research. He'll know which players he wants to keep at City, and which he doesn't. And, let's face it, thinking that overhauling Leicester and finishing ahead of Arsenal worries Guardiola is frankly a bit odd.

John: I can't work out whether City need a bit of tinkering or a complete reconstruction.

Joseph: There are some quick wins for Guardiola, no doubt. Defensively, City haven't been any good for ages. They've conceded an average of 39 goals per season in the last three campaigns, as many as they did under Keegan and Stuart Pearce in 2004–05.

John: Seriously? I guess Guardiola could emulate Pearce and stick David James on up front for a bit as well. Neuer tried but just wasn't brave enough.

Joseph: And going forward, there's been a steady decline in goals, 102 in 2013–14, 83 in 2014–15 and 71 last season. Basically they're increasingly reliant on Agüero, who's provided 17%, 31% and 34% of the goals respectively. And when you're reliant on Agüero you're reliant on his fitness and you probably don't want to be reliant on that.

John: So, sign some defenders, sign someone to take the load off Agüero, turn Sterling into the future of English football, unleash Kevin De Bruyne and he's onto another winner.

Joseph: Pretty much. He's even got the upper hand over new neighbour José Mourinho. Three defeats in 16 games. Nothing can go wrong.

John: Hmm, maybe. We'll see. All aboard the Pep Express, let's see where we end up.

Guardiola at Barcelona:
- Only manager to win six titles in a year (2009: La Liga, Spanish Cup, Champions League, Spanish Super Cup, European Super Cup and FIFA Club World Cup)
- 16 consecutive wins in La Liga in 2010–11
- 12 away wins in a row in La Liga in 2010–11 (including two in previous season)

Honours
- La Liga champions: 2008–09, 2009–10, 2010–11
- Champions League winners: 2008–09, 2010–11
- Copa del Rey winners: 2008–09, 2011–12
- FIFA Club World Cup winners: 2009, 2011
- European Super Cup winners: 2009, 2011
- Spanish Super Cup winners: 2009, 2010, 2011

Guardiola at Bayern:

Best Bundesliga coaches: points per game			
Rank	Coach	Games	Points/game
1	**Josep Guardiola**	102	**2.52**
2	Sascha Lewandowski	45	2.04
3	Ottmar Hitzfeld	461	1.98
4	Louis van Gaal	63	1.94
5	Franz Beckenbauer	17	1.88

Best Bundesliga managers: goals per game

Rank	Coach	Games	Goals/games
1	**Josep Guardiola**	102	**2.49**
2	Helmut Benthaus	102	2.33
3	Martin Wilke	30	2.30
4	André Schubert	29	2.24
5	Hennes Weisweiler	469	2.22

Best Bundesliga coaches: goals against per game

Rank	Coach	Games	Goals against/game
1	**Josep Guardiola**	102	0.57
2	Eckhard Krautzun	17	1.00
3	Ottmar Hitzfeld	461	1.02
4	Roberto Di Matteo	27	1.04
5	Louis van Gaal	63	1.05

- First manager to win the Bundesliga in each of his first three seasons
- Combined winning margin over the three title winning seasons of 39 points
- Earliest ever title win (27 games, 2013–14)
- 19 consecutive Bundesliga wins between October 2013 and March 2014
- Most clean sheets in Bundesliga history (22 in 2014–15)
- Fewest goals conceded in a Bundesliga season (17 in 2015–16)

Honours

- Bundesliga champions: 2013–14, 2014–15, 2015–16
- DFB-Pokal winners: 2013–14, 2015–16
- UEFA Super Cup winners: 2013
- FIFA Club World Cup winners: 2013

October–November

October

Liverpool's decision to replace Brendan Rodgers with Jürgen Klopp led to some of the most frenzied activity among the English footballing press for at least a week or two. But while some were tracking his flight in real time from Dortmund to John Lennon Airport, others were revising the philosophy that had brought the ebullient tactician such success in the Bundesliga. Chief among his beliefs was the concept of 'Gegenpressing'. In his own words, 'the best moment to win the ball is immediately after your team just lost it. The opponent is still looking for orientation where to pass the ball. He will have taken his eyes off the game to make his tackle or interception and he will have expended energy. Both make him vulnerable.'

All well and good, but how quickly could the new man at Anfield instil such principles into a team which had laboured under Rodgers? The answer seemed to be: quite quickly. In Klopp's first game (a goalless draw against energetic Tottenham), they ran almost ten kilometres further than they had in their final game under Rodgers, and the trend continued in Klopp's opening weeks in charge. Proving that it is possible to get players to run more, simply by asking them to.

Date	Opponent	Result	Manager	Team distance (km)	Team sprints
09/08/15	Stoke City	W	Rodgers	105.5	389
17/08/15	Bournemouth	W	Rodgers	108.8	475
24/08/15	Arsenal	D	Rodgers	110.5	584
29/08/15	West Ham United	L	Rodgers	104.6	434
12/09/15	Manchester United	L	Rodgers	109.2	484
20/09/15	Norwich City	D	Rodgers	111.9	513
26/09/15	Aston Villa	W	Rodgers	105.9	457
04/10/15	Everton	D	Rodgers	106.5	458
17/10/15	Tottenham Hotspur	D	Klopp	116.0	614
25/10/15	Southampton	D	Klopp	117.8	566
31/10/15	Chelsea	W	Klopp	115.1	497
08/11/15	Crystal Palace	L	Klopp	112.8	521

Overall, by the end of the season Klopp's team had averaged 114 kilometres per game in the Premier League (compared to 108 kilometres under Rodgers), with about 70 extra sprints each match. But if football was just about running then the big game of the season would be the schools cross-country championships. As well as the extra effort, Klopp slowly but surely extracted more application from his team – taking them to finals in both the League Cup and the Europa League, with their comebacks against Borussia Dortmund and Villarreal in the latter competition a sign of things to come for the Reds under the new regime. The end-of-season poaching of Bayern's fitness coach Andreas Kornmayer and nutritionist Mona Nemmer only suggests that Klopp is planning to turn the volume of his heavy metal football up to 11 in 2016–17.

On the face of it, Newcastle's 6-2 thumping of Norwich in October was a welcome boost for Steve McClaren's stuttering outfit. Yet even big wins can be decided on the finest of margins. In the battle of the budget birds, the Magpies scored with all six of their shots on target against the Canaries. Only once in the past ten seasons has a Premier League team scored a higher total without seeing the opposition make a single save (Arsenal with seven against Blackburn in 2012).

There was another six-goal performance in the Premier League in October and this one came from Manchester City against Newcastle, led admirably by Sergio Agüero, a player who alternates almost weekly between crack and crock: you'll never get 38 games out of him but you might get 38 goals. In this match the Argentine became only the fifth player in Premier League history to score five goals in a single game, netting in the 42nd, 49th, 50th, 60th and 62nd minutes to leave Newcastle on their knees. Unsurprisingly, it was the quickest of the five fives, although Jermain Defoe deserves credit for being the only one to score all of his in a single half.

			Premier League five-goal hauls		
Date	**Player**	**Opponent**	**Min of first goal**	**Min of fifth goal**	**Gap**
03/10/15	Sergio Agüero	Newcastle United	42	62	20
22/11/09	Jermain Defoe	Wigan Athletic	51	87	36
19/09/99	Alan Shearer	Sheffield Wednesday	30	84	54
27/11/10	Dimitar Berbatov	Blackburn Rovers	2	70	68
04/03/95	Andrew Cole	Ipswich Town	19	87	68

Such displays from Agüero only consolidate the argument that he is the most effective forward yet seen in the Premier League, with his minutes-per-goal rate significantly better than any other player in the competition's history. An injury-free season or two and the City striker could even dip beneath the 100-minute mark, which is the sort of territory occupied by only the elite such as Lionel Messi. Agüero has even scored at the Britannia Stadium on a midweek evening. (Sadly, it was a Monday, rather than the statutory Tuesday.)

Player	Mins/goal	Goals
Sergio Agüero	107.76	102
Thierry Henry	121.79	175
Ruud van Nistelrooy	128.19	95
Daniel Sturridge	138.22	69
Luis Suárez	138.8	69
Robin van Persie	139.69	144
Edin Džeko	141.62	50
Alan Shearer	146.86	260
Ole Gunnar Solskjær	153.04	91
Michael Owen	153.55	150

José Mourinho's increasingly loose grip on the scenario unfolding at Chelsea was illustrated in the game against Southampton at Stamford Bridge. Willian had given the champions an early lead but shortly before half-time Ramires was booked for a foul, his fourth of the game, and Southampton proceeded to equalise from the subsequent possession. An infuriated Mourinho substituted Ramires for Nemanja Matić at the break, only to then take Matić off after 73 minutes, making the Serbian one of 284 players to come on and off in the same game, and one of 11 in 2015–16, more than you might have imagined, perhaps. One player in Premier League history, Keith Gillespie, has suffered this ignominy more than anyone else – four times, while the manager to employ it most often is Arsène Wenger (14 times, including Abou Diaby twice, possibly for injury-related reasons). As for Chelsea, Mourinho's tinkering in the Southampton game had no real effect, with the visitors winning the game 3-1 and not even allowing the Blues a shot on target in the second half.

Daniel Sturridge's fitness continued to mystify and torment Liverpool supporters in the autumn – brief cameos that reminded people of what he could do and then a retreat to the sidelines once more. In what would prove to be Brendan Rodgers' penultimate Premier League game in charge, Sturridge scored twice as his side edged past Aston Villa 3-2. Rodgers must have contemplated how much better his fortunes would have been had his main goal threat been able to play more frequently.

Just why Sturridge is revered so much at Anfield is shown by the table below. He has the best minutes-per-goal rate of any Liverpool striker in Premier League history, outpacing even Fernando Torres and Luis Suárez. As his technically superb goal in the Europa League Final demonstrated, a fit and focused Sturridge is something that any club would want.

Liverpool mins/goal – PL history	Mins/goal	Goals
Daniel Sturridge	118.51	43
Fernando Torres	121.32	65
Luis Suárez	138.80	69
Michael Owen	142.58	118
Robbie Fowler	158.33	128
Stan Collymore	185.42	26
Peter Crouch	207.95	22
Milan Baroš	213.21	19
Ian Rush	235.51	45
Emile Heskey	269.72	39

Data up until the end of the 2015–16 season.

October is stop-start domestically due to the spectre of international football but in 2015 England at least set a new record, namely ten consecutive wins in competitive games, a run that started immediately after the underwhelming display at the 2014 World Cup and encompassed the entirety of England's Euro 2016 qualifying campaign, with the standard of the teams in Group E not the greatest. Still, ten wins in a row is ten wins in a row.

November

Wayne Rooney's faltering form and the associated opprobrium from Manchester United fans reached a tipping point in November with another insipid display from the club captain in his team's 1-1 draw at Leicester. Whether Rooney's decline was entirely personal or partly down to the restrictive instructions placed on the team by Louis van Gaal was debatable, the depreciation of his contribution was not. As the table below starkly shows, Rooney's goal plus assist contribution in 2015 fell off a cliff, returning to a level last seen when he was a 16-year-old at Everton, when he often appeared as a substitute. There was a slight fall in 2014 after five years of excellent consistency from Rooney but the decline in 2015 was as inexplicable as it was dramatic, and his return to his normal level in the first half of 2016 only makes it stranger.

Wayne Rooney Premier League goal contribution by year

Year	Games played	Goals	Assists	G+A per game
2002	20	3	1	0.20
2003	30	7	5	0.40
2004	30	9	3	0.40
2005	36	17	7	0.67

**Wayne Rooney Premier League goal
contribution by year –** *continued*

Year	Games played	Goals	Assists	G+A per game
2006	34	14	9	0.68
2007	29	11	10	0.72
2008	31	11	9	0.65
2009	33	22	5	0.82
2010	23	13	7	0.87
2011	35	23	7	0.86
2012	**31**	**21**	**9**	**0.97**
2013	29	14	12	0.90
2014	28	16	5	0.75
2015	**31**	**6**	**2**	**0.26**
2016	13	6	5	0.85

By May 2016, Rooney had already matched his 2015 goal total and had three more assists than he had in the previous year, including a scooped peach for United's final goal of the season, at home to Bournemouth and converted by Ashley Young. The 2015–16 campaign was also the first time he had scored in the league, the FA Cup, the League Cup and the Champions League in the same season. Ensconced in his new, perhaps permanent, role in midfield, Rooney is still, according to the numbers at least, one of the most effective players in the Premier League. 2016–17 should see him become Manchester United's all-time record scorer, an honour he already holds for the national team.

Frustratingly patchy, yes, but Rooney's contribution and ability is in danger of being written out of history by those who see him not being able to match two of the best players of all time.

On 1 November, Everton's Arouna Koné scored a hat-trick against Sunderland, the eighth of the season so far at that point. If that seems quite a lot for that stage of the season then you're right, it is. In fact, only in 2011–12 had the eight hat-trick mark been reached sooner (29 October), and there have been four entire seasons (2001–02, 2005–06, 2006–07 and 2008–09) where there weren't even eight trebles in the whole campaign.

It wasn't only Wayne Rooney struggling at Manchester United as autumn turned to winter. The whole club seemed to be afflicted by an ennui that turned their once fearsome reputation to dust. Home games in particular were a bleak experience for the Old Trafford faithful (who were having to show faith at last), with five goalless draws at the Theatre of Dreams between 25 October and 28 December.

Occasionally there were brief glimpses of the former United. *'Manchester United never get beaten. We may occasionally run out of time but we never believe we can be beaten'*, former manager Sir Alex Ferguson once said, and he was true to his word. The table below shows all the occasions that Manchester United have won Premier League games via last-minute goals, and, by doing so at Watford in November, United did so for the first time in the post-Ferguson era. What once was commonplace now seemed like mere nostalgia.

As the table shows, there were a remarkable number of 90th-minute winners in the latter days of Ferguson's reign. Of course, the most famous of these goals is the first one on the list, the late, late Steve Bruce effort that edged Ferguson towards his first Premier League title and in doing so created the very concept of 'Fergie-time'.

Manchester United last-minute winners in the Premier League

Date	Opponent	For	Against	Venue	Winning goal time
10/04/93	Sheffield Wednesday	2	1	H	90
01/01/03	Sunderland	2	1	H	90
18/01/03	Chelsea	2	1	H	90
22/01/06	Liverpool	1	0	H	90
06/03/06	Wigan Athletic	2	1	A	90
03/03/07	Liverpool	1	0	A	90
06/12/08	Sunderland	1	0	H	90
17/01/09	Bolton Wanderers	1	0	A	90
05/04/09	Aston Villa	3	2	H	90
20/09/09	Manchester City	4	3	H	90
17/04/10	Manchester City	1	0	A	90
06/11/10	Wolverhampton Wanderers	2	1	H	90
26/02/12	Norwich City	2	1	A	90
02/09/12	Southampton	3	2	A	90
09/12/12	Manchester City	3	2	A	90
26/12/12	Newcastle United	4	3	H	90
21/11/15	Watford	2	1	A	90

Arsenal ended the month by continuing their tradition of flying to Norwich for their game at Carrow Road. The flight time is approximately 14 minutes, and yet the game itself saw the ball out of play for 37 minutes and three seconds, enough time for more than two and a half flights, or a sightseeing flyby over Thetford Forest.

★

At the time, as November drew to a close, Jamie Vardy's 11th consecutive game-scoring run was the biggest positive thing to happen for Leicester in the Premier League. Vardy had scored a late equaliser against Bournemouth on the Bank Holiday weekend in August, in what, at the time, looked like a valuable point between two teams who might well be contesting survival in May 2016.

Vardy then scored in Leicester's next game, another equaliser, this time making it 2-2 against Aston Villa in a game the Foxes went on to win 3-2, possibly the first inkling that this team under Claudio Ranieri had something different about them. Vardy, already notable as a player who clambered up the divisions from non-league football with Fleetwood to the English top flight, kept going as the leaves turned brown and then fell slowly to the ground. In three games in September, four games in October and three more in November, he put his name on the scoresheet, surely, but never slowly, hunting down Ruud van Nistelrooy's Premier League record of 2003.

Twelve years earlier, the Dutchman had scored in ten successive games, beating his own record set the previous year, with only Daniel Sturridge coming close to it in recent campaigns, scoring in eight successive games during Liverpool's helter-skelter 2013–14 campaign.

Date of final game in scoring run	Player	Nationality	Run of games scored in
28/11/15	**Jamie Vardy**	**England**	11
23/08/03	Ruud van Nistelrooy	Netherlands	10
19/01/02	Ruud van Nistelrooy	Netherlands	8
23/02/14	Daniel Sturridge	England	8

(continued)

Date of final game in scoring run	Player	Nationality	Run of games scored in
05/02/94	Mark Stein	England	7
23/11/94	Ian Wright	England	7
30/11/96	Alan Shearer	England	7
09/05/2000	Thierry Henry	France	7
11/02/08	Emmanuel Adebayor	Togo	7

By way of neatness, the goal that broke van Nistelrooy's record came against Manchester United and was a microcosm of the Midlands' side's season. A quick break (Leicester led the entire division in counter-attack goals in 2015–16), a defence-splitting pass by one of a myriad unsung heroes, in this case Christian Fuchs, and Vardy reaching the ball ahead of the opposition defence thanks to his unrelenting pace before squeezing it over David de Gea's right leg.

In total, during the 11-game run Vardy scored 13 times (54% of his seasonal total in the Premier League), hitting 23 shots on target and 49 shots overall. Between that weekend in August and that weekend in November, Vardy outscored eight teams, including reigning champions Chelsea, who scored 12 goals despite having 111 more shots than the Leicester player in that period.

But if Vardy was the score-man, his achievement also spawned a pretty tenacious straw-man argument. Firstly, his position as a *Premier League* record breaker was used to imply that, once again, all football that took place before 1992 was being deliberately ignored. Not so; rather, the further you go back, the less complete records are and the less certain we can be. Some sections of the press latched onto Jimmy Dunne's 12-game scoring streak for Sheffield United in the 1930s, as if there was some sort of collusion against him (mysteriously he wasn't mentioned in 2003 when van Nistelrooy set the ten-game mark). Ignoring the reality that even if all goalscoring runs back to 1888 could be properly verified (they can't), comparing Vardy with van Nistelrooy is a much fairer match-up, given the equipment, the rules, the tactics and the fitness levels of the game are considerably different from the 1930s. Even in the 1980s, before the Premier League had been created, people rarely used records from before the Second World War, recognising even then that football in sepia was largely a different game.

By mid-November, it was apparent that this was no average Premier League season. Five teams – Crystal Palace, Leicester, Stoke, Watford and West Ham – were enjoying their best ever starts to a Premier League season. Only Leicester and, arguably, West Ham maintained it for the rest of the campaign but Palace, Stoke and Watford achieved an FA Cup final appearance, another top-half finish and Premier League survival respectively. A job well done.

3.

Squeaky Glum Time: How Manchester United Fell Off Their Perch

'Your job now is to stand by the new manager'

Sir Alex Ferguson, May 2013

Manchester United reached one European Cup final in the first 21 years of Sir Alex Ferguson's time as manager, compared to three in his last six years, but it would certainly be a mistake to conclude that he left the club in a robust condition. Instead, the last few seasons of his reign were an acute display of his almost supernatural ability to extract the very last drops of talent and effort from players who might not have been the finest he had had at his disposal in his time at Old Trafford, but who did enough to extend the Ferguson legend. What came after his departure only reinforced his legacy. David Moyes and Louis van Gaal, two managers with different pedigrees, both had proven long-term ability to rebuild and shape clubs. But even they were left bereft as they tried to follow Ferguson.

Looking back at the closing act of Alex Ferguson's tenure, it was widely reported after he had departed that he had planned to end his time as manager in 2012 but was so stung by the late-season collapse that handed neighbours Manchester City the title that he stayed on for an additional season to regain the Premier League crown one last time. One final effort from a squad that looked like it needed updating and refreshing in certain areas but who were still ready to do their master's bidding.

RVP MVP

The one major arrival at Old Trafford in the summer of 2012 was Robin van Persie from Arsenal. The Dutch forward had enjoyed a highly productive 18-month period at the London side, and, perhaps fearing that he would never get a chance to win a Premier League title at the Emirates, was receptive to a move away in 2012, with both Manchester City and United eager to take him on.

As the table below shows, van Persie's first six seasons with the Gunners saw him suffer repeated injury absences, with his 28 appearances in 2008–09 his best figure (although he managed only 11 goals that season). The real transformation came in the 2010–11 season. An ankle injury in the autumn left van Persie in his familiar position on the sidelines but when he returned it was with renewed vigour. Starting from March, he began a highly unlikely sequence of 90 consecutive Premier League appearances without any absences, a run that ended five games after the departure of Ferguson from Old Trafford, whereby he sunk back into his old patterns.

Robin van Persie Premier League career

Season	Team	Games played	Goals	Goals/ 90	Shot conversion rate	Played game (%)
2004–05	Arsenal	26	5	0.46	14	68.4
2005–06	Arsenal	24	5	0.37	12	63.2
2006–07	Arsenal	22	11	0.68	21	57.9
2007–08	Arsenal	15	7	0.58	15	39.5
2008–09	Arsenal	28	11	0.45	13	73.7
2009–10	Arsenal	16	9	0.64	17	42.1
2010–11	Arsenal	25	18	0.92	21	65.8
2011–12	Arsenal	38	30	0.81	21	**100.0**

Robin van Persie Premier League career – *continued*

Season	Team	Games played	Goals	Goals/ 90	Shot conversion rate	Played game (%)
2012–13	Manchester United	38	26	0.75	22.03	100.0
2013–14	Manchester United	21	12	0.68	26.09	55.3
2014–15	Manchester United	27	10	0.43	15.15	71.1

Van Persie's goals-per-90 rate in 2010–11 was a career best 0.92 and, while it dipped in the subsequent four seasons, that period is what marked him out as a Premier League 'great', 96 goals in 149 appearances a notable improvement on 66 in the previous 131.

Ultimately, the decision by van Persie to move to Old Trafford rather than the equally interested reigning champions at the Etihad in summer 2012 was a crucial one for his new manager. City may have secured their first Premier League crown only on goal difference from United the previous season, but van Persie was democratically the best player in the league at the time (he had won both the PFA and Football Writers' player of the year awards in 2012). Adding him to either squad was almost certain to be as close as you can get to a guarantee of success in 2012–13, particularly as the player was now demonstrating hitherto unseen robustness to complement his sharpness.

And so it proved, with van Persie's Arsenal streak continuing straight through his first season at Old Trafford, and epitomised by the first-half hat-trick he scored in the home win against Aston Villa that sealed the Premier League title in April 2013. Twenty-six goals was four short of the total he managed in his final season with Arsenal but a winners' medal was decent recompense.

The Comeback Kings

Yet even with their new Dutch striker installed, Manchester United's progress in the Premier League was not the serene cruise to glory that the team's eventual 11-point winning margin suggests in retrospect.

An opening weekend defeat to Everton was followed by four successive wins, with van Persie scoring five times, but the manner of United's victories was notable – with comebacks required against Fulham, Southampton (where van Persie missed a penalty and still scored a hat-trick, with two of the goals coming in the final three minutes) and Liverpool. It was exciting, for both Manchester United supporters and the media, to get behind a team who looked like they would throw away points before van Persie or Wayne Rooney pulled them back from the brink. Sadly for the managers who were to follow Ferguson, it's a type of approach that's fundamentally unsustainable.

As the table below shows, by the end of the season, 29 of United's points had come from games in which they'd trailed at some point. Only Newcastle in 2001–02 (with 34 points) have ever recorded more in a single season. It wasn't just comebacks either, but also the sheer number of goals at both ends. Away at Reading in December, United trailed after only eight minutes but 34 minutes into the game they were 4-3 up, a scoreline that miraculously lasted until the end of the game. Up until Boxing Day, United kept only three clean sheets in 19 league games, and their halfway report showed a total of 76 goals (for and against). This was breathtaking, roiling football that lives in the memory (the final game of the season, against West Brom, was the first 5-5 in the top flight since QPR and Newcastle had shared ten goals in 1984). This kind of form, however, isn't particularly the sign of a good team.

Highest number of comeback points in a single PL season	Season	Wins	Pts
Newcastle United	2001–02	10	34
Manchester United	**2012–13**	**9**	**29**
West Bromwich Albion	2010–11	6	27
Arsenal	1999–2000	7	24
Manchester United	1999–2000	6	24
Everton	2002–03	7	24
Tottenham Hotspur	2010–11	6	24
Arsenal	2011–12	7	24

And yet the very concept of Fergie-time, as discussed elsewhere in this book, is a form of confirmation bias. So powerful are folk memories of United's comeback against Sheffield Wednesday at Easter 1993 that any future late surge from Ferguson's team was cast in a holy light, whereas other teams doing the same thing fade into the past. Technically if you're associating never-say-die attitude in the Premier League with a manager then it should be another knight, Sir Bobby Robson, who has the honour after that toing-and-froing in 2001–02 but he doesn't occupy that role. Say 'comebacks and Bobby Robson' to most fans and either Italia 90 as a whole or specifically England's quarter-final against Cameroon is what will come into the mind's eye, not a season in the early 2000s when Newcastle were good but not as good as they had been six or seven years earlier. We are not remembered by our deeds but by the deeds that are remembered.

Challenger Deficit

The league table doesn't lie. Over 38 games, the best team wins. Well, that's true: the team that gains the most points is the 'best' side, but the presence of a viable challenger (or challengers) makes it a much more memorable and worthy achievement. Think of United's battle with Manchester City a year earlier, or City's battle with Liverpool, Chelsea and Arsenal a year later for examples of how a close-fought race can elevate a season. Even Ferguson's first Premier League title saw his team pushed close by the gaudy spectre of former United manager Ron Atkinson at Aston Villa.

In contrast, 2012–13, while it was undeniably a title win, it was never really a *title win*. The announcement of the manager's forthcoming retirement in early May ended a spring of tedium. Having reached the halfway point of the season with a seven-point lead, the nearest it came to being pegged back was when United were held to a 1-1 draw by Spurs in late January and Manchester City closed to five points. Yet within three matches United were 12 points clear and all but home and dry.

Game	Points gap over second-place team
19	7
20	7
21	7
22	7
23	5
24	7
25	9
26	12
27	12
28	12
29	15
30	15
31	12
32	15
33	13
34	13
35	13
36	10
37	10
38	11

The final winning margin of 11 points was the second biggest of any of United's Premier League title wins, with only the monstrous effort of the reigning European champions in 1999–2000 (18 points) seeing a larger gap. That season ended, despite the domestic success, with Ferguson taking steps to reshape his side, convinced that future Champions League honours were impossible without a structural and philosophical reconstruction. He had taken similar steps in 1995 when jettisoning the likes of Paul Ince and Andrei Kanchelskis and promoting what would become the 'class of 92' to front-line duty. Put simply, Alex Ferguson was not the sort of manager to baulk from tearing up a proven blueprint when the time came. Yet in 2013, either because he was demob happy or because he truly believed what he was asserting, the outgoing manager was content to state that the team he had left his successor was more than capable of continuing where he had left off.

Title win under Ferguson	Winning margin
1992–93	10
1993–94	8
1995–96	4
1996–97	7
1998–99	1
1999–2000	18
2000–01	10
2002–03	5
2006–07	6
2007–08	2
2008-09	4
2010–11	9
2012-13	11

The Poisoned Legacy

'The quality of this league winning squad, and the balance of ages within it, bodes well for continued success at the highest level whilst the structure of the youth set-up will ensure that the long-term future of the club remains a bright one.'

The above quote from Alex Ferguson at the end of his tenure didn't strike anyone as outlandish when it was made. Manchester United's success in the 1990s and 2000s had been as much a product of their talent development as it had their power in the transfer market. Big-money signings had been made regularly but, of the European giants, only Barcelona had promoted more players from within. Once the Glazer family had leveraged the club to take full control in 2005 there was a reduced capacity, or desire, to pay the sort of transfer fees that had brought the likes of Juan Sebastián Verón to the club earlier in the decade. Ferguson, whether because it solidified his position within the new regime, or for other reasons, was happy to go along with this and thus the policy of promoting youngsters continued.

The problem was that Manchester United's 1990s crop was a once-in-several-generations yield, a gang of local lads (and Essex's David Beckham) who grew as players together and reached the first XI at roughly the same time. Youth development by big teams in the twenty-first century is more akin to gold prospecting than agriculture, with a vast number of prospects from a wide geographical area passing through clubs in the hope that a star will emerge. Often the best return is a fairly regular amount of transfer income from smaller teams happy to purchase players who have been educated at one of the giants. Often, though, their ability does not match their CV.

The table below shows all players at Manchester United to make between one and three Premier League appearances for the club in the period between August 2005 and May 2013, and is largely a list of the lost, with experiments such as Dong Fangzhuo now largely forgotten by most fans. Bebé is more memorable, mainly due to the size of his fee and his terrible performances at the club (he made two substitute appearances in the Premier League and was substituted back off in one of them). There were still talented players in the system, though, with the most obvious being Paul Pogba. However, his refusal to sign a new contract meant he joined Juventus in 2012 and United had let a gem slip through their fingers. Pogba, of course, typified the new era of youth development at big clubs, in that he was poached from La Havre when he was 16 and relocated many hundreds of kilometres north, in a different country. To expect the modern player to have the loyalty of, say, Paul Scholes, is wildly unrealistic.

Man Utd players with three or fewer PL apps (2005–13)

Player	Country	Games played	Date of birth
Will Keane	England	1	11/01/93
Ben Amos	England	1	10/04/90
Kieran Lee	England	1	22/06/88
Lee Martin	England	1	09/02/87
Dong Fangzhuo	China PR	1	23/01/85
Manucho	Angola	1	07/03/83
Liam Miller	Republic of Ireland	1	13/02/81
Tim Howard	USA	1	06/03/79
Nick Powell	England	2	23/03/94
Ezekiel Fryers	England	2	09/09/92
Bebé	Portugal	2	12/07/90
Richard Eckersley	England	2	12/03/89
Fraizer Campbell	England	2	13/09/87
Zoran Tošić	Serbia	2	28/04/87
Paul Pogba	France	3	15/03/93
Possebon Rodrigo	Brazil	3	13/02/89
Ritchie De Laet	Belgium	3	28/11/88
Danny Simpson	England	3	04/01/87

All of this meant that Ferguson's statement about the club being well set up for the future was a dubious one, as proved pretty quickly under his replacement David Moyes (known, in the infuriating habit of the English media since José Mourinho said he was the 'special one' in 2004, as 'the chosen one'. Jürgen Klopp at Liverpool, of course is currently inhabiting the role of 'the normal one').

Moyes' Boys

Despite well-worn stories about how Manchester United had struggled in the 1970s after the retirement of Sir Matt Busby, due to the impossibility of replacing a man who still had such influence and power at the club, Sir Alex Ferguson played a major role in deciding on his successor. He, and others, went for Everton's David Moyes, a fellow Scot who had given the Merseyside club 11 years of strong, if not spectacular, service. As is often the way with clubs who have had a manager in place for a long time, one of their main desires is to find a successor who may be able to install a similarly long dynasty. In this context, Moyes made more sense than, say, José Mourinho, even though the reality is that most managers are effective for only a short period and men such as Ferguson, Arsène Wenger and Guy Roux are absolutely the exception.

However, Moyes' bleak 51-game spell in charge of Manchester United was far worse than anyone had envisaged and, while not completely his fault, he did make errors that compounded the bad luck that hounded him at the club.

The most decisive thing Moyes did at Old Trafford was to immediately dispose of Alex Ferguson's backroom staff (Mike Phelan, René Meulensteen and Eric Steele) and bring in his Goodison lieutenants (Steve Round, Chris Woods and Jimmy Lumsden). Understandable, but when no new signings were made until the deadline day arrival of Marouane Fellaini from

Everton, it meant that you had Ferguson's team, with all its experience and memory of Premier League and Champions League titles, being managed and coached by four people who didn't have that experience.

Statistically there are a few key trends from the Moyes (almost) season. Firstly, as an example of both the turbulence at the club and the new manager's indecision, Manchester United played a unique starting XI in all 51 of Moyes' games in charge of the team. Fifty-one matches, 51 different combination of 11 players. It's not unheard of for teams to achieve success with such variation in their line-up (indeed, Manchester United themselves won the Premier League in 1996–97 while naming 38 unique starting XIs in 38 games), but as Leicester demonstrated so pointedly in 2015–16, a settled core can do wonders for your consistency and solidity.

Secondly, certain trends that affected Moyes at Everton continued in his time at Old Trafford. He had never been able to win away at any of the Big Four clubs who dominated the competition in the 2000s before the rise of Manchester City. This was explainable, perhaps, when you considered Everton's resources compared to these opponents. However, plenty of clubs much smaller than the Toffees enjoyed occasional victories at the cathedrals of the modern game, so it did start to look like an actual issue for the Scot.

But surely things would change once he was installed in the Theatre of Dreams? Well, no. He had only three games (obviously he couldn't win away at Old Trafford as Manchester United boss, although you suspect Ferguson would have found a way) to change his fortunes but couldn't do it, losing at Liverpool and Chelsea and playing out what the BBC described as a 'grim goalless stalemate' at Arsenal in February.

David Moyes away at the 'traditional Big Four'			
Opponent	**W**	**D**	**L**	**Pts/game**
Arsenal	0	4	9	0.31
Chelsea	0	6	7	0.46
Liverpool	0	6	6	0.50
Manchester United	0	3	8	0.27
Total	**0**	**19**	**30**	**0.39**

Crossfire Hurricane

By February the realisation that a top four finish was going to be unlikely was becoming more apparent. United were 15 points behind the leaders Arsenal and seven points adrift of the top four. A mini-revival over Christmas had been followed by more defeats to the likes of Stoke, and heading into the home match with Fulham on 9 February, the outlook was gloomy. In the Ferguson era, Fulham at Old Trafford had been the very essence of an easy ride (11 wins from 12 and an average of 2.6 United goals per game). This time, however, the Londoners were being managed (briefly as it turned out), by former United coach René Meulensteen, whose ejection from the club by Moyes seven months earlier surely still rankled. The game that ensued was an indictment of everything United had morphed into under their new manager.

Fulham took the lead after 19 minutes and then set out to defend their lead, knowing that Moyesian United had frequently been unable to break down stubborn opponents (after the comeback heroics in the final season under Alex Ferguson, United ended 2014–15 with a record of 12 defeats from the 19 Premier League games in which they'd trailed). United set about their task with the furrowed brows of put-upon yeomen, with their main plan of attack being that most English of weapons, the cross.

Over the course of the game, David Moyes watched his side put in 81 crosses – a record for any game from 2006 onwards. Getting on for one every minute of the match and neither of United's eventual goals came via that route. As you can see from the list of the five highest cross totals by a single Premier League team below, a combined 352 crosses produced just two goals. It's certainly a method, just not a very good one. Fulham's Dan Burn offered the ultimate, er, burn, when he commented, 'I was just saying to the lads that I've never headed that many balls since the Conference. But at the end of the day I'm happy for them to play like that.' From European champions to Conference tactics in six years, no wonder the fans were cross.

Date	Team	Opponent	Total Crosses	Goals From Crosses
09/02/14	Manchester United	Fulham	81	0
20/09/08	Liverpool	Stoke City	72	0
31/12/11	Manchester United	Blackburn Rovers	71	1
13/05/12	Manchester City	Queens Park Rangers	68	1
06/12/08	Manchester United	Sunderland	60	0

Two months later Moyes was gone. There were legitimate complaints about how he had been hamstrung in the transfer market with neither of his two major signings (Fellaini in August and Juan Mata in January) adequately filling any gaps in the squad. This looks valid, especially given the largesse that his successor, Louis van Gaal, was handed subsequently. But, more than anything, the Moyes experiment was a vicious circle where, with a few notable exceptions, including Wayne Rooney, he was managing players who were performing far below the level they had for Alex Ferguson. With each mini-slump, their confidence in their new manager faded as did his

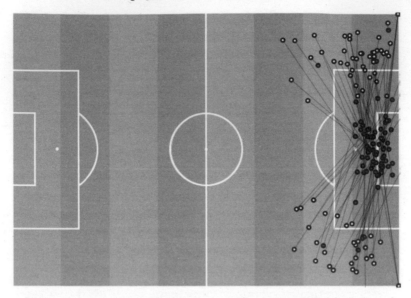

Manchester United crosses v Fulham, 9 February 2014

belief that these players were good enough for Manchester United. In that scenario, it's easier for a team to get rid of one man than gut an entire squad. So the club did something they had not done since autumn 1986; they fired the manager. The hope was that Moyes would act as a lightning rod for the post-Fergie blues, and that the new man would be able to start afresh. It didn't quite work out like that . . .

The Philosopher King

In an advert for the club's official wine supplier, Casillero del Diablo, in 2011, Wayne Rooney utters the words 'a new devil is arriving . . . they say he is a legend'. Was this a haunting prophecy of Louis van Gaal's advent as manager in 2014? Desperate people can latch onto the tiniest slivers of hope and the Netherlands' performance at the 2014 World Cup in Brazil, a tournament that came after their van Gaal had been confirmed as Moyes' replacement at Old Trafford, certainly restored hope to the United faithful that the good times were on their way back. Robin van Persie's celebration after his diving header against Spain, saw him run to van Gaal and high-five, well, more like middle-five, his manager, so he was clearly going to his top form again in 2014–15. While van Gaal's decision to replace goalkeeper Jasper Cillessen with Tim Krul ahead of the penalty shootout win against Costa Rica was hailed as the manoeuvre of a maestro. The £1.6 million in his salary for image rights indicated the heft of the man.

Unfortunately, the van Gaal who arrived at Old Trafford was not the Brazilian gambler but instead the more stoic version who had been ushered out of the manager's office at Bayern Munich a couple of months early in 2011. A win in America against Liverpool in the final of the International Champions Cup was as poor an indicator of future fortune for United (as it was for tournament top-scorer Stevan Jovetić). When the proper stuff began the outcome was a little less enticing. With an opening day home defeat to Swansea, it was the first time United had lost at Old Trafford on the first weekend of the season since 1972. Ninety minutes into his reign, van Gaal had managed to out-Moyes Moyes. It also meant that United had suffered ten home reversals in the Premier League in 495 days, with the previous ten losses coming over a period of 2562 days. If you wanted an illustration of how the post-Ferguson era differed from the glory years, there it was.

Throughout the autumn, things didn't improve for United's new Dutch supremo. The emergency glamour signing Ángel Di María was pitched straight into an agricultural battle against Burnley at Turf Moor in his first game, a match that eventually ended 0-0. United avoided starting the season with four winless games for the first time since 1986, by beating the fortunately hapless QPR 4-0 in September. Plunged into the second round of the League Cup for the first time in many seasons (the cruel fate of every Premier League team not involved in European competition), United promptly lost 4-0 to League One side MK Dons, not even managing a shot on target until the closing 20 minutes of the game.

Negative records were tumbling seemingly on a daily basis, with United's 5-3 defeat at newly promoted Leicester in their fifth league game being the first time in Premier League history that the 13-time champions had lost a match in which they had led by two goals. The fact that it came against a team which *looked* destined for relegation just made things worse. More on that later.

Like Moyes before him, van Gaal was quickly realising that the tools he had been left to work with were not really adequate in all areas. Although he had been allowed to plunder the transfer market in a way that Moyes hadn't, his signings, such as Di María, weren't really covering up the team's failings. By the first week of October United had already used 30 players in the Premier League, only three short of their record spread in a Premier League season (they ended the campaign matching that total of 33 and did so once again in 2015–16).

One small but happy consequence of the chopping and changing under the van Gaal regime has been the associated reliance on youth. In his two seasons in charge of the club, the Dutchman has given Premier League debuts to 13 players aged under 23, two more than any other club except Liverpool. For an institution so wedded to the heritage of the 'class of 92' the emergence of players such as Marcus Rashford and the introduction of potential superstars such as Anthony Martial (however steep the price) has at least freshened up a team which by the final season under Ferguson had reached an average age of almost 29. It was even more pronounced in 2015–16, with Manchester United responsible for nearly a quarter (23%) of all minutes played by teenagers in the Premier League in that particular campaign, just slightly ahead of Tottenham. But while Mauricio Pochettino's belief and trust in youth is well known, the nagging feeling with van Gaal is that, had United's squad been fitter, or more sensibly constructed, youth would not have been given its chance quite so readily.

Minutes played by teenagers in PL 2015–16

Club	Minutes played
Manchester United	2,638
Tottenham Hotspur	2,384
Everton	1,489
Liverpool	1,433
Manchester City	778
Aston Villa	628
Arsenal	573
Southampton	450
Chelsea	411
West Bromwich Albion	292
West Ham United	210
Leicester City	177
Newcastle United	67
Sunderland	52

If things had carried on under van Gaal the way they had started, the United board would have had to dispense with him even sooner than they had Moyes. Yet a six-game winning streak in November and December not only saved him in the short term, but set a pattern for his first two seasons. He would flirt with utter disaster, leading to situations where he sank into the abyss and faced imminent dismissal, only to pull himself free with an important result or two. The winter ended badly, but, from late February to early April, United won six consecutive league games, a run culminating in a 4-2 humping of neighbours City, pushing them to second place and within eight points of leaders Chelsea. More importantly, they were nine points clear of fifth place in the race for that commercially important Champions League qualification. The modern dream.

Then, just as talk turned to a concerted title challenge in 2015–16, van Gaal's team won one of their last six Premier

League games and finished fourth, 17 points adrift of José Mourinho's new champions. That run included three successive defeats without scoring a single goal, the first time that had happened since April 1989. Would the real Manchester United please stand up?

One final note on the 2014–15 season. United had to wait until mid-February to get their first penalty of the campaign in the Premier League. Of course, the image of the Ferguson era was that the team could summon penalties at will (even though the reality is that Liverpool have consistently led the division in this respect and indeed were the first team to reach 100), and while this is a wild exaggeration of the persuasiveness of Fergie's yellers, there has certainly been a spot-kick slowdown for the Red Devils.

Period	Games per pen	Games per pen conceded
Ferguson's last three seasons	5	13
Moyes/van Gaal era	9	11

As the table shows, in Ferguson's final three seasons United could expect a penalty every five games in the Premier League, while they conceded them at a rate of one every 13 matches. They haven't been conceding them at a vastly quicker rate under the Scot's successors, but they are waiting almost twice as long (nine games) to see the referee point sagely to the spot in their favour. Conspiracy lovers will, at this point, stroke their beards and nod knowingly but the team has entered the penalty area much less in the new era, so the chances of getting a penalty are, understandably, reduced.

Farce and Furious

For Manchester United and Louis van Gaal, 2015–16 was like 2014–15, only more so. A return to the Champions League, with a kindly group draw, looked like a solid platform for the manager to build on, while a dismal start to the league campaign by defending champions Chelsea meant the title was a more realistic opportunity, especially with the likes of Manchester City and Liverpool also in turmoil.

United began like a train, albeit one that goes quite slowly and in a repetitive circular route. A 1-0 win against Tottenham on the opening day looked, like a salad with E. coli, good at first glance but the solitary strike was an own goal from Kyle Walker and the home team didn't record an actual shot on target until the 65th minute. A paucity of shots on target became a theme as the new season progressed and, by January, all 91 other clubs in the Premier League and Football League had managed more shots on target at home. The Theatre of Dreams had become the Odeum of Tedium.

Just how rarely United hit the target compared to other elite clubs in 2015–16 is shown in the table below. Bayern and Real are hitting more than seven and a half shots on target per game, while United, across the big five European leagues, are down in 61st place (just behind Bournemouth). On the rare occasions that the team cut loose and attacked with something resembling vigour, the United fans were quick to get behind them. Too often, though, they were left rigid watching a team trapped in a philosophical straitjacket without a key.

Rank	Team	Shots, on target	SOT/game
1	FC Bayern München	246	7.69
2	Real Madrid	276	7.67
3	Barcelona	249	6.92
4	Tottenham Hotspur	241	6.69
5	Paris Saint-Germain	231	6.60
6	Borussia Dortmund	206	6.44
7	Napoli	225	6.25
8	Borussia Mönchengladbach	183	5.72
9	VfL Wolfsburg	181	5.66
10	Manchester City	202	5.61
61	Manchester United	135	3.86

A corollary of a lack of shots on target, combined with administrative errors that meant that Real Madrid didn't buy United's very talented goalkeeper on the closing day of the summer transfer window, is goalless draws. And Manchester United, as 2015 drew to a close, became very *very* good at goalless draws. By Christmas, van Gaal had clocked up the 11th 0-0 of his short reign with, incredibly, six of those coming since the end of October.

And while 2016 saw a reduction in United's 0-0 affliction, van Gaal remains the manager in the club's history most susceptible to 90 minutes of football and nothing to show for it. The table below shows all United managers with 50 or more games, with the Dutchman clear of Jack Robson who led the club in the 1910s. David Moyes isn't on the list for obvious longevity-based reasons but, if you're interested, his 0-0 rate was a mere 5.9%.

Manager	League games	% goalless
Louis van Gaal	73	11.0%
Jack Robson	116	10.3%
Dave Sexton	168	9.5%
John Chapman	206	9.2%
Tommy Docherty	188	9.0%
Ron Atkinson	223	9.0%
Frank O'Farrell	64	7.8%
Wilf McGuinness	65	7.7%
Ernest Mangall	330	7.6%
Walter Crickmer	98	7.1%
John Bentley	86	7.0%
Herbert Bamlett	188	6.9%
Sir Alex Ferguson	1035	6.9%
Scott Duncan	224	6.3%
James West	51	5.9%
Sir Matt Busby	985	5.2%

By the end of January United had mustered just two first-half goals at home all season, a figure players as varied as Matt Ritchie, Scott Sinclair and Mauro Zarate could match.

Endgame

The closing weeks of what would become Louis van Gaal's second and final season at the club were inconsistent, and thus maddeningly similar to his reign. United beat title-chasing Arsenal at home (via a Marcus Rashford league debut brace), but then lost at West Brom. They hauled themselves back into the race for fourth place by winning away at a weakening Manchester City but then were eviscerated by Tottenham at White Hart Lane. In their pomp under Ferguson, United would invariably win at Spurs, famously coming from 3-0 down to win 5-3. This time Tottenham's three-goal lead remained constant.

Nevertheless, ten points from their next four matches, combined with a pre-Guardiola slowdown from Manchester City, meant that United and van Gaal knew that wins in their final two games would secure a top four finish. Even four points could be enough if City drew their last game at Swansea.

Complicating matters was the fact that their penultimate outing also happened to be West Ham's last ever match at Upton Park/the Boleyn Ground (select your preferred moniker), and the Hammers were suitably motivated to end their days in this part of east London in raucous fashion. An energetic atmosphere outside the ground meant that the kick-off was delayed, with United's coach coming under attack, something that van Gaal later claimed affected his players. In fact, three of United's last seven Premier League fixtures failed to kick off at the allotted time; where once they were the masters of snatching something from games in the dying minutes, now their games never seemed to finish for more prosaic reasons.

If you want a snapshot of van Gaal's time at Manchester United, the West Ham game is the perfect example. In a match they realistically had to win, United managed just three shots in the entire game, yet still found themselves leading 2-1 at one point. No matter, two goals in four minutes late on sealed the three points for the Londoners and put fourth place out of United's hands once again. As the table below shows, in Premier League games for which individual shot totals are available (from 2003 onwards), five of United's ten lowest totals came in the torrid two years under their Dutch manager. Three shots in 90-plus minutes of football for a team assembled at great expense is poor. To do it more than once is a sign of a problem with the manager's tactical approach. To do it in a game that Champions League qualification is hinging on is abysmal.

Date	Opponent	Total shots	Manager
10/05/16	**West Ham United**	3	van Gaal
08/12/14	**Southampton**	3	van Gaal
18/09/05	Liverpool	4	Ferguson
10/04/16	**Tottenham Hotspur**	5	van Gaal
20/03/16	**Manchester City**	5	van Gaal
31/10/15	**Crystal Palace**	5	van Gaal
10/11/13	Arsenal	5	Moyes
20/01/13	Tottenham Hotspur	5	Ferguson
30/04/12	Manchester City	5	Ferguson
15/01/05	Liverpool	5	Ferguson

Manchester City's draw on the final day at Swansea and the unusual and semi-farcical postponement of United's game against Bournemouth meant that when they finally faced the Cherries two days later than planned, the game was up. Needing to win by 19 goals (no Premier League team has ever recorded more than 16 shots on target in a single game), the match was sparsely attended and had the air of the sort of celebrity charity games that Old Trafford hosts so often.

A 3-1 win ensured that United ended the league season with fewer than 50 goals for only the fifth time since the Second World War and their haul of 49 goals was only one more than they scored in cup games during the treble season of 1998–9. How times change. Furthermore, Bournemouth's late goal ended goalkeeper David de Gea's hopes of matching Arsenal's Petr Cech with 16 clean sheets, and claiming that most modern of prizes, the Golden Glove. De Gea, who had kept United in so many games during the campaign and often seemed to be fighting a one-man battle with the opposition, had seen his season, like a struggling business from the 1980s, start with a broken fax and end with a bouncing Cech.

Van Gaal did at least end his time with a trophy, winning

the FA Cup four days after the Bournemouth game, thanks to an extra-time comeback win against Crystal Palace (scoring twice from three shots on target, *plus ça change*). But when he replaced the injured Marcus Rashford up front with a winger (Ashley Young) while having strikers on the wing and in central midfield respectively (Anthony Martial and Wayne Rooney), it seemed as if the manager was determined to end his time in charge by bewildering the fans as usual. His time was definitely ending: as his players cavorted with the trophy, sources confirmed the imminent appointment of José Mourinho as United's third manager in three years, echoing the equally sudden departure of Manchester City manager Roberto Mancini after the FA Cup final in 2013. The showpiece occasion where managers walk out with their teams has turned into one where teams walk out on their managers.

Like Moyes, van Gaal is now a footnote in the club's adjustment post-Ferguson. In time they'll likely be lumped together as a disappointing double, although they were, as we've seen, subtly different. Moyes failed to get Ferguson's last squad to play for him in the same manner, while van Gaal was given the resources, and the time, to rebuild, yet found himself adrift in a Premier League that was, often literally, moving too fast for him. It wasn't his age – after all he's only two months older than Claudio Ranieri – but, rather, his rigid inflexibility in a league that prefers and cherishes anarchy.

December–January

December

When it came on 17 December, José Mourinho's sacking at Chelsea seemed as inevitable as those of all the other managers at Stamford Bridge who have been disposed of in the past decade. Yet the raw facts are still shocking. It was only a matter of months since Chelsea had won their fourth Premier League title, and their third under the Portuguese. As the first table shows, Mourinho's total of nine league defeats (from just 16 games) was considerably more than he had suffered in any previous campaign as a manager. By losing to nine different teams in the opening five months of the season he had matched the number of teams he lost to in his first three full seasons at the club between 2004 and 2007. In his first reign, he didn't lose a single Premier League home game. At the end of his second, Bournemouth (a League One team in Mourinho's heyday), were able to come to Stamford Bridge and waltz off with three points, the first promoted team to win at the reigning champions since Bolton at Old Trafford in 2001–02.

Mourinho League Defeats (Season by Season)

Season	League defeats for Mourinho
2015–16	9
2013–14	6
2001–02	5
2005–06	5

Mourinho League Defeats (Season by Season) – *continued*

Season	League defeats for Mourinho
2012–13	5
2008–09	4
2009–10	4
2010–11	4
2006–07	3
2014–15	3
2000–01	2
2002–03	2
2003–04	2
2011–12	2
2004–05	1
2007–08	1

Secondly, looking at the wider picture, Chelsea's title defence under Mourinho was staggeringly inept. Previously the worst defending champions in the Premier League era were a Blackburn team in 1995–96 that had lost manager Kenny Dalglish and were struggling to cope with the increased demands on their resources made by the Champions League. Chelsea, in contrast, started the season with the most successful manager in their history in charge and had a squad well used to fighting on multiple fronts. And yet by mid-December Chelsea were six points worse off than that Blackburn team 20 years earlier, and a monstrous 28 points behind their first ever title defence under Mourinho in 2005–06.

Reigning PL Champions – Title Defence Stats After 16 Games of Following Season

Reigning PL champions	Season	P	W	D	L	F	A	GD	PTS	Final pos
Chelsea	2005–06	16	14	1	1	35	7	28	43	1
Manchester United	1993–94	16	13	2	1	33	13	20	41	1
Manchester United	2000–01	16	12	3	1	41	10	31	39	1
Manchester United	2011–12	16	12	3	1	37	14	23	39	2
Manchester United	2003–04	16	12	1	3	32	10	22	37	3
Manchester United	1999–2000	16	11	3	2	40	21	19	36	1
Chelsea	2006–07	16	11	3	2	26	9	17	36	2
Manchester United	2007–08	16	11	3	2	29	8	21	36	1
Manchester City	2014–15	16	11	3	2	33	14	19	36	2
Manchester United	1994–95	16	11	2	3	31	10	21	35	2
Arsenal	2002–03	16	11	2	3	36	17	19	35	2
Manchester United	1997–98	16	10	4	2	40	12	28	34	2
Arsenal	2004–05	16	10	4	2	42	20	22	34	2
Manchester United	2009–10	16	11	1	4	34	14	20	34	2
Manchester City	2012–13	16	9	6	1	30	14	16	33	2
Manchester United	2008–09	16	9	5	2	27	10	17	32	1
Chelsea	2010–11	16	9	3	4	30	11	19	30	2
Manchester United	1996–97	16	7	6	3	31	24	7	27	1
Arsenal	1998–99	16	6	8	2	15	7	8	26	2
Manchester United	2013–14	16	7	4	5	25	19	6	25	7
Manchester United	2001–02	16	7	3	6	36	27	9	24	3
Blackburn Rovers	1995–96	16	6	3	7	27	19	8	21	7
Chelsea	**2015–16**	**16**	**4**	**3**	**9**	**18**	**26**	**−8**	**15**	**10**

Such is the force of José Mourinho's personality that he probably hung onto his job at least two or three weeks longer than another manager in a similar situation would have, but his departure does raise an interesting point about his wider influence on the league. Mourinho's original spell at Stamford

Bridge in the mid-2000s saw an increasingly defensive league where shots per game and goals per game declined, as the brief but powerful era of the 'Big Four' (Manchester United, Arsenal, Chelsea and Liverpool) stifled the domestic game but dominated the Champions League, with appearances in the final for those four clubs six times in five years.

Almost as soon as Mourinho departed Chelsea in 2007 the shots per game rate started to creep up, with even his former charges at Chelsea throwing aside their shackles under Carlo Ancelotti and winning the Premier League with a record 103 goals in 2009–10. As the table below shows, the period up until 2012–13 saw an above average number of shots per game in the Premier League, before a decline in 2013–14, coinciding exactly with Mourinho's return to Chelsea. His second-era team were clearly not as impressive as the Chelsea of the mid-2000s but it didn't stop Mourinho dominating the news agenda in a similar fashion. Can a single man influence the entire style of a league? Almost certainly not but the neatness of this apparent coincidence is quietly compelling.

Ultimately, the autumn under Mourinho cost Chelsea any chance of contesting the title again. They ended the season as

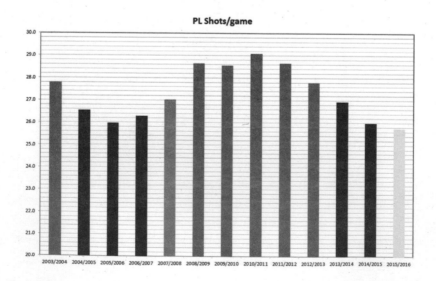

the first reigning champions to finish lower than ninth since Leeds in 1993 and the 20th team to do it overall. It's worth noting that of instances of reigning champions finishing tenth or lower, more than half came before the Second World War, with Manchester City in 1938 remaining the only title winners to be relegated in the subsequent season. Chelsea were bad, but that's a different level.

Difficult to reconcile with their disastrous last few weeks of the campaign, but Everton were doing OK before the New Year. In December, Romelu Lukaku scored in eight consecutive games in all competitions for the Toffees, the first person to do this since Dave Hickson in 1954. The Belgian also became the first Everton player to score 50 goals in 100 games or fewer since Joe Royle. Nevertheless, by the end of the campaign, Lukaku had bought into the depression at Goodison and failed to score in any of his final ten games of the season.

In a press conference shortly before Christmas, Arsenal manager Arsène Wenger pointed out that the season was different and that a 'new pragmatism' was affecting the league, partially demonstrated by the lessening importance of teams having possession. The figures backed up what Wenger was trying to show, with a steady fall in average possession for winning teams over the past five seasons. Indeed, 2015–16 was the first campaign in that period where winning teams almost averaged less of the ball than the opposition, something clearly influenced by the likes of Leicester but even by Arsenal in blitzkrieg home wins against Manchester United and Manchester City (38% and 37% respectively).

Average possession of winning teams in the Premier League (%)	
2011–12	52.8
2012–13	52.1
2013–14	52.1
2014–15	51.1
2015–16	50.3

Leicester's title win ended a bad record for the letter 'L' at Christmas. The previous instances of a team beginning with that letter being top on Christmas Day (Liverpool x4 plus Leeds) had all seen them fail to land the prize at the end of the campaign.

In 2014–15 Leicester City became only the third team in the Premier League era to be bottom of the table at Christmas and avoid relegation. One year later they topped the division, joining Norwich (in 1987 and 1988) as the only other team in English top-flight history to have engineered such an unlikely turnaround.

Teams bottom of the PL at Christmas who survived

Team	Season	P	W	D	L	Final pos
West Bromwich Albion	2004–05	18	1	7	10	17
Sunderland	2013–14	17	2	4	11	14
Leicester City	2014–15	17	2	4	11	14

But how instructive is looking at the Premier League table at Christmas? Does this arbitrary point in the season have any bearing on the final standings?

The table below shows movement from Christmas to the final standings in the Premier League era, and the largest unique proportion is teams staying in exactly the same position, with 16%. Adding in a movement of a single place, be that up or down, takes the combined proportion to 42%. Almost half of teams in Premier League history have ended the season either in the place they occupied at Christmas or one place different. Adding in the movements two places up or down takes this to 61%, and thus it's reasonable to take the table at Christmas as a guide to who will finish where when May comes around.

From position at Christmas	%
Stay the same	16
Rise one place	12
Fall one place	14
Rise two places	11
Fall two places	9
Rise 3–5 places	13
Fall 3–5 places	14
Rise 6+ places	6
Fall 6+ places	5

Of course, there will always be outliers, the likes of Norwich in 1994–95 (who fell 13 places, from seventh at Christmas to 20th, and relegation, by the end of the season) and Wimbledon/Fulham who climbed from 21st to 12th in 1992-93 and from 17th to ninth in 2010–11 respectively. However, slumps/recoveries are rare so if your team is doing better than expected as you festively open your presents, or your club's unexpected struggles are putting you off your turkey, then the good/bad news is that you'll probably be experiencing similar emotions five months later.

> Just how bad Aston Villa were, and possibly still are, is shown by the fact that by the end of 2015 they had picked up fewer Premier League points (25) in the entire year than Watford (29) had since joining the division in August.

Arsenal's routine home win against Bournemouth on 28 December was the 170th time that Petr Cech had kept a clean sheet in the Premier League, finally surpassing David James' record, set in 2009 when he was with Portsmouth, his fifth club in the top flight. By the end of the season, including Arsenal's 4-0 win on the final day that elevated them above Tottenham in the league standings yet again, Cech had another eight clean sheets, giving him an outside chance of reaching 200 by the end of next season.

Looking a bit more deeply at the goalkeepers Cech heads, you can, by observing the average number of games per clean sheet, see the glovesmen who are either a) very good, b) at a club with a good defence or c) a combination of a) and b). Cech's rate of a clean sheet every 2.06 games is exceptional, with the former Liverpool keeper José (Pepe to his friends) Reina not far behind with a figure of 2.13. David James, in contrast, has a high number of clean sheets thanks mainly to the huge amount of games he racked up in a 17-year Premier League career. Keepers with similar career paths to James in this list include Mark Schwarzer (a man who was at Chelsea in 2014–15 and Leicester in 2015–16, so knows what it's like to observe champions) and Jussi Jääskeläinen, who holds the exciting record as the overseas player to play the most games at a single club (Bolton). These are keepers who are good enough to get hundreds of games in the top division, but never quite good enough to get plonked behind a grade-A defence and enjoy the parsimonious benefits that brings.

Player	Games played	Clean sheets	Goals conceded	Games per clean sheet
Petr Cech	367	178	272	2.06
David James	572	169	665	3.38
Mark Schwarzer	514	151	653	3.40
David Seaman	344	140	291	2.46
Nigel Martyn	372	137	412	2.72
José Reina	285	134	247	2.13
Brad Friedel	450	132	567	3.41
Tim Howard	399	132	427	3.02
Edwin van der Sar	313	132	304	2.37
Peter Schmeichel	310	128	287	2.42
Joe Hart	302	119	303	2.54
Shay Given	446	113	593	3.95
Jussi Jääskeläinen	436	108	613	4.04
Thomas Sørensen	364	107	455	3.40

January

On a weekend dominated by Norwich and Liverpool's roller-coaster game at Carrow Road, Swansea snuck under the radar and finally recorded a league win against Everton. It was their first against the Toffeemen in their 22nd game against them, stopping them just three short of the all-time English league record, held by Blackpool against Arsenal. Back in the 1930s, the Seasiders had to wait until their 25th game against the London side before finally winning, a record that still stands. It capped off a bad Christmas for the Arsenal players, largely (or perhaps wholly) because they had to play Blackpool away on 25 December. They may have made the relatively short trip to Norwich in 2015–16 by plane, but Arsenal's travel arrangements in the 1930s were surely more rustic.

Team	Opponent	Games until first win	Year it happened
Blackpool	Arsenal	25	1937
Carlisle United	Hull City	24	1963
Rochdale	Brentford	22	1999
Swansea City	Everton	22	2016

When Leicester regained first place on 16 January it was the 33rd day they'd spent top of the Premier League in 2015–16, which is coincidentally the same number of days Tottenham have ever been top of the competition. In this season when Tottenham finally mounted a realistic title challenge, they spent longer in the relegation zone (one day) than they did on top (zero).

The end of January is now synonymous with the closure of the transfer window but it wasn't always this way. Until the 2002–03 season, transfers could be made until the end of March, which made for a far more interesting state of affairs. Notably, in 1997–98 workaday midfielder Andy Roberts managed to play against Arsenal four times in a single Premier League season, facing them for Palace in October and February, before transferring to Wimbledon and facing Arsenal in March and April thanks to the wonders of a rearranged fixture. Roberts remains the only player in Premier League history to come up against the same opponents four times in one season, and until the transfer regulations are altered he will surely be so for the considerable future.

On a related, mid-season transfer note, just two players have managed to score against the same team in three seperate games in one Premier League season, namely Dion Dublin against Southampton in 1998–99 and Mikel Arteta against Blackburn in 2011–12.

In delightful disciplinary news, Chelsea's 2-2 draw with West Bromwich Albion on 13 January was the first Premier League game to see both goalkeepers booked since a Portsmouth v Hull match almost six years earlier. The record for yellow cards collected by a goalkeeper in a single season remains eight by the superbly fractious Jens Lehmann in 2006–07. No other goalkeeper in the competition's history has ever collected more than four in a single campaign. I miss Jens.

Jamie Vardy's goal against Stoke in January ended a Premier League drought of ten hours and 17 minutes, and even included an operation on his groin (not that he missed any league games because of it). At this point, even with the barren spell he had just endured, Vardy was still ahead of the two men he would battle with at the end of the campaign for the Golden Boot, Harry Kane and Sergio Agüero.

As the graph shows, Vardy's run of scoring in 11 consecutive games made him the front runner until well into the New Year with Kane improving significantly as the season reached its climax. Agüero's path was much more unpredictable, with a slow start followed by a five-goal burst against Newcastle in Manchester City's eighth game. The Argentine, though, was

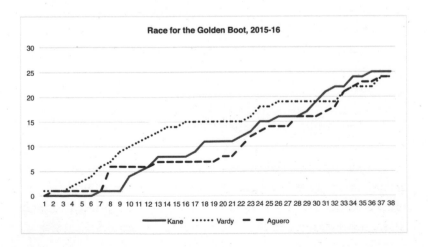

never ahead of Vardy or Kane in the scoring stakes at any point of the season, although he featured in fewer games than the English pair.

*

A chink of light in the mid-winter gloom, early January invariably sees the appearance of the third round of the FA Cup and all of the associated coverage of shocks, sensations, upsets and stunned big guns reeling as yeoman teams from the lower leagues go toe-to-toe with their inflated rivals. And yet the sense that this landmark on the football calendar has lost some of its lustre persists, partly due to the fact that January is also when the transfer window is open, and the cacophony of DONE DEALS drowns out the David v Goliath stories that used to dominate the new cycle.

People hark back to a golden era of cup shocks but, as the table below shows, the number of lower league/non-league teams knocking out top-flight clubs has hardly varied during the last seven decades. The 2010s have already seen 15 instances and look likely to at least match the 1980s and 1990s with 19.

Decade	Tier 3 or lower knocking out Tier 1
1950	22
1960	15
1970	16
1980	19
1990	19
2000	16
2010	15

Where you *can* argue that the cup has changed is in the actual make-up of the battles between the minnows and the giants. Before the 2000s it was very rare for a top-flight side to make any changes to their starting XI for an FA Cup game, even though this was the era of multiple replays. In the twenty-first century, though, Premier League sides will routinely rotate almost their entire side for FA Cup games against smaller opposition, thus surely improving the chance of a 'surprise' result. Think of it like this: was Bradford's 4-2 win against Chelsea in 2015 treated as a bigger shock than Wrexham beating Arsenal in 1992? Probably not, and it is the diluted nature of much of these early rounds that is the biggest danger to the longevity of the world's oldest competition.

Looked at positively, Portsmouth beating a team in the FA two divisions above them (in this instance, Ipswich) is a heart-warming tale of classic romance. Looked at realistically, it's more of an illustration of how the team that won the FA Cup as a top-tier side in 2008 have slipped so far down the divisions, one of only three teams to play in the fourth tier after being in the Premier League.

January 28th saw the retirement of Darius Vassell, briefly beloved of England manager Sven-Göran Eriksson in the early 2000s (Vassell actually scored six times for England, one more than both Sir Trevor Brooking and Sir Les Ferdinand) and a player who retains a niche record: Vassell scored in 46 different Premier League games and was not on the losing side in any of them.

4.

What's in a Name?

'Play for the name on the front of the shirt,
and they'll remember the name on the back'

Tony Adams

There are many ways to track the shifting essence of English football over the past 25 years but none show the passing of time better than names. Surnames, first names, known names, nicknames, double-barrelled names: they all indicate a gradual shift from one era to another.

And that's not a surprise, for there is a constant shift in names over time. As every parent knows, their collection of carefully considered name choices will almost certainly sound archaic, odd and probably downright stupid to their own parents, who in turn named their children in ways that the previous generation would have baulked at. Add in fashionable additions (you should consider that we may be only 15 years or so from the first appearance in the Premier League by a player named after a character from *Game of Thrones*) to the natural waxing and waning of historic names and you can see why there is such an ebb and flow, and why the glorious era of Kevins in the 1980s could yet be seen again.

That said, the list of the most popular first names by season in the Premier League shows a remarkable loyalty to David for the first 20 years, with it being the top or joint-top first name in 12 of the first 20 campaigns. Delightfully, the one season where David and James were the most popular names

(2010–11) was the first Premier League campaign in which goalkeeper David James did not feature.

Season	Most popular forename
1992–93	David
1993–94	David/Paul
1994–95	David
1995–96	David
1996–97	Steve
1997–98	David
1998–99	Steve
1999–2000	Paul
2000–01	Paul
2001–02	Paul
2002–03	David/Paul
2003–04	Paul
2004–05	Darren
2005–06	David
2006–07	David/Michael
2007–08	David
2008–09	Michael
2009–10	David/Michael
2010–11	David/James
2011–12	David
2012–13	James
2013–14	Steven
2014–15	James
2015–16	James

David is currently on its longest dry spell since the legendary Paul ascendency at the turn of the century. James is the current dominant name, but what this table doesn't show you is how the bunch has closed up on the leaders. There were more than 30 Davids in 1992–93 but James led the way in

2014–15 with only nine. Clearly some closer investigation is required.

The Decline of Alans

The Premier League's record scorer is an Alan. England's only World Cup winning team contained an Alan. But Alans are old and Alans are on the wane: we have the evidence. The seven Premier League seasons to take place entirely in the 1990s contained an average of 9.7 Alans per campaign, with 1995–96 seeing a peak (12: Wright, Shearer, Kimble, Thompson, McDonald, Stubbs, Reeves, Neilson, Moore, Kernaghan, Miller and Maybury). The 2000s saw a slow, steady decline of Alans and the last three Premier League terms have seen only Alan Hutton keeping the name alive in England's top flight. Alain Goma provided a brief cosmopolitan boost between 1999 and 2006 but with Aston Villa's relegation, 2016–17 could be the first Premier League campaign not to contain a single Alan. We mourn you, Alan.

But, happily, for every decline there must be a rise, and Jordan (and Jordon) was there to take up the slack. A lone representative at the tail end of the 1990s, in the form of Leicester's Jordan Stewart, was only the start of something special, with Jordan Henderson's arrival in the competition in 2008 the true dawning of the Jordanian era. 2010–11 saw three Jordans (Cook, Henderson, Spence) and the first Jordon (Mutch). Just five years later there were eight in the Premier League (Amavi, Henderson, Lyden, Pickford, Rossiter, Veretout, Ibe and Mutch). And the capital of Jordan appears to be Aston, not Amman, with Villa the only team (so far) to play three Jordans in a single Premier League match, alongside, of course, the sole remaining Alan. Their demotion to the Championship is even more haunting when you consider what we are about to lose.

We Need to Talk About Kevin

Like Alan, some names fall out of fashion in England, but unlike Alan they gain or retain popularity overseas. The Premier League's increasing reliance on overseas imports balances out the loss of local players. A good example of this is Kevin. Each of the first three Premier League seasons saw 11 Kevins take part, while there were ten Kevins, all of them UK-born, as recently as 2000–01.

By the mid-2000s the Kevins were dying out, with just two (Kilbane and Nolan) keeping the name alive in the English top flight. Time, surely, for Kevin to join Alan in the heritage zone . . . but no. Instead, the 2015–16 season saw six Kevins grace the Premier League (De Bruyne, Mbabu, Mirallas, Stewart, Wimmer and our old friend Nolan), with only two of them born in the UK. The others came from a narrow band of Europe where Kevin remains a viable naming choice (or at least it did so 20 years ago), namely Belgium, Switzerland and Austria.

Duncan, Duncan, Duncan and Big Dunc

Forgive the indulgence, but my own name, Duncan, has not had a chequered Premier League history. There have only ever been four in the competition's annals, dominated, naturally, by the imposing figure of Duncan Ferguson, one of a chosen few people to officially earn the right to put the word 'Big' before his first name (see also: Big Ron, Big Phil Scolari). There were two others in the 1990s (Duncan Jupp and Duncan Spedding) both managing only 31 Premier League appearances between them and soon disappearing from view. The final member of the club is a new entry in 2015–16, Sunderland's Duncan Watmore, son of the former Chief Executive of the FA, who is one of a rare group of Premier League players with a university degree. He also played for England

Under-21s in his breakthrough season, perhaps a glimpse at a future where he becomes only the second Duncan to play for England after the great Duncan Edwards.

Hyphens

When Chris Bart-Williams played for Sheffield Wednesday at Everton on the very first day of the Premier League in August 1992 he was the only UK player with a double-barrelled name to feature until Marc Bridge-Wilkinson did so for Derby in November 1998. Bridge-Wilkinson is younger than Ian Thomas-Moore but the latter did not acquire his fashionably extended name until he married in 2009, so can largely be discounted. The heritage of players with double-barrelled names stretches all the way back to the 1888–89 league champions Preston North End, who had a Welsh goalkeeper called Robert Mills-Roberts. (Incidentally, any opponents of the supposedly modern trend of squad rotation should note that in their 'Invincible' double season, where, unlike Arsenal in 2003–04, they didn't actually lose *any* games, Preston played Mills-Roberts in the FA Cup while fellow Welsh custodian James Trainer played the large majority of the league games.) England, meanwhile, featured six double-barrelled players in the 1800s, two in the 2000s (Alex Oxlade-Chamberlain and Shaun Wright-Phillips) but just one in the whole of the twentieth century (Ian Storey-Moore with a single appearance in January 1970).

So using England as a rough guide to the prevalence of hyphenated surnames, it seems that the practice has returned after a fallow period in the 1900s, and the Premier League seems to bear that out. As the table below shows, almost 42% of the UK-born double-barrelled players to have featured in the Premier League were born in August 1993 or later. Arcane cynics might point out that August 1993 was also the exact moment that squad numbers were introduced to the Premier League, along with the money-spinning practice of fans paying extra, and by the letter, to have their heroes' names printed on the back of the shirts. Sometimes though, correlation really doesn't imply causation.

UK/Irish players with double-barrelled names to feature in the Premier League	Country	Date of birth
Rushian Hepburn-Murphy	England	28/08/98
Jake Clarke-Salter	England	22/09/97
Ainsley Maitland-Niles	England	29/08/97
Cameron Borthwick-Jackson	England	02/02/97
Reece Grego-Cox	Republic of Ireland	12/11/96
Ruben Loftus-Cheek	England	23/01/96
James Ward-Prowse	England	01/11/94
Alex Oxlade-Chamberlain	England	15/08/93
Jay Emmanuel-Thomas	England	27/12/90
Hal Robson-Kanu	Wales	21/05/89
Sylvan Ebanks-Blake	England	29/03/86
Bradley Wright-Phillips	England	12/03/85
Nigel Reo-Coker	England	14/05/84
Shaun Wright-Phillips	England	25/10/81
Gary Taylor-Fletcher	England	04/06/81
Gifton Noel-Williams	England	21/01/80
Marc Bridge-Wilkinson	England	16/03/79
Ian Thomas-Moore	England	26/08/76
Chris Bart-Williams	England	16/06/74

The Brotherhood of the Vowels

Nothing announced the glamour of the modern era in English top-flight football more than players whose names end in vowels. There are a fair few 'English' names that end in 'e', but a's, i's and o's are invariably the preserve of the prestigious over-seas brigade.

Just look at the top-scoring players whose surname both begins and ends in a vowel: Anelka, Agüero, Ekoku, and . . . Robbie Earle. Special mention to Ugo Ehiogu who is the top-scoring Premier League player whose first name and surname both begin with a vowel. Compare those with the figures of Shearer, Rooney and Lampard, the top-scoring consonant yeomen.

Let's go deeper and ask who is the top-scoring player whose name contains all five vowels? That would be former Charlton man Talal El Karkouri who scored eight times in the English top flight. If you're not satisfied with the two parts to his sur-name then you should plump for Maynor Figueroa who scored four times for Wigan, including one from his own half against Stoke, which gave Potters goalkeeper Thomas Sørensen enough time to recite the entire alphabet before it looped over him.

Win Percentages

Let's imagine you're about to have a baby boy and you want him to enjoy a successful and satisfying career in the Premier League. What name should you choose to help him on his way? Well, if you're Dutch then Arjen would be a good start, thanks to Arjen Robben's brief but impressively successful spell in England in the mid-2000s. The winger was victorious in 55 of his 67 Premier League outings which not only makes Arjen the winningest forename in the competition but also gives Robben the best win rate of any player in the competi-tion's history who has played 50-plus games.

But 67 is a tiny sample size (and encompasses just one, bald, man) so we need to expand the search, moving past highly successful but limitedly spread names such as Nemanja, Patrice and Sergio.

Putting in a minimum of 1000 Premier League appearances,

we are left with a top three of Ryan (49% win rate), Frank (47%) and Wayne and Ashley (43%), but even these are obviously dominated by notable single players with historic Premier League careers.

We need, then, to push the margin even further, by putting a minimum of 3000 Premier League appearances. Yes, we'll rule out most of the names ever seen in the division but we'll be left with what can be exclusively called 'the big ten' and we'll be able to see just how they rank.

Name	Win %age
John	39.6
Michael	39.4
David	37.1
Mark	35.7
Gary	35.7
Steve	35.5
Paul	34.4
Chris	32.2
Kevin	31.8
Andy	29.8

The result is sensational news for John as he sneaks the title by just 0.2% ahead of Michael, with the ever-reliable David in third place. At the other end of the table it's sad news for Andy which is the only one of the big ten names not to record a win rate of at least 30%, while the arrival of the glamorous European Kevins has not yet caused a winning surge, although this could change as time moves on.

Of course, as discussed earlier, none of these names are currently fashionable (only David and Michael were in the top 100 boys' baby names in the UK in 2015, in 50th and 52nd respectively), so in the unlikely event that you were actually planning to name your children on this evidence, the advice would be: don't.

Length

Name length is obviously affected by the naming conventions in the place you originate and there have been some hefty entries in Premier League history. Technically leading the way is Greek midfielder Georgios Charalambos Georgiadis who usually didn't use the middle of those three names but clocks up a decent 31 characters, 21 more than the number of appearances he made in England's top flight.

Second is Jan Vennegoor of Hesselink, who, to English ears, sounds like a respectable, if occasionally violent, medieval squire but actually has a name that dates back to the seventeenth century when two farming families from the Enschede region of Holland intermarried, and chose to keep both names. Rather than hyphenating them, they used the word 'or' (which is 'of' in Dutch), leaving subsequent generations with a literally questionable surname.

Longest names in PL history

Georgios Charalambos Georgiadis
Jan Vennegoor of Hesselink
Kévin Théophile-Catherine
Cameron Borthwick-Jackson
Giovanni van Bronckhorst
Johannes Karl Gudjonsson (Joey)
Anderson Silva de Franca
Jimmy Floyd Hasselbaink
Alex Oxlade-Chamberlain
Florent Sinama-Pongolle
Jean-Claude Darcheville

Another notable player in this list is Jimmy Floyd Hasselbaink, one of the finest goalscorers in Premier League history. The Jimmy part of his name is only a nickname, albeit one that has stuck (his real first name is Jerrel, so would add one extra letter to the total), and when he joined Leeds in the 1990s he wanted it on the back of his shirt instead of Hasselbaink, but the Premier League refused. It doesn't seem to be a hard and fast rule, though, as players such as Javier Hernández (Chicharito), Sergio Agüero (Kun Agüero) and the late Christian Benítez (Chucho) have all played in the division with nicknames on the back of their shirts.

Looking at the shortest names to feature in the Premier League is less easy, due to the proliferation of nicknames and single-named players. Former Manchester City and Everton forward Jô could be argued to take the win, but his full name is João Alves de Assis Silva so the purists naturally recoil.

Using the highly unscientific basis of players with a forename and a surname, we arrive at this list:

Shortest names in PL history
Li Tie
Ben Mee
Ian Cox
Aly Dia
Joe Cole
Joe Hart
Ruel Fox
Ian Rush
Tim Krul
Neil Cox
Ian Woan
Alex Rae
Demba Ba
Wim Jonk
Emre Can
Idan Tal
Amr Zaki

Shortest names in PL history – *continued*

Eric Roy

Tom Ince

Andy Dow

Tim Ream

Jay Tabb

Lee Todd

Dan Burn

Jes Hogh

Phil Gee

Lee Camp

Ben Amos

So former Everton (a club which clearly places a high value on short-named players) midfielder Li Tie is at the top of the list with just five characters. Followed closely by the six character trio of Ben Mee, Ian Cox and Aly Dia, who convinced then Southampton manager Graeme Souness that he was George Weah's cousin and earned a brief but memorable substitute appearance at The Dell. Following them is a significant haul of 24 players with seven-character names ranging from current England internationals like Joe Hart to former Danish centre-half Jes Høgh who made a handful of appearances for Chelsea at the turn of the century. Finally, a small hat tip to Amr Zaki who is the only player in this table to stretch his name to four syllables, an admirable feat with only seven letters to play with.

(NB: the average number of characters in a Premier League player's name is a respectable 14.)

Managers

Unlike the vast influx of overseas players to the Premier League, and despite the longevity of Arsène Wenger at Arsenal, the spread of managers in the competition's history is far more parochial and the names reflect that.

Name	Number
Steve	8
Alan	7
Brian	6
David	6
John	6
Paul	6
Kevin	5
Tony	5
Alex	4
Billy	4
Chris	4
Ray	4
Roy	4

The predominance of Scottish managers for much of the UK's football history means that names such as Billy and Alex stand out here more than they do for players, but the overall impression is that you could walk into any pub in England in 1983 and shout one of these names and someone would turn around and look.

As it stands, Steve is the outright leader, helped by a couple of caretakers with a single game. But despite their prevalence, no Steve has yet brought much to the table in the Premier League era. Steve Bruce's sheer number of games can be respected, but overall the impression is one of mediocrity. There are certainly Jobs for Steve but, as yet, no Apple-like innovation.

Steves	Games	Wins	Win %age
Bruce	392	110	28.1
McClaren	216	70	32.4
Coppell	146	42	28.8
Kean	59	13	22.0
Clarke	55	17	30.9
Wigley	16	1	6.3
Holland	1	1	100.0
Perryman	1	0	0.0

5.

The Decline of Cristiano?

'I don't listen to what the press say.
The statistics and numbers don't lie'

Cristiano Ronaldo

The reaction above came from Cristiano Ronaldo after Real Madrid lost 1-0 at home to neighbours Atlético in February 2016, a defeat that left his team ten points behind Barcelona and, at the time, looked like it would ensure that Real would fail to land the league title for a fourth successive season. Instead the team reacted well under rookie manager but experienced superstar Zinedine Zidane and not only contested the championship with Atlético and Barcelona until the final day, but also saw off their city rivals in the Champions League final, for the second time in three years. Nevertheless, 2015–16 also marked the first time that there had been a consistent level of criticism aimed at the team's star forward, which on the face of it looks ridiculous, given how incredibly consistent he has been over the past decade.

It's impossible to get a grasp of how Ronaldo's career will look in ten or 20 years' time. Co-existing at the same time as Lionel Messi has both elevated the two men and almost certainly caused the Portuguese some contemplative moments, given that the Argentinian is generally ranked that iota higher than him in the great church of opinion. At least Ronaldo will have most if not all of his great moments available online for future generations. Maradona's are limited at best, and we've all seen Pelé tackled by Bobby Moore.

What does look increasingly likely, though, is that Ronaldo's peak was, roughly, a ten-year stretch from 2006 until 2016. Starting with the first of the three successive Premier League titles he drove Manchester United towards, and ending with Real Madrid lifting a second Champions League in three seasons in May 2016, he enjoyed an extraordinary and prolonged scoring spree that at some points seemed to result in a new record every week. Just a small handful are listed below:

- Most goals scored in the UEFA Champions League group stage in a single season: 11 goals in 2015–16.
- Most goals scored in Champions League history: 93 goals
- Most penalties scored in Champions League history: 11 penalties
- Most goals scored in a European Cup season: 17 goals
- Real Madrid's all-time top goalscorer in La Liga with 260 goals
- Real Madrid's all-time leading goalscorer with 364 goals
- Most goals scored in a single La Liga season for Real Madrid: 48 goals in 2014–15.

Goals in game	Instances
0	129 times
1	122 times
2	61 times
3	30 times
4	5 times
5	Twice

Ronaldo goal breakdown at Real Madrid

Surely the only player in football history to score against the true Axis of Evil (Iran, North Korea, Millwall), Ronaldo's

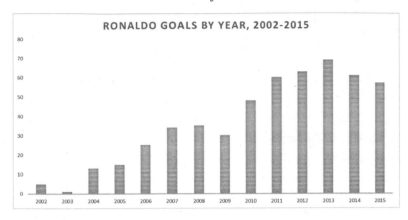

RONALDO GOALS BY YEAR, 2002-2015

evolving goalscoring prowess through his career can be seen in the above graphic.

Four successive years with 60-plus goals between 2011 and 2014 is a rate that few players in the history of football have ever managed. Indeed, there are numerous clubs that would be glad to have totals like that. For example in 2011–12 Ronaldo hit more shots on target in La Liga than Stoke managed in the Premier League, and their shots on target per game rates (a single man versus an entire club, remember) have followed a pleasingly similar pattern over the past six seasons.

But we'll need to delve deeper into Ronaldo's career to get a true picture of his achievements, any flaws he may possess and any signs of decline. To do this it's probably fair to divide his time into four distinct periods. Firstly there's the initial years at Sporting and Manchester United (from 2003 to 2006), when he was a talented winger. Inexperienced, yes, but ripe with potential. The second period dawned after his 'part' in getting Wayne Rooney sent off at the 2006 World Cup (spoiler: Rooney managed it all by himself). Ronaldo returned to the Premier League having added muscle and power to his hitherto stepover-based game and played a significant part in leading United to three successive league titles and two successive Champions League finals.

The third period is his initial spell at Real Madrid from 2009

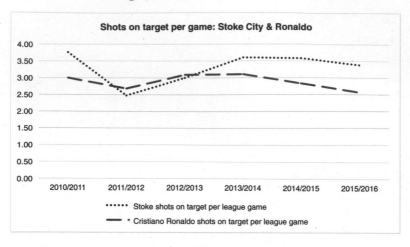

Shots on target per game: Stoke City & Ronaldo

· · · · · Stoke shots on target per league game

— · Cristiano Ronaldo shots on target per league game

until 2013, the point at which his goalscoring went supersonic particularly under the tutelage of José Mourinho. During this time Ronaldo essentially became 'wide left-forward', creative duties shelved in favour of amassing giant, pre-war, goal totals. Finally, there is the period from 2013, where age and injury have certainly reduced Ronaldo's mobility, and have seen him occupy a more central role in the Real side, with the likes of Ángel Di María and then Gareth Bale doing much of the running that Ronaldo used to do himself. The goals have kept coming, in fact the rate at which he has scored has increased, but the raw menace has subsided a little.

The Young Contender

The Ronaldo for whom Manchester United paid Sporting Lisbon £12 million in 2003 was clearly a prospect (the signing of Brazilian Kléberson, announced at the same time, was arguably a bigger deal, given he had appeared at the World Cup a year earlier) but at 19 he was not seen as someone who would make a decisive impact in his debut season.

He arrived in Manchester as United hit arguably their lowest ebb under Sir Alex Ferguson. They were reigning champions, but had lifted the trophy thanks to a combination of an improbable run of 15 wins in their last 18 games, and an ever-so-slightly more probable collapse by 2002 title winners Arsenal. The Gunners made amends in Ronaldo's debut Premier League campaign, with United finishing a distant third (although they did knock out the 'Invincibles' in the FA Cup semi-final), the same place they occupied in 2004–05 as Chelsea won their first title under José Mourinho. These two third places were, along with 2002, the only times that United finished outside the top two in the Premier League under Sir Alex Ferguson, a record made only more impressive by their finishes under his successors.

The world that Ronaldo was ushered into was both difficult, in the sense that his new team were unused to be being outpaced so regularly by rivals, and helpful, in that his arrival was one of the founding bricks in the construction of Ferguson's third great side. Joined by Wayne Rooney a year later, and supplemented by the likes of Edwin van der Sar, Patrice Evra and Nemanja Vidić soon after that, Ronaldo had found an environment in which he could both grow as a player and be given responsibility as the manager increasingly trusted him. (Just how much Ferguson trusted what Ronaldo was and would become is illustrated by the fact that he was willing to sell Ruud van Nistelrooy, scorer of 95 goals in 150 Premier League games, at the end of 2005–06 after the Dutchman's relationship with his team-mate had broken down.)

PL/CL combined	Minutes played	Gls/90	Shots/90	Ass/90	Ch/90	Chances/ shots
2003–04	1839	0.20	3.57	0.20	1.71	0.479
2004–05	2925	0.15	4.40	0.12	1.69	0.385
2005–06	2790	0.29	4.03	0.19	1.71	0.424

The above table is an overview of Ronaldo's first three seasons at Manchester United, and we'll use these categories for the other parts of his career as well. The main metrics here are goals per 90, shots per 90, assists per 90 and chances created per 90. Finally, there's a number which is the relationship between the chances Ronaldo created and the shots he took. As he changed from a winger with creative responsibilities to an all-round menace and finally to a goal machine, this relationship should have changed accordingly.

The first thing that you notice from the first three seasons at Manchester United is that although the goals did not flow for the young man, he still averaged around four shots per game in each campaign. Only one Manchester United player in 2015–16 got close to hitting four shots per 90 minutes (Memphis Depay with 4.13), partly due to the meagre philosophy imposed by Louis van Gaal but even in the more expansive Ferguson era it should be remembered that Ronaldo's first three seasons at the club were a low ebb and that he was not a mainstay of the team, coming off the bench 14 times in his debut campaign.

It should also be noted that 2003–04 was not only his first season in England but also the highest number of chances created in relation to the number of shots. This Ronaldo was an eager youngster, happy to perform his pleasing tricks on the touchline and then whip the ball into a team-mate (not always, though; just ask van Nistelrooy, whose major issue with Ronaldo was reportedly the inconsistency of his deliveries). Ronaldo also showed early promise in big games, too, scoring in the 2004 FA Cup final victory against Millwall, which was, until 2016, the last time United had won the old trophy, and the 2006 League Cup win against Wigan, his side's only two honours in this relatively troubled time. The Lions and the Latics weren't giants of the game then, and aren't now, but it was an early sign that the callow Portuguese forward was deserving of the attention his manager was showing him.

This support was no better illustrated than in the aftermath of Wayne Rooney's red card for England against Portugal in the 2006 World Cup. Ronaldo was understandably cautious about how he'd be received when he returned to his adopted home, and it took some trademark Ferguson backing for him to happily return to Old Trafford ahead of the new season. Ronaldo's performance in the subsequent campaign fully justified his manager's faith in him. It was the dawn of Ronaldo mark II.

EPL MVP

There weren't many people tipping Manchester United for the title in August 2006. In fact, on the season previews that are still easily accessible, it's near universal backing for two-time reigning champions Chelsea. Chelsea had landed the title in José Mourinho's first season by losing only once and conceding just 15 goals, before retaining it with relative ease in 2005–06, eight points clear of their rivals, despite losing the last two matches of the season, both of them dead rubbers.

United had finished second in 2005–06 but it wasn't enough to sway the opinion makers. Ronaldo had ended the season with nine goals (level with Stelios Giannakopoulos) and six assists (level with Dean Whitehead). But there were a few signs of both his and his team's nascent recovery, most obviously in a run of nine successive wins between February and April, with Ronaldo scoring in each of their first three. Even so, to predict that this team would win the next three titles and reach two of the next three Champions League finals (United had finished bottom of their group in 2005–06, scoring just three times in six matches) would have seen you filed as 'eccentric'.

But that's exactly what happened and Cristiano Ronaldo was the beating heart of the team that achieved it.

Season	Minutes played	Gls/90	Shots/90	Ass/90	Ch/90	Chances/ shots
2006–07	3749	0.48	5.81	0.31	1.78	0.306
2007–08	3761	0.93	5.50	0.17	1.70	0.309
2008–09	3759	0.53	6.06	0.19	1.77	0.292

The first thing to note from Ronaldo's data in his three great seasons at Manchester United is just how consistent his playing time was. The amount of minutes he played between 2006–07 and 2008–09 in the two main competitions varied by just 12 minutes across three seasons. Obviously, as a player grows older and grows in consistency he will naturally play more, but Ronaldo post-2006 was a bigger, stronger man. Football has seen myriad talented players but the true greats are the ones that can a) avoid injury and b) recover quickly from any knocks they do pick up. Both Ronaldo and Lionel Messi have been blessed in this respect, and the Portuguese's revamped physical form in 2006–07 proved much harder to handle for Premiership (and, for the super-pedants out there, 2006–07 was indeed the last time the English top-flight was named 'The Premiership') defenders.

Dividing the three title wins into simple baskets is both facile and extremely tempting, so here goes:

2006–07: The team effort. Ronaldo was the top scorer in the Premier League for United with 17 goals but Wayne Rooney ably supported him with 14, with the Englishman also supplying 11 assists. United's squad was still slightly short in areas, illustrated by the unexpected and not altogether impactful loan signing of Henrik Larsson in January. Ronaldo swept the board in terms of awards, winning PFA player of the year, the Football Writers' player of the year, the PFA young player of the year and the PFA fans' player of the year.

2007–08: The Ronaldo show. Forming part of a freewheeling front three with Rooney and new arrival Carlos Tévez, United briefly adopted the Roma-inspired 4-6-0 formation with no central striker to speak of, although any attacker could fill in there as and when required. Ronaldo became the first and so far only non-centre-forward to score 30-plus goals in a Premier League season and added eight more in the Champions League as United landed the trophy for the second time under Ferguson. This was the season that Ronaldo convinced the watching world that he was a great, and Real Madrid's interest in him was activated.

2008–09: Case for the defence. Convinced to stay for one more season on the understanding he could move to Madrid in 2009, a slightly less enthusiastic Ronaldo once again top-scored for United in the Premier League with 18 goals. Only two of those came away from home, and although they reached the Champions League final once more, hopes of becoming the first team to retain the European Cup since Milan in 1990 fell in Rome as Barcelona, in their first season under Pep Guardiola, outmanoeuvred the defending champions. Arguably, the team's real star man in 2008–09 was veteran goalkeeper Edwin van der Sar who set a Premier League record of 1311 minutes without conceding a goal as part of a 14-game clean-sheet spell for the team.

*

One of the main developments in Ronaldo's game in his final three seasons at Manchester United was his free-kick technique. Fans at Old Trafford had enjoyed the best of David Beckham's prowess with the dead ball, but the Englishman's success was based around a mainly traditional approach, curling the ball (admittedly more than most people had managed before or have since) after approaching it with a tightly angled run. Ronaldo's technique was something else altogether, comprising of a virtually straight run-up and a connection with the ball on the valve, which all but eliminated the spin and instead caused the ball to veer and dip, often unpredictably. His first direct free-kick goal came in November 2003 against

Portsmouth (a cross-cum-shot from the left flank that evaded both his team-mates and the Pompey defence). But it wasn't until 2007–08 that he really seemed to hit a rich seam, scoring four and then following up with four more in 2008–09. Ronaldo's direct free kick conversion rate of 11% in 2007–08 remains the best he has recorded, almost certainly a combination of the newness of his technique combined with some wayward goalkeeping.

As the table below shows, he kept up a decent free-kick rate once he moved to Spain, scoring seven goals in his first two campaigns with Madrid, although the conversion rate was slowly starting to fall. A nadir in terms of success rate came in 2011–12, with a record 55 attempts from direct free-kicks but only two goals. Such was the overall importance of Ronaldo to the team, though, that no one was going to try and persuade him to hand over or at least share responsibilities with a team-mate. There's bravery on the football pitch and then there's disagreeing with CR7.

Cristiano Ronaldo direct free-kicks 2006–present (domestic league data)

Season	Team	Free-kick goals	Free-kick shots (incl. blocked)	Conversion (%)
2006–07	Manchester United	1	30	3.3
2007–08	Manchester United	4	38	10.5
2008–09	Manchester United	4	50	8.0
2009–10	Real Madrid	3	37	8.1
2010–11	Real Madrid	4	53	7.5
2011–12	Real Madrid	2	55	3.6
2012–13	Real Madrid	4	49	8.2
2013–14	Real Madrid	3	30	10.0
2014–15	Real Madrid	2	33	6.1
2015–16	Real Madrid	1	26	3.8

Recent campaigns have seen fewer Ronaldo goals from direct free-kicks and his failures in Portugal's opening game at Euro 2016 took him to 34 taken, zero scored in major international tournaments. But it remains a decent weapon to be unveiled on occasion (although, thanks partly to imitators, it will never again have the visceral impact it did in the Premier League in the late 2000s). And even though Ronaldo only played in the English top flight for a relatively short period, his total of 11 direct free-kicks remains one of the highest hauls in the competition's history, with only doyens of the genre Beckham, Gianfranco Zola and Thierry Henry ahead of him. Indeed, the vintage nature of the names in the list hints at a golden era of free-kick speciality that is now a dying art. Appreciate any CR7 stunners while you can.

All-time Premier League	Free-kick goals
David Beckham	15
Gianfranco Zola	12
Thierry Henry	12
Cristiano Ronaldo	11
Sebastian Larsson	11
Laurent Robert	11

*

The great oddity of Ronaldo's Premier League career is the lack of hat-tricks. Although the metamorphosis from a winger into a bona fide scoring forward took place in his time at Old Trafford, he registered only one hat-trick. Once upon a time that would have been unremarkable, with icons such as Eric Cantona, Dennis Bergkamp and Marlon Harewood all ending their Premier League careers with a single treble. But we know what happened when Ronaldo moved to Spain; the world changed and goals became as common as insects, with endless hat-tricks as a corollary.

It's not like he didn't come close to a glut in the Premier League, though. As the table below shows, he hit two goals in a game on 21 different occasions. If he is now known (he isn't) as the (occasionally) smiling assassin in Spain, in England Ronaldo was definitely the man with the braces. At least he did hit one hat-trick, though; his former team-mate Ryan Giggs holds the Premier League record for the most braces (11) without a single three-goal haul to his name.

Cristiano Ronaldo multiple-goal games in the Premier League

Date	Opponent	Venue	Goals
12/01/08	Newcastle United	Old Trafford	3
25/04/09	Tottenham Hotspur	Old Trafford	2
05/04/09	Aston Villa	Old Trafford	2
27/01/09	West Bromwich Albion	The Hawthorns	2
15/11/08	Stoke City	Old Trafford	2
01/11/08	Hull City	Old Trafford	2
29/10/08	West Ham United	Old Trafford	2
03/05/08	West Ham United	Old Trafford	2
19/03/08	Bolton Wanderers	Old Trafford	2
23/02/08	Newcastle United	St James' Park	2
30/01/08	Portsmouth	Old Trafford	2
23/12/07	Everton	Old Trafford	2
03/12/07	Fulham	Old Trafford	2
11/11/07	Blackburn Rovers	Old Trafford	2
06/10/07	Wigan Athletic	Old Trafford	2
30/12/06	Reading	Old Trafford	2
26/12/06	Wigan Athletic	Old Trafford	2
23/12/06	Aston Villa	Villa Park	2
11/02/06	Portsmouth	Fratton Park	2
04/02/06	Fulham	Old Trafford	2
31/12/05	Bolton Wanderers	Old Trafford	2
01/02/05	Arsenal	Highbury	2

Supersonic Goal Angel

A reported 85,000 people crowded into the Bernabéu to see Ronaldo unveiled as a Real Madrid player in early July 2009. Madrid had made many forays to the Premier League in the 2000s to acquire players, from McManaman to Beckham, Woodgate to Gravesen, but this was a different level altogether, both financially and theatrically. Ronaldo's sheer menace meant that great things were expected once he reached La Liga. He didn't disappoint.

Ronaldo's first four league games for Real saw him score once, once, twice and once respectively, leaving him with a goals to game rate of 1.25. It has barely dipped since.

As the table below shows, he played fewer than 3000 minutes of league and Champions League football in his first season in Spain, an ankle injury in the autumn leading to a rare spell in the treatment clinic for the usually perma-fit forward. Even so, Ronaldo still managed more than a goal per 90 and his rate of 7.49 shots per 90 is a career high (level with the 2012–13 season). Perhaps in an attempt to ingratiate himself with his new team-mates, Ronaldo's chances created per 90 rate of 2.59 goals per game is the best he has ever registered in his career. The man who arrived at Real was a goalscorer, yes, but also a supplier.

Season	Minutes played	Gls/90	Shots/90	Ass/90	Ch/90	Chances/ shots
2009–10	2920	1.02	7.49	0.22	2.59	0.346
2010–11	3922	1.06	7.41	0.34	1.97	0.266
2011–12	4284	1.18	7.10	0.32	1.79	0.251
2012–13	3798	1.09	7.49	0.26	2.01	0.269

The consistency Ronaldo showed in his first four seasons in Spain is remarkable. As the figures above clearly demonstrate, if you went to a game in this period you could roughly expect to see a Ronaldo goal and seven shots in your allotted 90 minutes of action. 'Selfish Ronaldo' still assists at a rate that all but a handful of players in world football would be delighted with. Between 2009 and 2015 he produced 65 assists, behind only Messi, Özil and Fàbregas in the top five European leagues.

It's genuinely difficult to thread a way through the records Ronaldo set once he had his feet under the table at Real (so numerous they are), but his two Ballons d'Or at Madrid (in 2013 and 2014) are almost numerically equal to the number of league titles and Champions Leagues he has won in his entire time there (one league in 2012 and European titles in 2014 and 2016 respectively). Yes, he has had to play in a division against a Barcelona team experiencing their own holy peak but, even so, he won more leagues/Champions Leagues in his final three seasons at Manchester United as he has in seven seasons in Madrid. He was the cherry on the cake at Old Trafford but often at Real he has had to be the sponge as well, soaking up both opposition attention and the criticism of the famously intolerant fanbase.

However you look at it, his goalscoring has come at a rate that was once deemed the preserve of the 1920s and 1930s when balls were heavy and pressing was light. The similarly extravagant returns by Lionel Messi at Barcelona have created a rivalry that will live on for decades, and almost certainly pushed both men to greater heights. Twenty-six goals in 29 games in his first La Liga season was followed by 40 in 34 in 2010–11, the first time any player had hit that number in a single season. A year later Ronaldo pushed the mark to 46 and finally claimed the league title, although Messi responded with 50 goals in 37 league appearances.

One trend that is interesting to note is the rise and fall of La

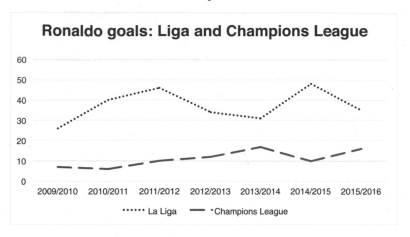

Ronaldo goals: Liga and Champions League

La Liga — •Champions League

Liga and Champions League goals in relation to each other. As the graph below indicates, as Real finally landed their tenth European Cup in 2014, Ronaldo set a Champions League record by scoring 17 times in a single campaign, while at the same time recording 'only' 31 league goals, his lowest total since his first season at the club. It also seemed that the 2015–16 season for Real Madrid was a write-off, with Barcelona seemingly unstoppable. But when an energetic Zinedine Zidane replaced Rafa Benítez, and Barca went four games without a win (losing three in a row), the gap at the top tightened. The La Liga title was only decided on the final day of the season – with Real finishing only a point behind their rivals. There was also a more concerted effort in Europe, which is once again reflected in the gap between Ronaldo's goal totals in each competition.

The most recent three seasons Ronaldo has played at Madrid have seen his latest, perhaps final metamorphosis. This time he is a less dynamic but arguably more dangerous forward, one who doesn't necessarily instigate counter-attacks but who will still punish any mistake and gobble up virtually any chance.

Season	Minutes played	Gls/90	Shots/90	Ass/90	Ch/90	Chances/shots
2013–14	3533	1.22	7.44	0.33	1.78	0.240
2014–15	4164	1.25	6.40	0.41	1.97	0.307
2015–16	3149	1.06	6.75	0.31	1.55	0.229

His goals per 90 rates in 2013–14 and 2014–15 were 1.22 and 1.25 respectively, which are by some way the best he has recorded in his career. Season 2014–15 is particularly telling as his shots per 90 fell to its lowest level since his final season at Manchester United yet the goal rate has never been higher. Let us not forget that football is a team sport, and it remains so even in the era of Ronaldo and Messi. When Ronaldo criticised his team-mates in February 2016, the contrast with Barcelona was stark. While Messi has dovetailed perfectly with Neymar and Luis Suárez, the very definition of being greater than the sum of their parts, Ronaldo has often appeared to be the one constant in the Real side, with injury and the club's often haphazard transfer policy preventing him striking up productive relationships. He was particularly critical of the club when they sold Mesut Özil and Ángel Di María to Arsenal and Manchester United respectively. By the end of the 2015–16 season, Ronaldo had posted his lowest chances created per 90 figure, his transformation from a creative player to a finisher finally complete. His last action of the club season was to strike home the winning penalty in the Champions League final shootout, a special moment for a person who, if he was in the NFL, would now be a special teams operative rather than leading the offence.

One final note on Ronaldo's goalscoring record, and it's something that comes up frequently on social media where his fans battle seemingly endlessly, and usually witlessly, with Messi supporters in a footballing cold war. Any mention of the Portuguese is guaranteed to elicit the taunt 'Penaldo' referring to the belief that the Madrid man's voluminous goal total is hepped up with penalties, as if somehow these are lesser goals.

The truth is less clear, with Ronaldo's total of 11 penalties in the Champions League indeed a record number, but only two clear of Messi, with both men having missed three each (a competition joint record along with van Nistelroy, Müller and Hazzard). Indeed, what is noticeable about both players' penalty records is that they're really not that impressive, with both missing at rates that in lesser men would have seen the duties handed to someone else.

Slow Decline?

Identifying plateaus and declines in footballers is something that clubs spend a lot of time doing, both when assessing their own players or weighing up potential signings. Identifying it in someone like Cristiano Ronaldo, undeniably one of the most effective and talented players in the history of the sport, is both difficult and probably unfair.

That said, looking for signs of it can still be an interesting exercise, and there definitely are some in this instance. The table below shows Ronaldo's touches and passes per game in La Liga and both have generally declined throughout his time at Madrid, with 2015–16 a career low in both metrics. Whether it's more down to a change in role, the ageing process or, more likely, a combination of both, the truth is that the great CR7 is slowly becoming more peripheral at Real Madrid.

Cristiano Ronaldo (La Liga)	2009–10	2010–11	2011–12	2012–13	2013–14	2014–15	2015–16
Games played	29	34	38	34	30	35	36
Touches/game	**68.2**	**61.5**	**60.2**	**51.6**	**53.6**	**53.9**	**46.8**
Passes/game	38.6	36.9	37	31.9	31.8	33.7	29.7

But, you cry, who cares about touches or passes? Ronaldo isn't about touches or passes, he's a goalscorer, he's a goalscoring *machine* and the goal rate is showing no significant decline. Well, that's both true and not true. As you can see below, in 2015–16, only a run of goalscoring in his final ten games of the season prevented it being the first season where Ronaldo had scored in fewer than half of his league appearances. He also failed to trouble the leading teams, scoring eight times in two matches against struggling Espanyol but registering just a single goal against Barcelona, Atlético and Villarreal. He still has the numbers but rub at the surface and it's not quite as shiny as it used to be.

Ronaldo % of games scored in

La Liga	Games played	Games scored in	Games not scored in	% failed to score in
2009–10	29	19	10	34.5%
2010–11	34	18	16	47.1%
2011–12	38	27	11	28.9%
2012–13	34	20	14	41.2%
2013–14	30	22	8	26.7%
2014–15	35	25	10	28.6%
2015–16	36	20	16	44.4%

*

Wherever Cristiano Ronaldo ends his career, be that at another European club, the MLS or even China, his place in the game's pantheon is assured. His goalscoring rate between 2006 and 2016 is one of the wonders of the modern game, a rapidly increasing crescendo that helped Real Madrid to become European champions for the tenth and 11th times. The Galáctico era that Real ushered in with the signings of Luís Figo and Zinedine Zidane in the early 2000s never really led to the dominance of European football that those in charge of the vision thought it would. However, it did establish the club as the team that would go out and pay the galactic transfer fees, of which Ronaldo was the ultimate purchase (hence the guilty fudging of the higher Gareth Bale fee to prevent their star man taking offence). He has repaid the faith in him by a huge margin but, as the data has hinted, there probably aren't going to be more than a couple of seasons left at the very top level. Soon the Ronaldo era will have passed into legend, a legend where, if you so wish, you can watch more than 500 goals from the man on YouTube. Dixie Dean, sadly, has to go without.

February–March

February

Leicester seemed to have as many caveats as they did fixtures in 2015–16, with periods where almost every game was tagged as 'the day that their unlikely title bid comes to an end'. A classic of the genre came at the start of February as they travelled to two-time Premier League winners and top four rivals Manchester City.

City's expensive hounds were expected to tear the uppity Foxes to bits but instead the visitors added another famous-yet-routine win to their glimmering seasonal CV. All very well for Claudio Ranieri's band of adventurers but for the home team it was a disaster and instigated a run of three successive Premier League defeats, the first time they had lost three in a row since November 2008.

Top 6 head-to-head record 2015–16	P	W	D	L	F	A	Pts
Arsenal	10	4	4	2	19	16	16
Tottenham Hotspur	10	4	3	3	16	10	15
Manchester United	10	4	3	3	10	13	15
Southampton	10	4	2	4	16	14	14
Leicester City	10	3	5	2	13	13	14
Manchester City	10	1	3	6	11	19	6

It also highlighted a particular weakness in City's approach in 2015–16, namely their struggles against direct rivals. They ended the season having won just one of their ten games against the top six, at least eight points fewer than any other side. It's also interesting to note that Leicester's go-to result against rivals was a draw, with half of their top six games ending level, while Arsenal's strength in games against title rivals reveals their implied weakness against teams lower in the table.

Compare City with their first Premier League title win in 2011–12 (below), when they claimed eight wins from ten games against the top six, including two against Manchester United who they only pipped to the title on goal difference. If United had managed just a slightly less embarrassing thumping at home to their local rivals (in the game that ended 6-1 to the visitors) then the Premier League trophy would have been making its more familiar journey to Stretford instead.

Top 6 head-to-head 2011–12	P	W	D	L	F	A	Pts
Manchester City	10	8	0	2	24	9	24
Manchester United	10	5	2	3	24	19	17
Arsenal	10	4	2	4	17	19	14
Chelsea	10	2	4	4	14	17	10
Tottenham Hotspur	10	2	3	5	16	23	9
Newcastle United	10	2	3	5	10	18	9

Manchester United found a new hero in February in the form of Marcus Rashford. The academy graduate scored two unexpected goals on his first-team debut in the Europa League v expected goals icons Midtjylland. He then followed it up a few days later with another brace, this time against crisis icons Arsenal. In doing so he became only the fourth teenager to score twice on his Premier League debut, joining colleague James Wilson as well as Robbie Keane and Kevin Nolan, who, like all of us, were young once.

Chelsea's performances in 2015–16 should form a case study on how players can play badly for one manager and then improve miraculously (clue: it's not a miracle) under his replacement. The arrival of emergency uncle Guus Hiddink at Christmas came shortly after José Mourinho publically gave up on his squad after their defeat away at Leicester.

The Dutchman had the desired effect on his temporary charges, guiding them to an unbeaten Christmas, New Year and into January and February. By the end of 2016's second month Chelsea were poised to return to the top half of the table for the first time since August, an incredible situation for the reigning champions.

Another prosaic-yet-necessary landmark was reached right at the end of February when Chelsea came from behind to win at Southampton. That triumph was the first time the Blues had won consecutive games in the Premier League all season. Again, an extraordinary scenario for current title holders.

The Southampton game was Chelsea's 27th of the season; only Leeds in the Premier League's opening season had to wait longer for two wins in a row.

Reigning champions	Season	Matches until they won successive games
Leeds United	1992–93	32
Chelsea	2015–16	27
Blackburn Rovers	1995–96	21
Arsenal	1998–99	11
Manchester United	2013–14	10

All five teams in this list have fairly obvious reasons for their struggles in the subsequent season. Leeds famously went through their entire title defence without a single away win, which naturally heavily reduces the chances of consecutive wins for a team. Chelsea, as we know, had their autumn trauma under Mourinho. Blackburn in 1995–96 had lost their guiding hand Kenny Dalglish and toiled in both the league and the Champions League.

Those are the three long runs, with Arsenal in 1998–99 still an early Arsène Wenger work in progress despite their unpredicted title win a season earlier. Finally, 2013–14 was Manchester United's first season after the departure of Sir Alex Ferguson. Sometimes a manager leaving can disrupt a club significantly. Sometimes, as we saw with Chelsea, the departure of the man in charge was just what was required.

2016 was a leap year so the end of February was a special moment for the four players in Premier League history to have had the misfortune/good fortune (depends if you like birthday parties) to be born on 29 February: Niklas Gudmundsson, Mike Pollitt, Darren Ambrose and Scott Golbourne. I hope you wished them well. If not, set a reminder for 2020.

If there was an award for the most-seemingly-scripted football club then Liverpool would surely scoop it. From unlikely European comebacks (latest instalment: Villarreal/Borussia Dortmund) to cup victories on penalties, the Reds have a template and they like to stick to it. But sometimes real life gets in the way, as it did at the end of February, when their Capital One Cup final against Manchester City went to extra-time (the third League Cup final in a row involving Liverpool to do so), before a penalty shootout. Liverpool had won all five previous cup finals they'd contested on spot-kicks. The most famous of which came in Istanbul in 2005, but this time reality bit hard, with City winning 3-1.

Liverpool penalty shootouts in cup finals

Season	Opponent	Pens for	Pens against	Shootout result	Competition
1983–84	Roma	4	2	W	European Cup
2000–01	Birmingham City	5	4	W	League Cup
2004–05	AC Milan	3	2	W	European Cup
2005–06	West Ham United	3	1	W	FA Cup
2011–12	Cardiff City	3	2	W	League Cup
2015–16	Manchester City	1	3	L	League Cup

The outcome meant that Jürgen Klopp had tasted defeat in a cup final for the fourth successive season, while the loss in the Europa League final in May ensured he was the first manager to lose two cup finals in his first season in England since Avram Grant in 2007–08. Fortunately for the German, his reputation seems more robust than that of the former Chelsea boss.

Dele Alli's stellar first season in the Premier League was an example to many of his rivals, and his goal against Norwich in early February saw him draw level with Jack Wilshere for Premier League goals, despite playing (at that point) 92 games fewer in the competition. It was something for them to talk about at the Euros, anyway.

March

Liverpool's slow metamorphosis into a Jürgen Klopp team gathered pace in early March as the Reds continued to close the gap on the top four with a late win at Crystal Palace on 6 March. Klopp's first defeat as Liverpool manager came in the reverse fixture at Anfield so the German would have been satisfied with this victory, especially as his team had been reduced to ten men in the second half (thanks to James Milner's second ever red card in the top flight).

Liverpool's win came courtesy of a 96th-minute penalty, a decision that led to Alan Pardew aggressively dispensing with his coat almost exactly two years after then Tottenham boss Tim Sherwood had done the same in a match against Arsenal. The number of English managers in the top flight may be declining but their ability to passionately de-cloak remains unparalleled.

The 2-1 win was Liverpool's 28th in Premier League history via goals scored in the 90th minute or later, which at the time was seven more than any other side, as the table below shows. Once again, reality doesn't necessarily match received wisdom as you can see that Manchester United (those inventors and beneficiaries of Fergie-time) and Tottenham (the club where fans curiously lament that generic bad luck in football is 'Spursy') both have 17 wins from 90th-minute goals. Don't believe the hype.

6 March 2016	Wins from 90+ min goals
Liverpool	28
Arsenal	21
Chelsea	20
Everton	20
Manchester United	17
Newcastle United	17
Tottenham Hotspur	17
Aston Villa	13
Wigan Athletic	12
Bolton Wanderers	11
Southampton	11
Blackburn Rovers	10
Manchester City	10

Excitement peaked at Aston Villa on 1 March as they ended a barren two-game run without winning a corner. Despite this, they still lost 3-1 in the third of 11 consecutive Premier League wins as they lurched towards and into the cold arms of relegation.

On the same weekend that Liverpool struck late at Palace, Chelsea stretched their unbeaten start under interim manager Guus Hiddink to 12 games, setting a new record for best loss-less beginnings by Premier League managers (a run they extended to 14 games before losing to Swansea in April). The previous holder of this record was Frank Clark at Nottingham Forest, in that brief, purposeful period where Forest came back up after their relegation at the end of the Brian Clough era. Chelsea's strength in the Abramovich era is reinforced by the presence of both José Mourinho and the much-maligned Felipe Scolari in this list. Big Phil may have been unbeaten in his opening games but 17 matches on he was fired. It's tough at the top, unless you're Guus Hiddink.

Date	Team	Manager	Unbeaten
27/02/16	Chelsea	Guus Hiddink (second spell)	14
22/10/94	Nottingham Forest	Frank Clark	11
10/02/01	Middlesbrough	Venables + Robson	10
21/10/06	Aston Villa	Martin O'Neill	9
18/10/08	Chelsea	Felipe Scolari	8
03/10/04	Chelsea	José Mourinho	8
12/09/92	Ipswich Town	John Lyall	8
01/10/2000	Leicester City	Peter Taylor	8

Mesut Özil may assist for fun (and also a salary) in the Premier League but in the Champions League it's a different story. Arsenal's exit at the hands of Barcelona saw him once again fail to create a goal, meaning his run without an assist in Europe stretches back to October 2014. Meanwhile, Arsenal have failed to progress in a Champions League knockout tie since Gordon Brown was UK Prime Minister, back in 2010.

A series of injuries at Old Trafford in the spring saw beleaguered manager Louis van Gaal turn to youth, with Marcus Rashford the most obvious example but the likes of Timothy Fosu-Mensah, Cameron Borthwick-Jackson and Anthony Martial also providing new blood, even if the latter player could end up with one of the biggest transfer fees of all time.

United's game against Watford in March saw them name their fourth youngest starting XI in Premier League history, notably the only one of the top five instances not in the experimental days of August or May. Furthermore, the bench named by van Gaal in that game must rank as one of the most inexperienced in United's recent history, comprising of Sergio Romero, Matteo Darmian, Jesse Lingard, Joe Rothwell, James Weir, Paddy McNair and Joe Riley. The days of Sheringham and Solskjær these were not.

Date	Opponent	Season	Venue	Years	Days
24/05/09	Hull City	2008–09	A	23	177
22/08/11	Tottenham Hotspur	2011–12	H	23	191
28/08/11	Arsenal	2012–13	H	23	197
02/03/16	**Watford**	**2015–16**	**H**	**23**	**222**
06/05/14	Hull City	2013–14	H	24	82

And it wasn't only Manchester United that were looking towards a new generation. Overall in the Premier League in 2015–16, 30 English players under the age of 20 appeared, which was the most in the division since the 2005–06 season and almost twice as many as there were as recently as 2012–13. With a player born in 2000 likely to appear at some point in the Premier League next season, 2016–17, we're all reliant on the millennials now. Pensions, energy solutions. World Cup glory. It's down to them now.

Season	English players under 20
2005–06	33
2006–07	26
2007–08	24
2008–09	27
2009–10	26
2010–11	27
2011–12	21
2012–13	17
2013–14	21
2014–15	28
2015–16	**30**

★

Everton don't head many rankings in the modern game but Kevin Mirallas's red card against West Ham in March also saw his team go from 2-0 up and end up losing 3-2. It was also the Toffees' 82nd in the competition's history (they would add two more before the end of the season), more than any other club and ahead of Arsenal (81) in second. Unsurprisingly, the burglar-taming icon Duncan Ferguson leads the way with eight reds, twice as many as any other Evertonian in the Premier League era.

Jermain Defoe earns his complimentary tins of custard. The former England striker was one of the main reasons for Sunderland's surprising-yet-inevitable survival in the Premier

League, scoring 11 goals after New Year, eight more than any other Black Cats player. His late equaliser at Southampton in early March not only gave his side a valuable point but was also his 23rd goal as a substitute, more than any other player in Premier League history, six more than anyone else.

Most goals as a substitute in PL

Player	Goals
Jermain Defoe	23
Nwankwo Kanu	17
Ole Gunnar Solskjær	17
Javier Hernández	14
Michael Owen	13
Darren Bent	13
Edin Džeko	13
Andrew Cole	13
Robbie Keane	13
Victor Anichebe	13
Daniel Sturridge	13
Tore André Flo	13

Defoe is 6 ahead of two players rightly and wrongly associated with substitute goals. Rightly in the case of Ole Gunnar Solskjær, who remains the only substitute ever to score four goals in a single Premier League game (at Nottingham Forest in Manchester United's treble-winning season). Wrongly in the case of Nwankwo Kanu, who, despite scoring 17 goals as a substitute, is invariably thought to have scored a hat-trick from the bench at Chelsea, while playing for Arsenal. While his three goals definitely did happen, Kanu was, equally, most definitely in the starting XI in that game.

Overall, there have been only six hat-tricks from substitutes in the Premier League, with one of them coming in 2015–16, namely Steven Naismith for Everton against Chelsea in September, something that a few months later earned him a transfer to Norwich and, ultimately, relegation.

Premier League hat-tricks as a substitute

Date	Player	Team	Opponent	Goals
06/02/99	Ole Gunnar Solskjær	Manchester United	Nottingham Forest	4
12/09/15	Steven Naismith	Everton	Chelsea	3
19/05/13	Romelu Lukaku	West Bromwich Albion	Manchester United	3
28/04/08	Emmanuel Adebayor	Arsenal	Derby County	3
19/03/05	Robert Earnshaw	West Bromwich Albion	Charlton Athletic	3
27/03/04	Jimmy Floyd Hasselbaink	Chelsea	Wolverhampton Wanderers	3

England's friendly with the Netherlands at the end of March was the clearest sign of Leicester's elevation to the upper echelons of the game. With both Danny Drinkwater and Jamie Vardy featuring (the latter scoring for his country for the second game in a row), it was the first time two current Leicester players had appeared for the Three Lions since Steve Guppy and Emile Heskey did so in 1999.

Amidst the debris of Brendan Rodgers departure from Liverpool in the autumn were plenty of articles bemoaning the club's well-publicised transfer committee. One in particular focused on the committee's decision to pay almost £30 million for Roberto Firmino, noting pointedly that the Brazilian played for a team, Hoffenheim, that had finished only eighth in the Bundesliga the previous season.

Hindsight is an easy weapon to deploy, but perhaps the better approach would be not to criticise players coming into English football within a few weeks of their arrival. Yes, some will fail to adapt, but many others just need some time, or perhaps a change in manager, in order to excel.

Firmino is a great example of this. He played only two Premier League games in March but provided two goals and an assist for the Reds, part of a total of 13 direct goal involvements in the Premier League in 2016. That was bettered by only two players (both of whom are out-and-out goalscorers) and level with the much-heralded Dimitri Payet at West Ham. It was also five more than the PFA player of the year, Riyad Mahrez, another player who took a while to settle into England's top division before finding his feet. It's almost as if that's a thing.

PL goal contribution January–May

Player	Goals	Assists	G+A
Sergio Agüero	17	1	18
Harry Kane	14	0	14
Roberto Firmino	**9**	**4**	**13**
Dimitri Payet	4	9	13
Jermain Defoe	11	1	12
Jamie Vardy	9	3	12
Dušan Tadic´	4	8	12
Diego Costa	7	5	12
Dele Alli	6	6	12

6.

Away With Your Complaints:
The Away Goals Rule

'Two English teams have gone out on away
goals and that should be questioned because it is an
outdated rule that has to be changed'

Arsène Wenger, 2015

Like a household boiler in the depths of winter, concerns about
the away goals rule only really surface when the system lets
you down. In England there was a mini-meltdown in spring
2015, when both Arsenal (to Monaco) and Chelsea (to PSG)
exited the Champions League on away goals at the same stage.
The result, other than meaning there was an absence of Premier League sides in the quarter-finals for the second time in
three years, was a fevered look at whether away goals were a
legitimate way of deciding a game in the twenty-first century.

The very concept seems to have been designed to be con-
fusing to the casual fan. 'Away goals count double' is the usual
explanation, but, of course, it should actually be 'away goals
count double if the two teams are level on aggregate at the end
of the two-legged tie'. It doesn't roll off the tongue as easily but
it does have the advantage of being accurate. Instead, we are
left with a world where in almost every game where the rule
applies commentators have to take time to explain – very
slowly – the scenarios that could unfold due to the infernal
clause. The sentence 'in many ways that goal has not changed
the other team's task one bit' has been used so often that it has
lurched into self-parody on social media.

More importantly, the rule has the potential to change the nature of games significantly, sometimes to the benefit of the match, but, equally, it can put the tie completely out of reach and thus end any interest in the game for anyone but supporters of the winning team. It is the latter scenario, combined with some sense of a good performance not counting, that tends to lead to periodic demands for its abolition.

History

Let's start with a reminder of why away goals were even considered in the first place. Before the rule was implemented, the most obvious (and logical) solution to two teams who couldn't be separated in the allotted time was a replay. The first competitive replay came in the second round of the FA Cup in 1871–72, when Barnes edged past Hampstead Heathens (a club named like one of your five-a-side teams), 1-0 in a rematch, while five ties in the competition's history took *four* replays to decide. Thankfully for travelling fans, this was removed from the rules in the 1990s.

When pan-European competitions began in the 1950s the same logic was applied, with the first 'deciding game' after a two-legged draw coming between Borussia Dortmund and Spora Luxembourg in September 1956, while later that autumn eventual European Cup winners Real Madrid were taken to three games by Rapid Vienna (under the away goals rule, Madrid would have exited in the first round, having conceded twice at home while scoring just once in Austria).

But the logistics of European travel in the 1950s were more difficult than choosing between the orange plane company or the blue one. Understandably, additional games were something that clubs were keen to avoid, so by the early 1960s they had been replaced by the coin toss, something that remains an integral part of the pre-match ritual but was now elevated to a game-deciding process.

The first such flick of a coin in a European game took place in a Cup Winners Cup match between Linzer ASK from Austria and Yugoslavia's Dinamo Zagreb. Zagreb progressed, thanks to their correct call of what, despite the best efforts of magicians, remains a 50/50 scenario. Over the next seven years a further 22 European ties were decided by a coin toss, with Zagreb adding another progression in 1966. Galatasaray and Leeds also progressed twice from a coin toss. The last coin toss in a European club game was one of the biggest, denying, as it did, Roma a place in the 1970 Cup Winners' Cup final. Instead, Polish side Górnik Zabrze progressed to face Manchester City, ultimately losing 2-1 in front of a meagre 8,000 spectators in Vienna.

By 1970, away goals had already been introduced to some stages of European competition. The first instances in the European Cup came in October 1967, with Glentoran and Jeunesse Esch exiting against Benfica and Valur Reykjavík respectively. The first English side to experience the rule in the European Cup were Everton in 1971, when they were knocked out after a 0-0 draw away to Panathinaikos and then a 1-1 draw with the Greeks at Goodison Park. (Incidentally, in the previous round against Borussia Mönchengladbach, the Toffees had taken part in the competition's first ever penalty shootout. It was truly a campaign of new experiences.)

Panathinaikos enjoyed their progression on away goals against Everton so much that they used the same method to dispose of Red Star Belgrade in the semi-final (before losing to Ajax at Wembley in the final). And on that note, a special mention should go to PSV Eindhoven in 1987-88 who won the European Cup despite needing the supporting arm of the away goals rule in the quarter- and semi-finals and then penalties in the final against Benfica. Three of their last four games in the competition that year ended 0-0, their last actual victory in a game came in early November and they ended the campaign with a record of W3 D5 L1.

The Case Against the Rule

The main thrust of the twenty-first-century complaints about the away goals rule is that it is outmoded. Travel conditions have improved, stadium conditions have got better, life, for both fans and players alike, is more homogenous. Any disadvantage playing away from home is now massively outweighed by the impact of scoring at your opponent's ground. Furthermore, since the European Cup transformed into the Champions League and multiple teams from the same country entered the competition, you can get situations like the 2003 semi-final where AC Milan progressed on away goals against Inter, a goal that took place in their own stadium, albeit in a game where they were designated as the away team.

Away goals in the European Cup

	Ties settled on away goals	Knockout ties	%
1970s	20	287	7.0
1980s	27	293	9.2
1990s	13	137	9.5
2000s	15	108	13.9
2010s	9	98	10.2

The above table shows the proportion of knockout ties decided on away goals in the European Cup from the 1970–71 season onwards, with the sharp decline in total knockout games once the group stages were introduced in the 1990s clearly obvious. The 2000s, by some distance, saw the highest proportion of games settled by the rule, and it is unlikely to be a coincidence that this is roughly when people started complaining about it.

But we'll need to look a bit deeper at the result data to draw any more conclusions, so the table below shows the average number of goals scored by away teams in knockout European Cup/Champions League games.

	Goals by away teams in European Cup knockout ties 1970–present	Games	Gls/game
1970s	577	586	0.98
1980s	527	588	0.90
1990s	289	276	1.05
2000s	204	216	0.94
2010s	**213**	**196**	**1.09**

Although there are jumps in goals per games from away teams between the 1980s and 1990s and again from the 2000s and 2010s, both covering eras when the structure and shape of the tournament was tinkered with, the number of away goals has remained remarkably steady throughout the away goals rule era. Away teams have scored around 37–38% of goals in European Cup knockout ties in each of the last three decades.

	Goals by away teams in European Cup knockout ties 1970–present	Total goals	% of goals
1970s	577	1732	33.31%
1980s	527	1644	32.06%
1990s	289	776	37.24%
2000s	204	543	37.57%
2010s	**213**	**548**	**38.87%**

The number and proportion of away goals in knockout games, therefore, has not radically changed in the past five decades, so we need to dig a bit deeper.

One of Wenger's points was that where once a 0-0 draw at home in a first leg was a 'bad' result, in that you had to travel away to your opponents without having landed a blow, such is the improvement of performance on the road that that o-o at home is now an excellent result, as it allows you 90 minutes (or 120) of play at your opponent's ground with the chance to score an away goal of your own.

	European Cup knockout ties where first leg ended o-o	Home team in first leg progressed	%
1970s	26	11	42.3
1980s	23	6	26.1
1990s	14	5	35.7
2000s	16	6	37.5
2010s	8	1	12.5

As the table above shows, the data doesn't really support the theory. The 1970s, when the away goals rule was supposed to have worked, actually saw the highest proportion of teams which drew o-o at home in the first leg go on to the next round after the second leg (42.3%). Compare this to the current decade where so far there has been only one instance of a team drawing o-o at home in the first leg of a Champions League game and then progressing to the next round (that being Atlético Madrid against Chelsea in the 2013–14 semi-final). Just this season gone we saw Manchester City draw o-o at home to Real Madrid in the semi-final, which under Wenger's thinking gave the Premier League side the advantage. But City's insipid performance in the second leg ensured that Real were never really under any sort of threat, across virtually the entire 180 minutes of the tie.

There may be an element of confirmation bias taking place with Wenger as Arsenal progressed against holders Milan in exactly this fashion in 2008, drawing o-o at the Emirates but then winning 2-o in the return leg in Italy. It's instructive to read the match reports from the first leg in 2008, where Arsenal were deemed to have wasted a good opportunity against the reigning champions and that they would now face a difficult second game at the San Siro. As it turned out, Wenger's side dominated that match, and although their goals in the 2-0 win came late on, it's not inconceivable that this match plays a major part in their manager fetishising the power of a 0-0 draw at home. That was certainly the case in 2016, when Arsenal were looking reasonably comfortable in their home tie against Barcelona, only to let in two late goals to nemesis Lionel Messi. To Wenger, the all-important 0-0 at home was so close, even though logic and form would suggest that Barcelona would have still cruised through a second leg tie at the Camp Nou.

The other factor to consider is that Arsenal have made such a habit of finishing second in the Champions League group that they have had to play their Round of 16 first leg game at home in seven of the last nine seasons. Such repeated exposure to that particular scenario is bound to make an impression on anyone closely involved, such as, ah yes, the manager of the team.

Next, let's look at teams which have conceded at home at any point of a two-legged European Cup match, and here we can detect a slight shift in the modern game, although it is one that goes counter to the argument that away goals are proving more decisive.

	Conceded at home in either leg	Eliminated	%
1970s	319	216	67.7
1980s	312	218	69.9
1990s	154	107	69.5
2000s	134	86	64.2
2010s	**125**	**78**	**62.4**

As you can see, the period between the 1970s and the 1990s saw the elimination of more than two-thirds of teams who conceded at home at some point of a European Cup tie, but the twenty-first century has seen a decline, with the 2010s recording a significantly lower proportion, of around 62%. Put simply, conceding at home in a tie is less disastrous in the modern game than it was in the 1980s or 1990s. Again, the argument that away goals hold too much power under the current rules is not helped here. Incidentally, 62% is roughly the proportion of teams eliminated under the same conditions in the 1950s and 1960s, in other words the era before the introduction of away goals.

What about teams which lose at home? Not only have they let the opposition score an away goal but they also surrender an aggregate advantage. If we exclude second legs (because occasionally teams that have won handsomely away from home in the first leg relax in the second game, or rest key players) then we see that it has always been extremely rare for teams to come back from such a dire situation halfway through a two-legged tie.

	Lost first leg at home	Progressed	%
1970s	59	0	0.0
1980s	71	1	1.4
1990s	28	2	7.1
2000s	22	0	0.0
2010s	31	1	3.2

Only four times in the away goals era in the European Cup has a team lost the first leg at home and still progressed to the next round, yet three of those have come in the Champions League era, again not really fitting the theory that away goals are becoming too powerful.

Teams to lose at home and still progress to next round

Team	Opponent	Season	Round
Nottingham Forest	Dynamo Berlin	1979–80	Quarter-final
Steaua Bucharest	Dinamo Zagreb	1993–94	First round
Ajax	Panathinaikos	1995–96	Semi-final
Internazionale	FC Bayern München	2010–11	Last 16

The Victims

Perhaps it's all as simple as the teams that have suffered the most are the ones that are making the most noise. The list of countries whose clubs have exited the competition on away goals most often is led by England and Germany, both of which have teams and media who aren't afraid of complaining when they have been eliminated, by fair means or not. Interestingly, Italy have had only half as many exits on away goals, which could be pure luck or it could be a natural flair for doing just enough to get through. *Catenaccio*, but for numbers.

The team with the most exits on away goals in the European Cup are predictably stellar, with Real Madrid leading the way on five, followed by Manchester United and Inter on four each. Inter account for four of the five Serie A away goal defeats, with all four coming in the past 13 years, so they have a case for being the most unlucky team, or alternatively the team that struggle most with the rules that are clearly set out before the competition commences each season.

At the other end of the scale, the three teams to have progressed on away goals in the European Cup most often are

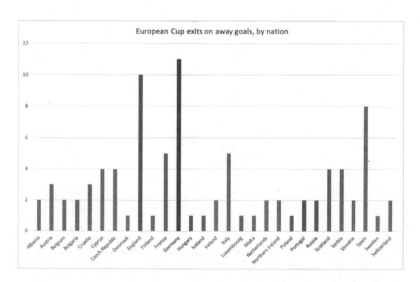

Barcelona and Bayern Munich (five times each) plus Monaco on four, the latter club taking an approach to the concept of aggregate in the same way they deal with taxes.

Conclusion

It is easy to understand the antipathy that the away goals rule attracts; it's an imperfect solution to a problem that would ideally be solved by additional games, games which the congested football calendar, and no doubt an army of frowning sports scientists, won't allow. But like the penalty shootout, the current system is probably still the best option. An alternative could be to apply the rule only after a period of extra-time is played in the second leg, as happens in the English League Cup, but while this may extend the interests of teams in certain scenarios, it will also mean a reduction in the type of games where home teams know they have to attack their opponents but with the jeopardy of knowing that any goal they concede will have dire consequences. Yes, it penalises the home team, but ultimately that's the very point of the rule. Furthermore, it's likely that future reconstructions of the Champions League will actually reduce the number of knockout games and instead expand the league section, so in some senses Wenger may get his wish, as the frequency of games ending on the away goals rule reduces and his own *bête noire*, the Round of 16, is consigned to history.

7.

The Goalscorers

'Well done, lad, but remember,
you're still only half as good as I was'

Dixie Dean

Unfortunately for those who like to cry 'football wasn't invented in 1992', that year is undeniably the point at which the Premier League was created, and the breakaway division is by its very existence a separate and unique competition. So, no, football wasn't invented in 1992 but handily a new league was, for which we have complete goalscoring records. That means not just totals, but minutes played, venues, precise ages of players and, for the past ten years, shot locations. So who is the greatest goalscorer in Premier League history? The traditionalists would suggest Shearer, simply because he scored the most goals, and, yes, he may well be the correct choice, but here we'll go beyond simple totals and use all the available data to make a compelling case for a number of men. Ultimately, there is no correct answer but everyone mentioned in this chapter has made a significant contribution to the highlights reels that play on, both digitally and in our minds, forever.

New Era, New Hero

Other than the formation of the Premier League, something else happened in 1992. A man called Alan Shearer signed for

Blackburn Rovers from Southampton for an English transfer record fee of £3.3 million. Shearer came to epitomise the first decade of the Premier League, his rustic combination of pace and power simply too much for most defences to handle. For 14 years Shearer plugged away at an extraordinary rate, ending his career with 260 Premier League goals, 283 including his spell in the old First Division with Southampton. Only four players have scored more league goals than Shearer: Jimmy Greaves (357), Dixie Dean (310), Steve Bloomer (309) and Gordon Hodgson (287). His position in the pantheon of greats is assured.

Most goals – Premier League	Goals	Games played
Alan Shearer	260	441
Wayne Rooney	193	435
Andrew Cole	187	414
Frank Lampard	177	609
Thierry Henry	175	258
Robbie Fowler	163	379
Michael Owen	150	326
Les Ferdinand	149	351
Teddy Sheringham	146	418
Robin van Persie	144	280

But there are a few factors that mean it's not an open and shut case in the Premier League. Firstly there's the penalty issue: Shearer took (and scored) a lot of spot-kicks. As his career reached its autumn in the 2000s, the proportion of his goals that were penalties increased, with at least 40% of them coming via that method in his final two campaigns. They're a perfectly valid way to score – Shearer's side-netting hungry technique throughout his career was exemplary – but it did give him a considerable advantage over certain other players. In particular, a certain Andy Cole.

Alan Shearer	Team	Goals	Goals (penalties)	% pens
2005–06	Newcastle United	10	4	40
2004–05	Newcastle United	7	3	43
2003–04	Newcastle United	22	7	32
2002–03	Newcastle United	17	2	12
2001–02	Newcastle United	23	5	22
2000–01	Newcastle United	5	2	40
1999–2000	Newcastle United	23	5	22
1998–99	Newcastle United	14	6	43
1997–98	Newcastle United	2	0	0
1996–97	Newcastle United	25	3	12
1995–96	Blackburn Rovers	31	3	10
1994–95	Blackburn Rovers	34	10	29
1993–94	Blackburn Rovers	31	3	10
1992–93	Blackburn Rovers	16	3	19

Cole the Goal

Discarded as a youngster by Arsenal, Andy Cole bounced back to have one of the most outstanding careers seen in the Premier League. Only one of his 187 top-flight goals came from the penalty spot, and that was late in his career at Fulham. He helped Newcastle to promotion in 1992–93 and then exploded into the top flight in the following season. His total of 34 goals in 1993-94 remains the highest scoring performance by anyone in their debut PL season and so it was understandable that as Newcastle became the pre-eminent challengers to Manchester United's early hegemony (along with Shearer's Blackburn) the Old Trafford club made a move to sign Cole. That didn't lessen the shock value at the time, though. In a globe where the World Wide Web was something pored over by obscure scientists, I can recall people refusing to believe Cole had moved

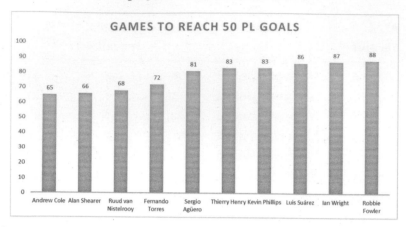

clubs until they got home and the stark truth faced them in cyan on Ceefax. It remains rare for players at top clubs to move to a rival, particularly mid-season, and this one was a transfer that was undeniably successful (Cole's eventual partnership with Dwight Yorke being one of the driving forces behind Manchester United's treble in 1998–99).

The graph above shows the players who reached 50 Premier League goals in the smallest number of games. Cole (65 games) did so in one game fewer than Shearer (66) and remains the fastest player to reach a half-century. Curiously, going into his 65th game, Cole had scored only 45 goals. He then became the first player in the Premier League to score five times in one match, something that Shearer then emulated a few years later, to clock up his rapid half-century. Cole's final total of 187 goals was for a long time second only to Shearer, before Wayne Rooney caught up with him in 2015–16, but Rooney's absence from this fastest to 50 goals table is instructive. In cricket terms, Cole was the twenty20 player, able to hit the ground running and smash out the runs, Rooney the calm Test opener who picked up the pace once settled at the crease.

Games to	Cole	Rooney
50 goals	65	146
100 goals	185	247
150 goals	286	330
187 goals	399	415

Another benefit of the fastest to 50 table is that it doesn't rule out excellent players who, for whatever reason, did not spend their whole careers in the Premier League. The presence of Fernando Torres (4th) Sergio Agüero (5th) and Luis Suárez (8th) is testament to their successful impact in the league.

No Penalties

While Andy Cole can boast that only one of his Premier League goals came from the penalty spot, the players in the table below are the top scorers not to boast a single spot-kick. Les Ferdinand ended his top-flight career with 149 Premier League goals; a single successful conversion would have given him a neat 150. Second is Emile Heskey, a player who in the latter stages of his career received more than his fair share of mockery yet for a decent spell in the late 1990s and early 2000s was one of the most effective and dangerous forwards in the league. A worthy mention to Luis Suárez, too, who scored 69 times in only 110 Premier League games, despite his captain Steven Gerrard monopolising the Liverpool penalty duties.

Penalty-less	Goals	Games played
Les Ferdinand	149	351
Emile Heskey	110	516
Ole Gunnar Solskjær	91	235
Kevin Campbell	83	325
Gabriel Agbonlahor	73	312
Luis Suárez	69	110

Incidentally, the reverse of this (i.e. players to have scored only penalties in the Premier League) is led by another former Liverpool midfielder, Jan Mølby, with seven. The big Dane's career pre-dated the Premier League, of course, and included that rare delight, a penalty hat-trick, against Coventry in the League Cup in November 1986.

Minutes Per Goal

So far we've looked only at quantitative categories. To make the process fairer we have to identify other metrics. Should Shearer win merely by his longevity? Minutes per goal is one of the more common ways of looking at effective goalscorers, and currently one man is significantly ahead of all others, namely Sergio Agüero. Manchester City's Argentinian forward, since arriving in England in 2011, has been one of the most effective finishers ever seen in the nation's top flight and this proves it. Scoring at a rate of a goal every 109 minutes, Agüero has already fired his team to two Premier League titles and in 2015 became only the fifth player to score five times in a single Premier League game. Thierry Henry was for a long time the best minutes-per-goal man in the division and, when allied to his significant haul of 175 goals, this also gives him a great shout of being the competition's greatest scorer. Unlike Agüero, Henry was rarely injured, playing more than 30 games in each of his first seven seasons at Arsenal. In fact he is the only striker to play more than 30 games in his first seven seasons in the Premier League, an impressive feat for someone who relied so much on those two elements so beloved of the English game: pace and power.

Other players of note in the ranking include Ruud van Nistelrooy and Luis Suárez in third and fourth respectively. Both men came into the division, scored at exceptional rates and then left for clubs in Spain. Daniel Sturridge is in fifth place, hugely impressive given his relatively slow scoring rate at the likes of Manchester City and Chelsea before hitting his stride at Liverpool. And Shearer? He is eighth, which, given how long he played in the Premier League, allied to the slowdown in his latter years at Newcastle, is hugely impressive.

Player	Goals	Mins/Goal
Sergio Agüero	102	107.8
Thierry Henry	175	121.8
Ruud van Nistelrooy	95	128.2
Daniel Sturridge	69	138.2
Luis Suárez	69	139.8
Robin van Persie	144	139.7
Edin Dzeko	50	141.6
Alan Shearer	260	146.9
Ole Gunnar Solskjaer	91	153.0
Michael Owen	150	153.6

Quality of Opponent

Theoretically it should be easier to score against teams from the lower reaches of the table than those at the top. That's a simplification, of course, but it is possible to assign players points (based on their opponent's position in the standings) for each goal. We are, therefore, looking for the lowest average figure, denoting that a player's goals have come against teams placed higher in the league.

Unsurprisingly there is not much variation among the leading scorers, their large hauls meaning that their average position figures all come in around 11. Of the top ten, Robbie Fowler has the lowest figure, helped by his habit of scoring so often against Arsenal.

1992–93 to 2014–15	Goals	Avg opponent pos per goals
Alan Shearer	260	11.6
Andrew Cole	187	11.5
Wayne Rooney	185	11.5
Frank Lampard	177	11.6
Thierry Henry	175	11.5
Robbie Fowler	163	11.0
Michael Owen	150	11.7
Les Ferdinand	149	11.3
Teddy Sheringham	146	11.3
Robin van Persie	144	11.6

Looking at this data another way, namely the players with the lowest average position per goal (players with 20-plus goals), reveals a few more interesting names. The majority played for clubs in the lower reaches but at the top of the pile is Chelsea's Diego Costa whose goals in his debut season for the club came against teams with an average position of 7.9. Danny Murphy also deserves mention, as the only player in this list with 50 goals, his average position helped by his superb record of scoring against Manchester United at Old Trafford. The Sturridge family are also happily represented once again, with Daniel's uncle Dean in eighth place here.

1992–93 to 2014–15	Goals	Avg opponent pos per goals
Diego Costa	20	7.9
Mick Quinn	25	8.3
Egil Østenstad	29	8.5
Francis Jeffers	25	8.5
John Fashanu	20	8.8
Danny Murphy	50	8.8
Steven Pienaar	20	8.9
Dean Sturridge	38	9.1
Henrik Pedersen	22	9.2
Efan Ekoku	52	9.2

Away Goals

Home advantage is becoming less pronounced in modern football (as we saw in the previous chapter) but it remains harder for a player to score away from home than it does on home turf. Who, then, are the players who have done best on the road in the Premier League?

Looking at the players to score 100-plus goals, only one has been more productive away from home: Ryan Giggs. He scored 109 goals, with 54% of them coming away from Old Trafford. That seems to make sense for a player who, in his early days at least, relied on pace and was therefore more effective away from home on the counter-attack. That said, no player loved a fast break more than Thierry Henry and he has the lowest proportion of away goals in this list, with just 55 of his 175 coming on the road. Understandably, Henry remains the only player to score 100 goals at a single ground (Highbury) until Rooney recently joined him in 2015–16 with his 100th at Old Trafford.

Player	Goals	Away goals	% away
Alan Shearer	260	87	33%
Wayne Rooney	**193**	**86**	**45%**
Andrew Cole	187	83	44%
Frank Lampard	177	85	48%
Thierry Henry	**175**	**55**	**31%**
Robbie Fowler	163	60	37%
Michael Owen	150	70	47%
Les Ferdinand	149	56	38%
Teddy Sheringham	146	64	44%
Robin van Persie	144	67	47%
Jermain Defoe	**143**	**56**	**39%**
Jimmy Floyd Hasselbaink	127	50	39%
Robbie Keane	126	49	39%
Nicola Anelka	125	56	45%
Dwight Yorke	123	51	41%
Steven Gerrard	120	51	43%
Ian Wright	113	51	45%
Dion Dublin	111	52	47%
Emile Heskey	110	54	49%
Ryan Giggs	**109**	**59**	**54%**
Paul Scholes	107	48	45%
Darren Bent	106	45	42%
Didier Drogba	104	35	34%
Sergio Agüero	**102**	**41**	**40%**
Matthew Le Tissier	100	44	44%

Also interesting is the fact that Alan Shearer has a low away goal proportion, with only 33% coming away from either Ewood Park in his Blackburn days or St James' Park in his time at Newcastle. Overall the average for players in the 100 goal club is 42%, which is probably about what you'd expect, basing it not on the numbers but on that gentle enemy of numbers, 'the hunch'.

Next let's look at players who have been particularly likely to score away from home. Using a minimum of 20 goals, we end up with this:

Player	Goals	Away goals	%
Michael Bridges	22	15	68
Marcus Bent	40	27	68
Paul Scharner	21	14	67
Roque Santa Cruz	26	17	65
Hernán Crespo	20	13	65
Javier Hernández	37	24	65
Peter Ndlovu	34	22	65
Rod Wallace	45	29	64
Aaron Ramsey	28	18	64
Edin Džeko	50	32	64
Efan Ekoku	52	33	63
Tore André Flo	38	24	63

It's a good list, made up of a range of different types of players. There's the hot prospect whose career was curtailed by injury (Michael Bridges), the reliable journeyman (Marcus Bent), the one-season wonder (Roque Santa Cruz) and the curiously underrated overseas players (Hernán Crespo, Edin Džeko). In case you were wondering, on the same basis (20-plus) goals, the player with the lowest proportion of away goals is Michael Carrick (17%), followed by Szilárd Németh, Jonatan Johansson and Graziano Pellè (all 22%).

Age Before Bounty

For many, your twenties are a period of both learning and frivolity. For footballers reaching the end of their third decade, the good times are all but over. There are exceptions, of course, but with the increasingly athletic requirements demanded of modern footballers, the days of players extending their prowess into their mid-thirties look numbered.

Here we can see top scorers split into three handy sections: goals before turning 22, goals before turning 30 and goals after 30. The first of these is a pretty stellar list, with Liverpool's 1990s fortune of having both Robbie Fowler and Michael Owen come through their youth system clearly evident. The pair scored 82 and 73 goals respectively before they were 22, with fellow Merseysider Wayne Rooney in third on 59. Rooney regularly gets compared with younger rivals or team-mates, with the inference that he will be eclipsed by the new generation. Fifty-nine goals at an age when most of these players have barely reached double figures suggests not.

PL – goals before turning 22	
Robbie Fowler	82
Michael Owen	73
Wayne Rooney	59
Chris Sutton	46
Romelu Lukaku	41
Cristiano Ronaldo	33
Emile Heskey	31
Jermain Defoe	28
Ryan Giggs	28
Nick Barmby	27
Alan Smith	27

Furthermore, Rooney heads the list of goals scored before turning 30. As befits a man who burst onto the scene at 16 with the body of a Greek wrestler, Rooney has plundered heavily and reached his fourth decade 11 goals ahead of Alan Shearer (who obviously suffered due to the Premier League not even existing when he was 16). Michael Owen's position in fifth place is a salutary lesson in how careers can start fast and end on the bench at Stoke. When he left Liverpool for Real Madrid in 2004, Owen had scored 118 goals in 216 games (0.55 per game), but after his return to England he added just 32 more in 110 matches (0.29). The man who never managed to score 20 league goals in a single season still had a reasonable career but it could (and probably should) have been a whole lot better.

PL – goals before turning 30	
Wayne Rooney	187
Alan Shearer	176
Thierry Henry	174
Robbie Fowler	152
Michael Owen	146
Andrew Cole	136
Robin van Persie	122
Robbie Keane	121
Jermain Defoe	116
Dwight Yorke	107

The list of top-scoring players in their thirties is headed by Ian Wright, a man who was not signed by a league club until he was 22 and who did not play in the top flight until he was almost 26. Whether that inauspicious start to his career spurred Wright on or not, he remains arguably the most effective player after his 30th birthday. Yes, Alan Shearer is there in second place, but his stellar days were his twenties, by this stage he had evolved into a not overly mobile penalty king, Wright in contrast was as good as ever as he single-mindedly hunted down Cliff Bastin's Arsenal goalscoring record. Though he scored 10 times in 1997–98 as the Gunners won their first Premier League crown under Arsène Wenger, he was an unused substitute as they landed the FA Cup and left for West Ham. In less salubrious conditions he still managed nine goals in 22 appearances.

Also worth a mention here is Frank Lampard, who is not only the top-scoring midfielder in Premier League history but maintained his standards until he left the competition for America in 2015. Eighty-two goals as a midfielder in your thirties, even one who takes penalties, is outstanding.

PL – goals after turning 30	
Ian Wright	93
Alan Shearer	84
Frank Lampard	82
Teddy Sheringham	77
Gianfranco Zola	59
Peter Beardsley	58
Didier Drogba	57
Les Ferdinand	57
Paolo Di Canio	54
Andrew Cole	51

Conclusion

There is, of course, no way to make a conclusive judgement on who is the Premier League's finest goalscorer. Alan Shearer stands alone on 260 goals and is unlikely to be passed in the next decade. His total is arguably less impressive than the way he reinvented himself in his thirties, once the toll of a career as a battering ram and a succession of knee injuries made their mark. For many, his latter days scoring largely from the penalty spot detract from the swashbuckling escapades of youth but that only matters if you place absolute importance on the number of goals scored. As we've seen in this chapter, there are myriad other ways of looking at quality (as well as quantity). Sergio Agüero's minutes-per-goal rate is surely as impressive as Shearer's monster haul, while Frank Lampard's combination of goals in his thirties and goals from midfield is unlikely to be repeated any time soon.

A lot of the names that have come up here might be either long forgotten to older readers or mysterious folk memory names to youngsters. It's good to remind or inform people about how impressive the likes of Les Ferdinand, Robbie Fowler and, yes, even Mick Quinn (who shone briefly but oh so brightly), were. The current stars will fade in time too, but what something like expected goals shows is that new ways to assess players will continue to be invented and will develop over time. One day Shearer's 260 goals will seem as isolated and information-less as Jimmy Greaves' 357, fine totals but with little context.

April–May

April

Categorised equally as 'squeaky bum time' by Alex Ferguson and 'the cruellest month' by T. S. Eliot, April is near enough to the end of the season to mean that if you are top of the table, then you should stand a good chance of landing the trophy. Does that stand up, though? The table below shows the team which topped the Premier League on 1 April in each season, with 17 of the 23 instances before 2015–16 seeing that side land the title. The only team to fall out of the top two were Norwich in 1992–93, and Leicester, who, ending the season with a winning margin of ten points, never looked likely to join the Canaries.

Premier League top 1 April	Team	Final pos
1992–93	Norwich City	3
1993–94	Manchester United	1
1994–95	Blackburn Rovers	1
1995–96	Manchester United	1
1996–97	Manchester United	1
1997–98	Manchester United	2
1998–99	Manchester United	1
1999–2000	Manchester United	1
2000–01	Manchester United	1
2001–02	Arsenal	1
2002–03	Arsenal	2

(continued)

Premier League top 1 April	Team	Final pos
2003–04	Arsenal	1
2004–05	Chelsea	1
2005–06	Chelsea	1
2006–07	Manchester United	1
2007–08	Manchester United	1
2008–09	Manchester United	1
2009–10	Manchester United	2
2010–11	Manchester United	1
2011–12	Manchester United	2
2012–13	Manchester United	1
2013–14	Liverpool	2
2014–15	Chelsea	1
2015–16	Leicester City	1

April 13th, a Wednesday, saw a delicious crop of games, with matches in the Champions League, the Premier League and the FA Cup all on the same day, the first time this had happened since 7 March 2003. Meanwhile, the following week saw six consecutive days of Premier League action, just two days short of the competition record of eight, back in the heady days of April 1995.

Watford's admirable commitment to rehabilitating goal-keepers who had spent some troubled time with a north London side (original case study: Manuel Almunia) is continuing apace with former Tottenham glovesman Heurelho Gomes. Gomes, despite occasional decision-making that in the goalkeeping lexicon is invariably classed as 'antics', remains one of the most effective penalty savers in the modern game.

Watford's away game at West Brom in mid-April could have been a case of 'can't shoot, won't shoot' but the home side mustered a healthy 17 attempts, including four shots on target. Look closer, though, and you'll see that half of these shots on target came from the penalty spot, and both resulted in saves

Date	Team	Player	Opponent	Penalties saved
02/03/94	Aston Villa	Mark Bosnich	Tottenham Hotspur	2
18/12/99	Sheffield Wednesday	Pavel Srníček	Aston Villa	2
02/02/05	Fulham	Edwin van der Sar	Aston Villa	2
09/09/06	Blackburn Rovers	Brad Friedel	Sheffield United	2
22/10/06	Bolton Wanderers	Jussi Jääskeläinen	Blackburn Rovers	2
03/04/10	**Tottenham Hotspur**	**Heurelho Gomes**	**Sunderland**	**2**
16/04/16	**Watford**	**Heurelho Gomes**	**West Bromwich Albion**	**2**

from Gomes in the Watford goal. It meant that the Brazilian, at that point, had saved 32% of the spot-kicks he had faced in the Premier League, the best rate of any goalkeeper to face 20 or more in the competition.

It was also only the seventh time in the Premier League era that a goalkeeper has saved multiple penalties in a single game, with Gomes the first player to do it since . . . Heurelho Gomes for Tottenham almost exactly six years earlier. (As a footnote, Watford conceded another two penalties in their next game, becoming only the second team in Premier League history to concede four spot-kicks in two games.

★

On sunnier shores, Barcelona won 8-0 and 6-0 in the space of four days in late April, reigniting their title charge after an under-par spell that had seen them exit the Champions League at the hands of La Liga rivals Atlético Madrid. A goal difference of plus 14 over two matches is, as you'd expect, fairly unusual, with the most recent instance of this happening within a single season in the English leagues coming back in 1962–63 when Oldham Athletic pummelled Southport 11-0 on Boxing Day and then beat Lincoln 4-1 in their next outing. Oldham didn't even have MSN, it possibly still doesn't.

★

The problem with being, for want of a better term, an 'ASSIST KING' like Mesut Özil is that you are reliant on your team-mates actually being able to tuck away the cavalcade of chances that you're handing to them. Like an award-winning chef whose waiters cannot carry plates of food without dropping them on the floor, Özil was stuck with the non-scoring Olivier Giroud and the almost non-existent Theo Walcott during the spring, his delicately prepared football menu going largely uneaten.

PL 2003–04 to 2015–16	Player	Chances created (incl. assists) in single season
2015–16	**Mesut Özil**	**146**
2008–09	Frank Lampard	134
2015–16	**Dimitri Payet**	**119**
2010–11	Florent Malouda	117
2006–07	Cesc Fàbregas	116
2012–13	Leighton Baines	116
2009–10	Frank Lampard	114
2007–08	Cesc Fàbregas	112
2006–07	Mikel Arteta	108
2015–16	**Christian Eriksen**	**115**
2012–13	David Silva	104
2006–07	Ryan Giggs	104
2007–08	Steven Gerrard	104
2011–12	David Silva	104

Anyone who enjoys the shrill sound of a referee's whistle should have been at Selhurst Park on 9 April as Crystal Palace took on Norwich. The ball was in play that day for only 45 minutes and 39 seconds, in a game that lasted for more than 98. Forty-five minutes each way? There's only one way in south-east London.

*

Records involving Lionel Messi have, like gold and Viennettas, been devalued in recent years. So keen are fans and compilers to usher along the next Messi humdinger that in the past they have used games and goals that they simply shouldn't have. Friendlies, B-team games, youth matches, it wouldn't be a complete surprise if someone was counting goals Messi had scored while playing FIFA with his friends. Thankfully, in April Messi finally reached a bona fide landmark, and one that very few players can ever celebrate, namely 500 goals.

As if to ratchet up the excitement a little bit more, Messi had gone on what was described as a scoring drought (four games without a goal.) Which, for Messi, was little short of a disaster.

Competition	Goals
La Liga	309
Champions League	83
Copa del Rey	39
Spanish Super Cup	11
European Super Cup	3
Club World Cup	5
Copa América	3
Friendly	27
World Cup	5
World Cup Qualifier	15

Scored with	Goals
Left	406
Right	71
Head	21
Other body part	2

Goals in game	Goals
1	184
2	98
3	33
4	4
5	1

The breakdown of his 500 goals can be seen above, with his thaumaturgic left foot accounting for more than 400 of them. And despite being only 170cm tall, Messi has scored 21 goals with his head, as many as Andy Carroll has scored in the Premier League. Yes, Carroll is probably better when the ball is chucked into the box in injury time, but overall I'd usually take Messi.

His seasonal totals are just as staggering, with 2011–12 his absolute peak with an astonishing 82 goals in a single season. Eighty-two goals. Eighty-two. That was three more than Liverpool managed that season in all competitions. Now, Liverpool have won the European Cup five times and are one of the best-supported clubs on the planet, but overall I'd usually take . . . you get the idea.

Season	Goals
2004–05	1
2005–06	10
2006–07	19
2007–08	21
2008–09	41
2009–10	48
2010–11	57
2011–12	82
2012–13	69
2013–14	48
2014–15	62
2015–16	45

*Table includes all of Messi's goals in 2015–16 so comes to more than 500. This excludes the 2016 Copa America.

The Cambridge University Footlights may be a good breeding ground for light entertainment, but the city's biggest football team have a more sinister effect on the industry. On 19 April, Cambridge scored seven goals in a Football League game for the first time since March 1999, the day before Ernie Wise died. Neatly, the team which took a hammering in 2016 were Morecambe, but surely that was the end of it. Sadly not, because on 20 April, Victoria Wood, who had played Eric Morecambe's mother in a BBC film in 2011, passed away. Next time the U's go goal crazy at the Abbey Stadium, someone keep an eye on the national treasures.

Back when the world was their oyster, Arsenal used to rule London with an iron fist. There's a long-standing theory that it's harder for London sides to win the title as they have to play many more local derbies than the northern powerhouses, but that ignores the fact that every team raised their game when facing Liverpool or Manchester United in their pomp.

In any case, Arsenal's points totals from London derbies in their three Premier League title-winning campaigns are 22 from ten games in 1997–98, 21 from ten in 2001–02 and 18 from eight in 2003–04. Last season the Gunners managed just seven points, with just a single win from eight matches, the first time this had happened since 1963–64. Indeed, it's not outlandish to say that their final ten-point gap to champions Leicester would have been overturned had Arsène Wenger's team performed more successfully in local battles.

Premier League London derbies 2015–16

Pos	Team	P	W	D	L	F	A	Pts
1	West Ham United	8	4	3	1	16	13	15
2	Tottenham Hotspur	8	3	4	1	13	8	13
3	Chelsea	8	3	3	2	12	8	12
4	Arsenal	8	1	4	3	9	13	7
5	Crystal Palace	8	1	2	5	8	16	5

And while the Gunners did fractionally better than Crystal Palace, topping the capital in 2015–16 were West Ham, who picked up points against London rivals as easily as they inherited Olympic stadia.

★

Though it wasn't quite the final nail in the coffin, Tottenham's 1-1 draw with West Brom on a Monday in late April certainly excavated a large hole into which their title dreams were lowered. It was the start of a four-game winless run that took them from title outsiders to outside the top two. Just a week earlier Spurs had smashed Stoke 4-0 to ignite hope, but faced with maximum Tony Pulis at home they didn't manage a single shot on target after the 20th minute of the game, their 33rd-minute goal coming courtesy of Craig Dawson. File under: squibs, damp.

May

The first weekend in May saw the first team promoted from the Championship, in the form of Burnley, who spent May 2015 being relegated to the Championship. The Clarets have now been promoted to the Premier League on three occasions, with only Crystal Palace, Sunderland, West Brom and now Middlesbrough having done it more often. Burnley are also the 19th team to bounce straight back from a Premier League relegation, something which is more common than you might think. Only in 2009–10, 2004–05, 2003–04 and 1997-98 have the teams coming up to the Premier League not contained a recent departure. Sometimes the parachute opens in time.

Team	Years promoted to PL
Birmingham City	2002, 2007, 2009
Bolton Wanderers	1995, 1997, 2001
Burnley	**2009, 2014, 2016**
Crystal Palace	1994, 1997, 2004, 2013
Leicester City	1994, 1996, 2003, 2014
Middlesbrough	**1992, 1995, 1998, 2016**
Norwich City	2004, 2011, 2015
Sunderland	1996, 1999, 2005, 2007
Watford	1999, 2006, 2015
West Bromwich Albion	2002, 2004, 2008, 2010
West Ham United	1993, 2005, 2012

*

Tottenham's Premier League title chase blew up in fantastically violent fashion against Chelsea. Two-nil up and set to prolong Leicester's wait for at least another five days, Spurs capitulated in terms of goals in the second half but not in terms of commitment, with Mauricio Pochettino's team conceding a series of aggressive fouls that would grace any football game or street brawl. Referee Mark Clattenburg demonstrated restraint/weakness (delete as you see fit) by not sending off any Tottenham players but did hand out nine yellow cards to the team in white, which set a new Premier League record, beating West Ham's eight in their trip to QPR in October 2012. West London, it can drive you mad, you know.

All-time Premier League

Date	Team	Opponent	Yellow cards
02/05/16	Tottenham Hotspur	Chelsea	9
01/10/12	West Ham United	Queens Park Rangers	8
26/11/2000	Arsenal	Leeds United	7
03/02/01	Derby County	Sunderland	7
24/11/02	Leeds United	Tottenham Hotspur	7
25/03/06	Everton	Liverpool	7
02/02/08	Manchester United	Tottenham Hotspur	7
21/09/08	Manchester United	Chelsea	7
28/08/10	Wolverhampton Wanderers	Newcastle United	7
02/01/11	Aston Villa	Chelsea	7
23/10/11	Chelsea	Queens Park Rangers	7
09/11/13	West Bromwich Albion	Chelsea	7

Anyone looking to understand football rivalry, and why the game cannot be boiled down in blogs to mere numbers, should watch the closing stages of Chelsea's 2-2 draw with Tottenham that ended the visitors' title ambitions. Chelsea, the reigning champions, were running the ball into the corner to use up time, essentially fast-tracking the end of their own time as the champions of England to inflict misery on their old rivals from north London. Schadenfreude remains the lifeblood of the game.

Manchester City's limp exit from the Champions League semi-final at the hands of Real Madrid was both unsurprising and a missed opportunity. It was the first time City had navigated this far in the competition but with a lame-duck manager in charge they failed a test that on another day they could well have passed. Real are one of the most feared teams in Europe for their attacking prowess rather than their defensive solidity (they went into this second leg having conceded more goals than any other team in La Liga's top four). Conversely, while City's defending has been often lacklustre under Manuel Pellegrini, they do have offensive talent.

Pellegrini referenced this after the match, noting that 'both games were close, but we are usually a team which creates a lot of chances and we didn't do that tonight'. But the evidence in fact shows a steady decline from the heights of Pellegrini's Premier League title winning season in 2013–14.

Season	Shots/game
2013–14	17.09
2014–15	16.98
2015–16	16.16
After Guardiola announcement	14.07

Back then City were hitting more than 17 shots per game, but by 2014–15 this had fallen by almost one per match. Furthermore, there was a significant fall from February onwards, which coincidentally happened to be the moment that City announced Guardiola as their new manager for 2016–17. Shooting may result in lame ducks, but it seems lame ducks cannot inspire shooting, and for Pep, unlike when he arrived at treble winners Bayern, he has plenty of room for improvement at the Etihad.

For the first time in Premier League history (and possibly all time, but, come on, everyone deserves a rest sometimes), 2015–16 saw not a single club with an English manager in the top half of the league table at the end of the season. An indictment of both coaching standards and the opportunities afforded to native managers, a full-time English boss hasn't even finished in second place since the 1990s (by live TV meltdown specialists Ron Atkinson in 1993 and Kevin Keegan in 1996).

Chelsea responded to Tottenham's nine yellow cards by picking up one of their own inside a minute against Sunderland, Gary Cahill the culprit. It was one of only two yellow cards shown inside 60 seconds in the Premier League in 2015–16, contravening the unwritten and unsubstantiated rule that 'refs will let one go early doors'. Special mention to Raheem Sterling who was booked for simulation inside four minutes on Boxing Day. Truly the spirit of Christmas.

Date	Player	Team	Opposition	Venue	Offence	Time
29/08/15	Max Gradel	Bournemouth	Leicester City	Home	Foul	00:37
07/05/16	Gary Cahill	Chelsea	Sunderland	Away	Foul	00:44
03/10/15	Mark Noble	West Ham United	Sunderland	Away	Foul	01:44
20/09/15	James Milner	Liverpool	Norwich City	Home	Foul	02:12
29/08/15	Moussa Sissoko	Newcastle United	Arsenal	Home	Foul	02:52
09/04/16	Andy Carroll	West Ham United	Arsenal	Home	Foul	03:13
26/12/15	Raheem Sterling	Manchester City	Sunderland	Home	Dive	03:51
09/08/15	Ibrahim Afellay	Stoke City	Liverpool	Home	Foul	03:56

West Brom aren't very good at penalties. Perhaps because the Hawthorns is the highest ground in England and West Brom's players struggle to process oxygen? Or perhaps it's because their technique is, um, bad. But, the truth is, their failure to convert one at Bournemouth in May was the fourth time from five attempts in 2015–16 that they had failed (including two in one match against Watford). When discussing penalty shootouts, managers often like to say 'we didn't practise penalties because you cannot recreate a game scenario in training', but some teams should just practise them anyway. Run up and kick the ball into the net. It's easy when you know how.

2015–16 PL	Penalties taken	Penalties saved	Penalty success rate (%)
West Bromwich Albion	5	4	20.00
Arsenal	2	0	50.00
Manchester City	8	0	62.50
Southampton	3	1	66.67
Bournemouth	4	1	75.00
Everton	4	1	75.00
Chelsea	4	0	75.00
Leicester City	13	2	76.92
Crystal Palace	5	1	80.00
Watford	6	1	83.33

> Talking of penalties, Leicester's pair against Everton in their coronation game took them to four for the season against the Toffees, which equalled a Premier League record held by Blackburn (v Bolton in 2006–07) and Sunderland (v Tottenham in 2009–10). To put it into perspective, Leicester's four spot-kicks against Everton in 2015–16 is more than seven teams were given in total, including Manchester United, Arsenal and Liverpool.

★

When Mesut Özil recorded his 16th assist of the Premier League season on 28 December it looked almost certain that Thierry Henry's competition record of 20 set in 2002–03 would be shattered. But the New Year saw a downturn in Arsenal's form and as a consequence, Özil added just another three in 2016 (an assist on the final day of the season was like a fresh cherry on a stale cake) as both he and his club ended a season which could have ended in a fourth league title for Arsène Wenger. As the table shows, in both October and December, Özil was providing more than one assist per 90 minutes of play. If you had suggested then that the German would not make it into the PFA team of the season, you would have almost certainly triggered the considerable online support he enjoys into their default attack mode. But he didn't and he and the Gunners will have to wait until 2016–17, or maybe even later, to mount a serious challenge.

Mesut Özil	Mins	Assists	Assists/90
August	263	1	0.34
September	249	2	0.72
October	335	6	1.61
November	270	2	0.67
December	432	5	1.04
January	267	0	0.00
February	360	2	0.50
March	253	0	0.00
April	530	0	0.00
May	88	1	1.02

★

When Roberto Martínez was relieved of his duties at Everton on 12 May he became the first Premier League manager to depart a team with one match to go since Avram Grant was sacked by West Ham in 2011, after a 3-2 defeat to . . . Roberto Martínez's Wigan Athletic. The story is old, but it goes on.

Newcastle went down but they took Tottenham with them, Hotspur sinking like an armoured medieval knight into a river. All Spurs needed to secure second place and finish above Arsenal for the first time in 21 seasons was a draw. A measly draw at a team already condemned to the Championship, but also strangely cock-a-hoop at the prospect of retaining glamour boss Rafa Benítez for trips to the likes of Burton Albion. Still, Tottenham had the best defence in the competition heading into the final day, and even without suspended fulcrums Dele Alli and Moussa Dembélé, they would surely have enough to see off the Magpies.

Instead, Tottenham's afternoon in the North East turned into a fully-fledged nightmare as Newcastle ran out winners by five goals to one, becoming only the seventh relegated team in top-flight history to score five or more goals in their final game, a last hurrah for fans preparing for a new life in a lower division. Additionally, Newcastle became only the second team in Premier League history to score five or more goals in a game where they had had a man sent off. The result was that Tottenham slipped out of the top two and once again ended the season underneath their old rivals. Champions League qualification has never felt so bitter.

Date	Team	Opponent	F	A	Season
10/04/1897	Burnley	West Bromwich Albion	5	0	1896–97
21/04/1906	Wolverhampton Wanderers	Derby County	7	0	1905–06
03/05/1930	Burnley	Derby County	6	2	1929–30
06/05/1933	Bolton Wanderers	Leeds United	5	0	1932–33
05/05/1951	Sheffield Wednesday	Everton	6	0	1950–51
30/04/1955	Sheffield Wednesday	West Bromwich Albion	5	0	1954–55
15/05/2016	Newcastle United	Tottenham Hotspur	5	1	2015–16

A mixed night for Wayne Rooney in Manchester United's rearranged final game against Bournemouth. His goal in the first half meant that he became only the second player in Premier League history to score 100 goals at a single ground (at Old Trafford, with Thierry Henry having scored 114 times at Highbury), while his failure to add two more goals meant that he failed to reach double figures for the first time at United, ending a run of 11 consecutive campaigns of ten or more goals, a Premier League record. He ended the season in midfield, of course, but that never stopped Frank Lampard.

The days of the 4-4-2 formation, that cornerstone of English football, continue to pass into the mists of time. Only three teams, Watford, West Brom and title winners Leicester, had 4-4-2 as their most used formation in the Premier League in 2015–16, a sad decline for the former go-to playing stance of choice. Leicester obviously fashioned it in a very successful way, but Watford, while lauded for their striker partnership of Troy Deeney and Odion Ighalo in the first half of the season, saw the latter player fade significantly in the New Year, with Quique Sánchez Flores (named manager of the month in December) relieved of his duties in May.

Pressure at the foot of the table was indicated by the fact

that Aston Villa used a 5-3-2 formation five times (pack the defence!) and Sunderland used 5-4-1 twice (pack the defence even more!). Meanwhile, the league showed that diamonds are not forever as the once-loved jewel-based formation was used just twice, once by Liverpool, once by Swansea City.

Most common formations – Premier League 2015–16

Team	Starting formation	Times used
Arsenal	4-2-3-1	38
Aston Villa	4-3-3	11
Bournemouth	4-1-4-1	16
Chelsea	4-2-3-1	38
Crystal Palace	4-2-3-1	17
Everton	4-2-3-1	28
Leicester City	4-4-2	34
Liverpool	4-2-3-1	13
Manchester City	4-2-3-1	24
Manchester United	4-2-3-1	25
Newcastle United	4-2-3-1	24
Norwich City	4-4-1-1	23
Southampton	4-2-3-1	22
Stoke City	4-2-3-1	32
Sunderland	4-1-4-1	19
Swansea City	4-2-3-1	22
Tottenham Hotspur	4-2-3-1	36
Watford	4-4-2	29
West Bromwich Albion	4-4-2	10
West Ham United	4-3-3	13

8.

Out of the Foxhole: The Baffling Glory of Leicester City

'Getting LCFC promoted and the greatest escape ever,
Pearson is sacked? Are the folk running football stupid? Yes'

Gary Lineker, June 2015

Leicester City's rise and rise and rise (and rise) from the dark days of spring 2015 to the almost preposterous scenes of May 2016 is going to produce enough content to last humanity for a good few years. Just what changed last year will probably never be completely and satisfactorily explained but we can at least have a try. If you were bullet-pointing key moments for the Foxes over the past few years then the first would be the purchase of the club by Thai billionaire Vichai Srivaddhanap-rabha in 2010, shortly after the club had clambered out of the third tier. Another would be a second promotion in 2014 and a statement from the owner that the club would finish in the Premier League's top five at some point in the next three years. Fanciful claims from excitable chairmen are part of the game's fabric, and this looked like just another entry in that list.

At the end of winter 2014, the Foxes looked very much like the standard over-promoted Championship team. Marooned at the foot of the table, the club was making headlines thanks to manager Nigel Pearson rather than the players on the pitch. In early February he, for reasons still unknown, wrestled with Crystal Palace's James McArthur on the touchline; his team lost 1-0. In late March, the last Plantagenet king of England, Richard III, was respectfully buried at Leicester Cathedral after spending most of the previous 500 years festering under the town centre. A few days later the city's football team went on a winning streak that not only saved them from certain doom in 2014–15 (they spent longer at the bottom of the table than any other non-relegated team in the competition's history) but then continued under Pearson's replacement, Claudio Ranieri in 2015–16, and drove them to one of the most unlikely successes in football history, namely the Premier League title.

King Arthur, King Richard, King Claudio, King Power.

Put simply, the last few months of the 2014–15 season were tumultuous but they put in motion something that a new manager was able to harness and improve on. This chapter will try and identify some of the elements behind Leicester's monumental achievement, although, as always, neither the data nor the anecdotes will be able to fully explain what happened in the East Midlands in the mid-2010s.

The Historical Parallels

The twenty-first century has been awash with statements bemoaning the supposed passing of meritocracy in top-level football, and, while there are many things that support that view, there are others that do not. Provincial teams like Wigan and Bournemouth have reached the Premier League and prospered (relatively), and now Leicester have become the first new champions of England since the 1970s. Just like Sheffield Wednesday in the late 1920s, Leicester escaped relegation by a fine margin and finished 14th, then followed it up a year later with the biggest prize in the country.

As the table below shows, the 1960s and 1970s both saw two new champions, with the incomparable Brian Clough responsible for both Derby and Nottingham Forest's maiden wins (Derby won another title under Dave Mackay after Clough had left in classically acrimonious scenes). Going back further, the 1950s saw three first-time title winners (Chelsea, Wolves and Tottenham), while even the war-ravaged 1940s saw Portsmouth win their first title in 1949.

Season	First time title winner	Seasons since promotion
2015–16	Leicester City	2
1977–78	Nottingham Forest	1
1971–72	Derby County	3
1968–69	Leeds United	5
1961–62	Ipswich	1

But since 1978: nothing. The 1980s were dominated by Liverpool, the 1990s by Manchester United and the twenty-first century by a group of English super-clubs, the traditional (sic) Big Four, as well as the addition of the newly enriched Manchester City. The chances of anyone breaking into that group were both limited by and reliant on large amounts of cash. Indeed, one persuasive view of the financial fair play rules that were introduced in the 2000s is that, rather than level the playing field, they were designed instead to protect the market leading position of the long-established clubs and prevent any more cash-infused arrivistes nibbling at the pie.

Leicester are neither a traditional big club nor particularly financially boosted. While it is true that they are owned by a billionaire, their wage bill (and wages remain one of the best guides to finishing position for a team) is one of the lowest in the division. Their title challenge is arguably the most unpredictable thing ever to happen in English football. When Nottingham Forest won the title as a newly promoted team in 1978 you could see that the momentum and winning mentality from the second tier had been carried through to the top flight. Leicester were dead and buried in March 2015 yet fifteen months later were the champions of England.

Other nations have seen comparable performances in the last 30 years. The most obvious is Hellas Verona in Serie A in

1984–85, securing their first and so far only league title. That season is notorious for being one where the organisers introduced randomly selected referees to games, as part of an attempt to clean up the reputation of the league, only to see a provincial team outstrip the usual suspects in what could have been a coincidence, or perhaps not. Like Leicester, Verona were a team which had bought well in the seasons leading up to their stellar campaign, and were also very organised (their defensive record was the best in the league, with 19 goals conceded), losing twice all campaign. One factor that shouldn't be underestimated, though, is that with only 16 teams in Serie A in this era, they needed to play eight games fewer than Leicester did in 2015–16. Just as cups can usually throw up bigger surprises than league competition due to the smaller number of wins/performances required, this much shorter league campaign certainly favoured the Italian side.

A more recent example is the 2011–12 season in France, where Montpellier landed the title ahead of nascent superpower PSG, despite having only been promoted to the top division in 2008–09. Like Leicester, Montpellier, a town known more for its rugby team, had finished 14th the previous season and no one had fancied them to mount a title challenge, let alone maintain one. Also, like the Foxes they were led by a native striker who had risen from the lower leagues (for Jamie Vardy read Olivier Giroud) while the creativity came from a North African (for Riyad Mahrez read Younès Belhanda). When La Paillade landed their unlikely trophy in 2012 the congratulations were accompanied by think-pieces stating that it was a 'freak season' and that the 'growing financial might of European super-clubs' could mean a similar feat was never seen again. In some senses that's been proved right, with PSG having won the title in each of the subsequent four seasons. On the other hand: Leicester City.

One final thought on the sheer unlikeliness of Leicester winning the title and the fact that it seemed so unthinkable in England. The table below shows the last first-time winner in a range of European countries (before 2015–16). England, before Leicester, had waited the longest for a new champion, followed by border pals Scotland, who last saw a new champion in 1983 when Dundee United won the SPL. In a neat coincidence, the Tangerines were relegated from the Scottish top flight on the same night that Tottenham failed to beat Chelsea, handing Leicester the title. Montpellier, as discussed above, are in there, while even leagues as dominant and cash-rich as those in Germany (Wolfsburg, 2009) and Spain (Deportivo, 2000) have seen new title winners this century.

Last first-time top-flight title winners

Country	Year of title win	Team
Belgium	2015	Gent
Denmark	2015	FC Midjylland
France	2012	Montpellier
Czech Republic	2011	Viktoria Plzeň
Norway	2011	Molde
Netherlands	2010	Twente
Turkey	2010	Bursaspor
Germany	2009	Wolfsburg
Russia	2008	Rubin Kazan
Sweden	2008	Kalmar
Portugal	2001	Boavista
Spain	2000	Deportivo La Coruña
Switzerland	1992	Sion
Italy	1991	Sampdoria
Poland	1991	Zagłębie Lubin
Greece	1988	AE Larissa
Scotland	1983	Dundee United
England	**1978**	**Nottingham Forest**

The Recovery

We know how the story ends, but the beginning remains shrouded in mystery. Nevertheless, it's worth a reminder of just how badly off Leicester were heading into their final ten games of the 2014–15 season, seven points from safety and nine points behind Hull (the team which eventually went down alongside Queens Park Rangers and Burnley). They had also been rock bottom at Christmas, triggering the real-but-declining-in-effectiveness rule that propping up the Premier League on 25 December ensured a team would go down (West Brom in 2004–05, Sunderland in 2013–14 and subsequently Leicester in 2014–15 are the exceptions).

Premier League – 16 March 2015						
Pos	Team	P	W	D	L	Pts
15	Hull City	29	6	10	13	28
16	Aston Villa	29	7	7	15	28
17	Sunderland	29	4	14	11	26
18	Burnley	29	5	10	14	25
19	Queens Park Rangers	29	6	4	19	22
20	**Leicester City**	**28**	**4**	**7**	**17**	**19**

Delving into the trends behind the data is one way to shine a light on what happened in the closing weeks of 2014–15, and the table below shows Leicester's expected goals and expected goals conceded rates by quarter and the leap in the final quarter of 2014–15 is the very definition of stark. (NB: you can also see how they key to Ranieri's good start as the Foxes manager in 2015–16 was the maintenance of the ~1.8 xG per game rate they hit in the final ten games under Nigel Pearson.)

Without getting too technical, remember that in essence expected goals are a guide to how a player or team should do with their shots, based on the historical norm from that particular position on the pitch. For the first three-quarters of 2014–15, Leicester's underlying data was that of a struggling team, but the five quarters since then have been championship form, with both scenarios playing out exactly that way in real life. It may be a results business but even a chef needs to know what ingredients he has in his kitchen.

What is particularly striking about the figures below is that Leicester recorded their best figures in all three areas in the final nine games of 2015–16. In the matches that secured them the title, they were performing best of all. At the exact time many people expected them to crumble under pressure, they actually became better than ever before.

	Quarter	Matches	xG	xG against	Avg pts
2014–15	1	9	1.00	1.60	1.00
	2	10	0.90	1.35	0.40
	3	9	0.90	1.50	0.70
	4	10	1.90	1.30	2.20
2015–16	1	10	1.80	1.32	1.90
	2	10	1.80	1.26	2.10
	3	9	1.83	1.06	2.11
	4	9	1.92	1.02	2.33

Jumping back to the end of the Pearson regime, Leicester essentially added an (expected) goal per game to their play in the final 10 games of 2014–15, an enormous boost to any team, but especially one rooted to the foot of the table. Their first game of that final ten-game spell, interestingly given the title race in the following season, was a 4-3 defeat at Tottenham, their attack rebooted but the defence uncharacteristically plundered. Nevertheless, Pearson's team went on to keep five clean sheets in their remaining nine matches, with 13 points garnered from them. Leicester's 5-1 hammering of relegated

QPR on the final day was almost universally filed under 'struggling team who survived the drop cutting loose on the last day of term' but in fact it was a portent of just what was to come in the new campaign.

Caen Do Attitude

Claudio Ranieri's appointment at Leicester was met with the familiar and over-publicised sense of dismay (from most Leicester supporters) and mild derision (from many journalists and pundits who could remember the Italian being ditched one year into the Roman Abramovich era at Chelsea and who had managed, largely unsuccessfully, in Spain, Italy and France. Most recently he endured a dismal spell as Greece national manager, which ended summarily after a home defeat to northern giants the Faroe Islands).

Yet his arrival at the King Power stadium was significant for reasons that only became obvious later in the season. Firstly, it allowed Leicester to continue with their owners' ongoing project for the club. Ranieri's stock wasn't so high that he could demand to tear up existing plans and embark on his own personal vision. Instead he was happy to take control of Nigel Pearson's survivalists and add a few new players, largely on the basis of the club's excellent scouting networks, led by head of recruitment Steve Walsh. A key example of this was N'Golo Kanté, signed from Caen in summer 2015. The Malian midfielder had led Ligue 1 for tackles made (178) in 2014–15 and was in the top five for interceptions. Crucially, he played for a team that were very similar in approach to his new side. Slotting into the Leicester team was not a gamble, and his influence on the side is illustrated in the table below. His inclusion in the PFA team of the season for 2015–16 should be of no surprise. His fellow professionals were easily able to spot the critical role he played in allowing Drinkwater to spring the attacking gazelles Riyad Mahrez and Jamie Vardy (incidentally, it's worth noting the success Leicester have had at importing players such as Kanté and Mahrez from French football, something overlooked in the stampede to criticise clubs such as Aston Villa for relying on imports from, oh yes, French football). The sheer amount of work Kanté got through – and it's worth noting that his pass completion of 82% was the best of any Leicester regular in 2015–16 – allowed the likes of Mahrez and Vardy to concentrate solely on offering an effective attacking threat.

N'Golo Kanté

	Caen 2014–15	League rank	Leicester 2015–16	League rank
Tackles	178	1	175	1
Interceptions	110	5	157	1

Other than integrating Kanté into the team, Ranieri largely relied on the players who had served so well under the previous regime in spring 2015. The key difference this time was that those players hit the ground running from the very first minute of the very first game (after 25 minutes of the opening game against Sunderland Leicester were 3-0 up, with goals from Vardy and two from Mahrez setting the tone for the autumn, although nobody gave it any thought at the time).

Indeed, Leicester's defence at the start of 2015–16 was often as unreliable as it had been during the previous campaign's relegation battle, only this time their attacking players were able to pull the team out of trouble on a game-by-game basis. One crucial early result was a 3-2 home win against Tim Sherwood's Aston Villa. The visitors were 2-0 up and heading for a second win of the season, before Leicester scored three times in the closing 18 minutes. Not only did the win maintain Ranieri's unbeaten start, but it plunged Villa into a dark spiral that saw Sherwood lose his job and the club's second league win of the season eventually arrive as late as January.

Leicester's gung-ho approach in the early weeks, something that had been glimpsed under the Pearson regime in 2014–15 when they inflicted Manchester United's first ever Premier League defeat from a two-goal lead, quickly saw them installed as the neutral's favourites, and their end-to-end 5-2 home defeat to Arsenal in September (the only time they conceded more than twice in a league game all season) saw their unbeaten start to the season end. It also seemed to confirm that the Gunners would finally mount a credible title challenge in what was already shaping up to be a strange season, one in which the defending champions Chelsea were already well off the pace, while Liverpool and Manchester United were also treading water.

Behind the scenes Ranieri was making subtle decisions that impacted on his team and their chances of success. A relationship with the Mapei centre in Italy gave his new team a fitness parity with the likes of Italian giants Juventus. This improved physical prowess allowed Ranieri to get the most from players such as Mahrez and Vardy. Even when Vardy did succumb to injury, he managed to schedule groin surgery to coincide with the FA Cup, meaning he didn't miss a single Premier League game until his suspension for a red card in the closing weeks of the campaign.

The sheer consistency of selection that Ranieri enjoyed in 2015–16 is shown in the table below, with Manchester United in 1992–93 the only Premier League title-winning team in the competition's history to make fewer alterations to their starting XI than Leicester. A year earlier, José Mourinho had been criticised for a lack of rotation at Chelsea (something thought to have caused their slowdown in the New Year as they trudged morosely to the title). Yet Mourinho made more than three times as many changes as Leicester did in 2015–16. In a season where everything the Foxes touched turned to gold, having such a settled team was a key element.

PL champion	Starting XI changes (overall)	Season
Manchester United	26	1992–93
Leicester City	33	2015–16
Blackburn Rovers	47	1994–95
Manchester United	52	1993–94
Manchester United	68	1995–96
Arsenal	69	2003–04
Manchester United	71	2002–03
Arsenal	75	1997–98
Chelsea	78	2004–05
Chelsea	86	2014–15
Manchester United	94	1996–97
Manchester United	100	1999–2000
Arsenal	102	2001–02
Manchester City	106	2013–14
Chelsea	107	2009–10
Manchester City	108	2011–12
Chelsea	118	2005–06
Manchester United	118	2006–07
Manchester United	118	2007–08
Manchester United	123	2010–11
Manchester United	126	1998–99
Manchester United	127	2000–01
Manchester United	135	2012–13
Manchester United	140	2008–09

The Foxes ended the season having used only 23 players, fewer than any other Premier League team in 2015–16. It was still much more a collective effort than the last Midlands team to win the English title, Aston Villa in 1981. Famously, Villa used just 14 players all season, an incredible achievement by a title-winning side. Like their Leicester counterparts 35 years later, early exits from the League and FA Cups helped an unlikely title contender maintain their challenge. (It's worth noting that Leicester's total of 43 games in all competitions in 2015–16 is the lowest ever by a Premier League-winning team, beating Manchester United's 49 in 1995–6.)

Schmeichel, Morgan, Huth, Vardy, Drinkwater, Mahrez, Kanté, Albrighton, Fuchs, Simpson and Okazaki all played more than 2000 minutes in 2015–16, a remarkable maintenance of both fitness and form, even if Okazaki, Mahrez and Albrighton, in that order, were the most substituted players in the whole of the Premier League during the campaign. Indeed, only Steve Malbranque (26 times in 2009–10) has been substituted more in a Premier League season. The hall-of-fame back four of Fuchs, Simpson, Morgan and Huth were all on the pitch for 2242 minutes, the most solid of bases for Ranieri to build on.

Gathering Pace

If the image of Leicester before Christmas was an ecstatic Jamie Vardy wheeling away as he set a new Premier League record by scoring in 11 consecutive games, the growing realisation that Leicester could be at least a player in the title race was the undercurrent. A look at the ten-year Google search graph for 'Leicester City' would suggest that November was the point when the globe woke up to what was happening in the East Midlands, and the associated spotlight fell on them.

Perhaps the moment Leicester knew their title challenge was being taken seriously was when they started being criticised.

Graph of Google Mentions for Leicester City

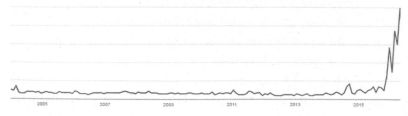

The end of 2015 saw the emergence of discussion about how Leicester 'were not playing like typical champions' and how their success was reliant on a counter-attacking game that would surely be nullified by tactically advanced teams in the New Year. A goalless draw at home to Bournemouth on 2 January meant the Foxes had gone three games in a row without scoring and their failure to dispatch a Cherries team who were about to stage their own recovery from relegation fears was seen as proof that the King Power blueprint had been compromised and that 2016 would see the traditional challengers come to the fore.

	Pass completion (%)	Avg possession (%)
PL champions 2007–15	83.2	57.9
Leicester 2015–16	70.5	42.4

It's true that statistically Leicester are unlike any previous winner of the Premier League this century. As the table above shows, their pass completion and average possession rates are far lower than the 'standard' output from title winners in the past ten seasons. In fact, if the league were sorted on pass completion alone, the Foxes would have ended the campaign in 19th place rather than first, but judging a team on a single metric is a) ridiculous and b) exactly the sort of thing people who are 'against stats' construct as a straw-man argument against them. In reality, winning the league title despite being the least accurate passers in the division is a fascinating development, with the only parallel in recent times being Zambia's triumph in the African Cup of Nations in 2012, where the Chipolopolo also recorded the lowest pass completion in the competition (instead utilising their pace on the break to overcome supposedly 'better' opposition).

Just how much of Leicester's approach was dependent on breaking at pace is shown in the table below. Almost 10% of their goals came from counter-attacks (defined as moves that begin in a team's defensive half of the pitch with the majority of the opposition players in that half, too), which was considerably more than any other team. Even as this method was nullified a bit in the second half of the season as teams sat deeper against the Foxes, they still came out on top.

Team	Counter-attack goals	% of goals on counter-attacks
Leicester City	**6**	**8.8**
Manchester City	5	7.0
Newcastle United	4	9.1
Arsenal	3	4.6
Southampton	3	5.1
Swansea City	3	7.1
Tottenham Hotspur	3	4.3

To a lesser extent, Atlético Madrid's win over Barcelona in the Champions League quarter final was another win for functional football over the snooty purists in 2015–16. Both their challenge to the traditional big two in Spain and Leicester's success in the Premier League show that there is no right way to play football; ultimately it's the result that counts. Unfortunately for aesthete fans of teams dedicated to playing 'the beautiful game', there's no room to engrave marks out of ten for perceived notions of style on trophies, and as yet you cannot convert dressing-room selfies into points.

Case for the Defence

Nevertheless, the predictions that Leicester's style of play in the first half of the season would have to change in the New Year were correct. They had to change; whether you're Leicester City or Manchester United, you will not win the title with a defence that leaks goals at a rate Ranieri's team were in the opening few months. You will win hearts but you will not land trophies. In Leicester's first 11 games of the campaign they let in 19 goals (1.73 per game) while the subsequent 27 matches saw them let in a miserly 17 (0.63 per game). The peak of their resilience came in the spell of five games in March/April when they didn't concede a single goal. It was the perfect response to losing at Arsenal on Valentine's Day, a match which seemed to signal a momentum shift in the title race but actually did nothing but act as another rallying point for Leicester to pause and renew their assault on glory, just as the home defeat to the Gunners in September had. Leicester, in the end, became the first title winners to have neither the best attack nor the best defence since Arsenal in 2001–02. A model club in so many ways, the Foxes showed how pragmatism at the back and up front can land you the biggest prize, if you get them working in tandem.

Evidence of Leicester's shift in style in the second half of the season is not too hard to unearth. If Vardy and Mahrez were the autumn stars, blazing a trail by ripping teams apart, and Kanté was the turnover bedrock of the entire campaign, the granite base on which the team's approach was anchored, then the defence came to the fore in the spring, just at the point when the team's attack was being figured out by the opposition. It seems apt that in a season where Arsenal surely blew their greatest chance of ending their long run without a Premier League title under Arsène Wenger, they managed to inflict two of Leicester's three defeats suffered by the champions before they secured the title, with 8.5% of the Gunners' entire points total in 2015–16 coming against the champions. As mentioned, the second Arsenal win against Leicester in February, via a last-minute winner from Danny Welbeck in one of his brief spells not in recovery, seemed to hand the initiative to the north London aristocrats. But it didn't. Instead, Ranieri's team went back to basics and seemingly flicked a switch marked 'DEFENCE'.

The table below shows the contrast between the first half of the season and the second, with improvements in key areas you need to control a game. The counter-attacking Vardy heyday in the autumn unsurprisingly saw the team cede more possession to the opposition, while the pass completion, although not high, crept up after the Christmas mini-slump. The crucial change here is the number of shots on target Leicester allowed their foes in the second half of the campaign: down from 4.3 per match to 2.8, a decline of 1.5 per game. As we saw earlier in the chapter, the number of shots the opposition was allowed (xG against) also saw a reduction.

This all translates into the holy grail of football: clean sheets. As Chris Anderson and David Sally pointed out in *The Numbers Game*, not conceding is more important than scoring when it comes to securing results. Leicester kept only four clean sheets in their helter-skelter opening 19 games but a massive 11 in the second half of the campaign. Vardy may have come close to the Golden Boot and Riyad Mahrez may have been voted by his fellow professionals as the player of the season but it was the defence that pushed the Foxes across the line. It is fitting that, in the fourth of Leicester's four successive 1-0 wins in March and April, Wes Morgan scored the only goal of the game to see off Southampton. For the third match in a row Leicester had taken the lead in the first half and then ground out the ultimate of scorelines. 1 (1) − 0 (0) × 3 = perfection.

Leicester 2015–16	First 19 games	Last 19 games
Possession	40.7%	45.5%
Passing accuracy	68.3%	70.3%
Shots on target faced	4.3	2.8
Clean sheets	4	11
Shots faced (incl. blocks)	13.5	13.5

We should also note the number of penalties that Leicester were awarded, 13, which equalled the Premier League record set by Andrew Johnson's Crystal Palace in 2004–05. In fact,

Leicester's total represented 14% of the spot-kicks awarded in the division in 2015–16 and (an increase of nine on the previous season) led to fans of other clubs complaining that they were getting some kind of special treatment from officials. Whether this had any influence on Jamie Vardy's second yellow card for simulation in Leicester's 2-2 draw with West Ham in April is unclear, but that game, and Vardy's red card, briefly gave Tottenham hope of hunting down Ranieri's men.

One subtle consequence of Leicester's patient, methodical second half of the season was the slow erosion of a long-term goal difference deficit. Like a government promising surplus and glory in the same budget, Leicester headed to Old Trafford in their 36th game of the season knowing (let's be honest they probably had no idea) that not only would a win guarantee them the title, but that a victory by one goal would take their all-time league goal difference non-negative for the first time since October 1977. Would fans who witnessed the Foxes slip into negative goal difference against Norwich at Carrow Road in 1977 have accepted 39 years of negative GD in return for the ultimate prize four decades later? You have to suspect they would. In the end, Leicester went positive in the 3-1 romp against Everton just before collecting the Premier League trophy. An unsighted cherry on a giant, delicious cake.

Points Win Prizes

There's no starker illustration of the unlikeliness of Leicester's transformation than the table below, which shows that they are the first team in English top-flight history (1888 onwards) to improve by more than a point per game in consecutive seasons in the top division. Previously (and this is based on three points for a win, which didn't get introduced to the English league system until the early 1980s but is applied universally here to allow a fair comparison) the biggest improvement season on season was by Arsenal in 1930–31.

Like Leicester in 2014–15, the Gunners had finished the 1929–30 season in 14th place but a season later landed their first title under Herbert Chapman, a year after winning the FA Cup. Arsenal also demonstrated a significant improvement in the early 1970s, bouncing back from a moribund 12th-place finish in 1970 to a league and FA Cup double in 1971, albeit in the lowest-scoring top-flight season of all time. The other two teams listed are Derby and Sunderland, in 1895–96 and 1891–92 respectively, worthy achievements, albeit in a world where cornflakes had just been invented. But Leicester City, of the twenty-first century, have outdone every other team to play consecutive seasons in the top flight. To say we may not see another title win like this in the next 100 years is conservative rather than outlandish.

Team	Season	Pts/game (3pts/win)	Improvement
Leicester City	2015–16	2.13	1.05
Arsenal	1930–31	2.24	0.98
Arsenal	1970–71	2.24	0.95
Derby County	1895–96	1.93	0.93
Sunderland	1891–92	2.42	0.83

The Final Frontier

We are where we are. Leicester City are the reigning Premier League champions and as such will enter the 2016–17 Champions League in pot one alongside the likes of Barcelona, Bayern, Juventus and Paris Saint-Germain. Even accounting for the Premier League's declining performances in continental competition in recent seasons, the Foxes will be an attractive draw for some of the big sides condemned to pots two and three by the recent seedings shake-up. Home and away games against Leicester look an easier prospect than two clashes with Barca, the European novices last playing a European game back in

2000. (Incidentally, 50% of Leicester's eight European games before 2016–17 came against Atlético Madrid, an opponent they could very well face in the Champions League group stage next season.)

And yet the Midlands has a proud heritage in the European Cup, the four clubs to represent England in it so far (Aston Villa, Derby, Nottingham Forest and Wolves) having a combined win percentage of 53% compared to the other First Division/Premier League teams, who are on 50%. Above all, Leicester will hope to avoid the fate of Blackburn Rovers in 1995–96, who probably offer the best comparison with Leicester's position going into 2016–17. As the last 'small' club to win the English title (although the spending power of Rovers in the 1990s made their victory much less of a surprise), Blackburn suffered the following campaign, with manager Ray Harford an inadequate replacement for Kenny Dalglish. They were also hampered by the Premier League's relative weakness in comparison to the rest of the major European leagues in the mid-1990s, the effects of the post-Heysel ban and arcane Uefa rules around native players which disproportionally penalised English teams who had to count Scottish and Welsh players as 'foreign', although I suppose Gary Walsh remembers it fondly.

Blackburn's Champions League nadir came in their penultimate group game against Spartak Moscow, a dead rubber with Rovers already rock bottom of the group with one point from four games. The game descended into farce when two of the visitors' players, Graeme Le Saux and David Batty, exchanged punches after a bad pass from the left-back. The Premier League was only three seasons from landing its first Champions League but at that point, in the barren Russian cold, European success seemed light years away. Few people will expect Leicester to challenge for the Champions League in 2016–17 but a decent showing in the group stage is desirable, especially given the Premier League's battle to retain its four qualification spots ahead of a semi-resurgent Serie A.

In the end, Leicester's winning margin of ten points went almost unheralded, yet only four Premier League seasons have seen a bigger winning margin. If results had gone a certain way on the final day, the Foxes could have won the title by 13 points, which would have been the joint second highest margin in English top-flight history. This wasn't a smash and grab title in the end, this was an annihilation of the other 19 teams in the division. It remains, and will continue to remain, the strangest and most compelling title win in the nation's history.

9.

The 2015–16 Awards

Football loves awards and award-based ceremonies. Sometimes football celebrates at the wrong time of the year (stop your calendar year-based awards, awards people), and sometimes football celebrates the wrong things. This chapter is designed to fix both of those. So, without further ado, let's look back at the 2015–16 season and at the things that *really* matter in the modern game.

The Handy Timing in East London Award: West Ham, in their final season at Upton Park, went on their longest ever unbeaten home league run in the top flight (15 games). Then a lot of black cabs drove onto the pitch and out stepped Matthew Etherington. Special memories for all involved.

The Services to Tedium Award: Not only did the Crystal Palace v Norwich game have the lowest ball-in-play time in the Premier League in 2015–16, it also had the fewest passes (616) and the fewest successful passes (360). It is tempting to buy a recording of the game just to see what the players were actually doing.

The TripAdvisor Early Holiday Award: Stoke like mid-table, and the mid-table likes Stoke. With safety assured and European qualification almost out of reach, the Potters went on a run of three games in April where they conceded four goals in each match, only the third time in Premier League history that a team has done this, after West Ham in 2008 and Wigan in 2010.

The Rory Delap Memorial Award: We have come a long way since Delap enchanted the Premier League by hurling the ball into the box as if he were besieging a Norman castle. But there are still a band of players secretly committed to throwing the ball long, and this season it was led by Leicester's Christian Fuchs, who did so 199 times. A decent effort, but still some way short of Delap's monster haul of 345 in 2009–10.

Giving Up Gold Award: Aston Villa's fightback in the New Year didn't really come to much. Was their hard-fought win against drop-zone rivals Norwich in February the start of an incredible recovery? No: they lost the next 11 games to set the second longest run of defeats in Premier League history and end their spell of consecutive top-flight campaigns at 27. Oh.

Giving Up Silver Award: Crystal Palace started 2016 in fifth place in the Premier League, but picked up just two points from their next 11 league games to slide down the standings like a sad raindrop. Reaching the FA Cup final was ample consolation, though.

The Jedi Mind Trick/Sleight of Hand Award: Guus Hiddink steadied Chelsea's ship after they were forced to sack title-winning José Mourinho for a second time. The Blues' 15-game unbeaten run between December and April was the longest in the top-flight this season yet it hid a dark truth, Hiddink won only one of his ten home league matches in charge of the club. Stamford Bridge used to be a bastion of domination for the only London club to win the Champions League but recently it's been little short of easy street for visiting sides, not that anyone's noticed.

The Most Niche Potential Sanction: When Manchester City fans booed the Champions League anthem ahead of their game against Sevilla, UEFA stated that they 'could be sanctioned under regulation Art. 16 (2) (g) DR 'disruption of a competition anthem'. It later transpired that they were not sanctioned.

Landmark of the Season: In October Theo Walcott made his 50th Champions League appearance, which took him ahead of the great Johan Cruyff for appearances in the European Cup

(Cruyff made 49). The Dutchman, who died just months later, defined an era and was arguably the most important player in the game's history, although Walcott did record a video diary at the 2006 World Cup.

The Disinformation Award: In the autumn it was reported by scurrilous online sources that Mesut Özil was close to breaking the 'all-time assist' record, despite being 'only 26'. They got his age right but the rest was nonsense. The vast majority of professional football was never recorded and when even goal records (hello Pelé) are debatable, claiming an all-time assist record when the metric didn't really gain popularity until the 1990s is risible. Don't believe the hype.

The Disinformation Runner-Up: Zinedine Zidane had a good season, taking over at Real Madrid, guiding them to yet another European Cup title and almost snatching the league title from Barcelona. But the French playmaker carries a dark legacy, namely the belief, one that is perpetuated almost daily on social media, that he was never caught offside in his playing career. Not only is it nonsense, but to even think this was possible for an attacking player not renowned for his pace shows a loose grip on the game's rules, at best.

Millennium Bug of the Year: In the year that Prince died, West Brom's Jonathan Leko became the first player born in 1999 to make a Premier League appearance, at 16 years and 344 days. It was a very unusual move by WBA boss Tony Pulis, who had never previously been a fan of the New Power Generation. Leko was the first player under 20 he had ever named in a Premier League starting XI at any of the clubs he has managed to a staid-but-safe mid-table finish.

Early Bird Fails to Catch the Worm Award: Manchester United were three goals down after 19 minutes at Arsenal in October, the first time they'd ever conceded three inside the opening 20 minutes of a Premier League game. On the plus side, the remainder of the game was a solid 0-0.

The Monkey on Their Back Hartlepool Tribute Award: Life has never been easy for Hartlepool fans, with their club's Wikipedia page not even bothering to include an honours section. The seasons of struggle have taken their toll and a 4-1 defeat at Bristol Rovers in March took their league goal difference to minus 1052, an all-time record by any club in English league history. A spring revival pushed them slightly closer to zero but sadly another disastrous trip to the West Country on the final day saw them lose 5-0 to Plymouth, putting them back on minus 1052 ahead of the 2016–17 campaign. Just how low can they go?

Nominative Determinism Gold Award: On 15 August and 16 January, Southampton's Matt Targett lived up to his name and mustered a shot on target. Given that he ended the season with 33 clearances, though, he should really consider a change.

The Alphabet Pioneer Award: Newcastle's relegation from the Premier League (combined with the composition of the three teams coming up) means that next season the English top flight will not have any teams beginning with 'N', 'O', 'P', 'Q' or 'R' for the first time in its entire history. Not even an entirely positive season for the letter 'M', either, with Leicester's title win bringing 'L' (22) to within two of 'M' (24) in the all-time title wins list.

G.O.A.L Hero Award: Talking of letters, 2015–16 was, in hindsight, a poor one for Aston Villa's Gabriel Agbonlahor. His team were relegated, he was sent to a special fitness camp and, finally, he was suspended by the club for repeated 'breaches of discipline'. Even so, he remains the second highest goalscorer in Premier League history, of players whose name contains each of G, O, A and L. Leading the way, if you hadn't guessed, is Ole Gunnar Solskjær, with Gianfranco Zola in third place.

The Horrors that Lurk Beneath the Trap Door Gold Standard Award: It's not how you dance, it's who you're dancing with when the lights go off. Sunderland, proud survivors in the Premier League, actually spent 237 days in the drop zone, four more than Aston Villa, who claimed only 17 points all season and were, well, Aston Villa. Big Sam should be renamed Big Sum, as he has clearly solved some extraordinary mathematical conundrum to keep the Black Cats in the top flight.

Defenders of the Earth Award: Crystal Palace's slow fade-out in the league after Christmas was not an ideal environment for forwards and, as a result, they had the unusual scenario of a defender ending the campaign as a (joint) top scorer, in the form of Scott Dann. This is only the second time this has happened in the Premier League, with the previous defensive threats coming from Julian Dicks at West Ham in 1995–96.

Inexplicable Americanism Award: Newcastle's Aleksandar Mitrović ended the season with a delightful treble of a goal, an assist and a red card in his team's final match of the campaign, becoming only the sixth player in Premier League history to do this. The publication of this information led to an influx of Americans chattering about 'Gordie Howe Hat Tricks', which it turns out is an ice hockey term for when a player scores, assists and gets into a fight. Gordie Howe? Geordie How, more like.

Minding Your Own Business Medal: Has Mark Hughes sanitised Stoke City? The team, famous under Tony Pulis for their agricultural approach, have mellowed under their replacement Welshman, but perhaps so much that they are the least memorable team in the division. Too good to slip into the relegation battle, too inconsistent to make a challenge for a European place, Stoke's finishes under Hughes have been 9, 9, 9. There's no emergency but the Potters could do with a bit more drama in their life.

The Stewart Downing Memorial Award: In his first season at Liverpool in 2011–12, Downing ended the campaign as the player with the most shots without scoring a goal and the most chances created without an assist. And in 2015–16 we found a true successor in the form of Watford's José Manuel Jurado. A man with Real Madrid on his CV, Jurado ended the campaign with 35 shots and no goals, and 41 chances created and no assists, both league high figures (his Hornets team-mate Étienne Capoue matched him on the shots front). Whether it was shooting or creating, in 2014–15 it was no way José.

Spider Keeper Gold Shield: For connoisseurs, goalkeepers doing things they aren't meant to is the very height of football. Paul Robinson lives on as a Premier League custodial legend, a goalkeeper who scored, assisted and won a penalty in his top flight career although sadly not in the same match. In European football in 2015–16 this award goes to Sporting Gijon's Iván Cuéllar who not only created four goalscoring chances, but saw two of them converted. His total of two assists was as many as Robert Lewandowski managed for Bayern in the Bundesliga and should be applauded. Leicester's Kasper Schmeichel created the most chances, five, but none of them were converted. Does this devalue his team's title win? That's for you to decide.

Hat-trick Heroes of the Year: Luis Suárez shook off the heavy yoke of Messi and Ronaldo by scoring more hat-tricks (6) than they did combined (5) in league football this season. In fact, the Uruguayan's haul represented 9.4% of all hat-tricks scored in the big five European leagues in 2015–16. Impressive. Arguably, Steven Naismith and Nabil Fekir achieved something even more impressive, though, by scoring only four goals all season but still registering a hat-trick. The dream, of course, is for a player to score all of his goals in hat-tricks but sadly that hasn't happened since Mounir El Hamdaoui did so for Malaga in 2013–14.

The Coventry Award for Being Coventry: Once again, Coventry scooped this one, recording yet another league campaign in which they finished outside the top six. Incredibly, unless you live in or support Coventry, they haven't finished in the top six of any division for 46 years, well clear of Fulham (15 years) in second place. Next time you're dismayed by your team's slump in the league, think of Coventry and smile.

Best of the Beatles Award: At the end of the 2015–16 season the all-time Premier League appearance records of players with the same names as the Beatles stood at:

Lennon 471
McCartney 193
Harrison 18
Starr 0

Hamburg-era purists might want to note that players called Best currently number 32 appearances.

The Chatty Men Award: Chelsea may have put up a terrible defence of their title but they didn't go quietly. The Blues picked up 12 bookings for dissent in 2015–16, more than any other Premier League side, but it was only two more than they did in their successful 2014–15 season. It appears that, win or lose, you get it in the ear from the Blues.

The Services to Longevity Award: One minor consequence of the dummy training bomb that was discovered at Old Trafford before Manchester United's last home game against Bournemouth on the final day of the season was that it meant that the 2015–16 season was the longest campaign in Premier League history. Lasting 283 days from 15 August 2015 until 17 May 2016, it beat four other seasons on 281 days. In fact, the only season in English top-flight history that has lasted longer is the 1946–47 campaign, which remains the only season to have seen games played in June, thanks to an exceptionally cold winter that decimated the fixture list. Cold, yes, but not as big as the chill that went down the spine of the person responsible for leaving a replica bomb at the Theatre of Dreams when he realised what had happened.

Cleanliness Award: Fans who attended the Dortmund v Eintracht Frankfurt game in December certainly weren't complaining about the referee, or, if they were, they clearly prefer stringent officials, as there were only seven fouls in the entire game, a match that contained five goals. That's a goal to foul ratio of 0.71, which although a concept invented just moments ago, by me, is a very strong figure. Well done Dortmund and Frankfurt (particularly the latter, who conceded three fouls compared to Borussia's hideous total of four).

The Tony Pulitzer: Welsh tactician Tony Pulis is a safe choice. Having never overseen a relegation at any of the clubs he has managed, Pulis has kept Stoke, Crystal Palace and West Brom in the Premier League at various points. His methods, though, are quite austere, and in his time with WBA he has seen his team fail to record a shot on target in nine of his 57 league games in charge, with a further 14 games seeing only one or two on target. Meagre fare, but his teams continue to dine at the top table, and that, at least in the short term, is deemed the main consideration.

The Unorthodox Goalkeeper of the Year: 2015–16 was not a vintage season for Manchester football, but both teams' goalkeepers continue to redefine what goalkeeping can be. United's David de Gea led the Premier League in saves with his feet, with 20, while Joe Hart eschewed his head and his shoulders and instead used his body, i.e. his chest, to stop eight shots. Joe Heart, more like.

The Own Goal as a Metaphor Award: In a season that saw a number of metaphorical own goals, from Chelsea's pitiful defence of their crown, to Arsenal's feeble title challenge and Manchester United's endlessly dreary attempts to play football, it was apt that the season both started with an own goal (by Kyle Walker) and ended with one too (by Chris Smalling). Even better, both came at the same stadium (Old Trafford) and even in the same goal, while Leicester were one of only four teams not to score an actual own goal. Sometimes life is almost too neat.

10.

Euro 96: The Missed Chance

'Not only the cows are mad in England.
The English press is also infected'

El Mundo Deportivo *(before the England v Spain, quarter-final)*

England's latest European Championships experience in 2016 brought up 50 years since the World Cup was lifted in late July 1966. Since then? Nothing. (Ignoring minor pleasantries such as 1997's Le Tournoi a forerunner of the modern Confederations Cup.) We are now only ten years away from it being as long since Skinner and Baddiel first sang about '30 years of hurt' as they were from England's World Cup win. The possibility of a future world where there isn't anyone alive who has ever seen England win a major trophy gets ever nearer.

Ask the average person when it was that England came closest to ending their empty existence since 1966 and most will point to the European Championships they hosted in 1996. Terry Venables' plucky troops reached the semi-finals and 'Euro 96' is now a trigger for a series of memories. Gazza's goal against Scotland, Gazza inches away from the ball in extra-time against Germany, Southgate's penalty and that dizzy game where the Netherlands were cut to pieces in perhaps the last joyous evening at the old Wembley.

But are we viewing that golden summer of 1996 through the rosiest of spectacles? With access to every single data point from the entire tournament it is possible to identify whether England were unlucky not to triumph or they wasted a clear opportunity to win the European Championships. For eventual winners Germany this tournament was sandwiched between awful World Cups for them, while France, the coming team in world football, were still a work in progress, even though Zinedine Zidane made his tournament debut in Euro 96. By looking at factors such as England's performance in the lead-up to the competition, the lack of creativity among attacking players once the finals began, the true contribution of Paul Gascoigne and the team's historical performance in penalty shootouts, a more nuanced view can be teased out.

The Squad

Squads of 22 players were required for Euro 1996, including the statutory three goalkeepers. It's interesting to note that there was a considerable lack of international experience in England's squad, partly due to Terry Venables' desire to rebuild the team after the Graham Taylor era. As the table below shows, the average number of caps for each squad member was 16.5, considerably below recent tournaments and especially the very experienced World Cup 1990 squad. As we'll see later, Venables makes the almost unheard-of decision in the semi-final to play 120 minutes (including penalties) with the 11 players who started the game (most of whom had played 120 minutes in the quarter-final just four days earlier). This decision looks slightly less baffling when you see just how inexperienced most of the squad was when playing for England. Teddy Sheringham, a veteran and one of England's best players in the five games had appeared only 15 times, fewer than Raheem Sterling ahead of Euro 2016, while penalty villain Gareth Southgate had featured just four times before the tournament began.

Total caps going into tournament	Total	Players	Avg per player
Euro 96	**362**	**22**	**16.5**
World Cup 1966	505	22	23.0
Euro 2016	534	23	23.2
World Cup 2014	657	23	28.6
Euro 2012	675	23	29.3
World Cup 1990	711	23	30.9

Goalkeeper	David Seaman	Tim Flowers	Ian Walker
Club team	**Arsenal**	**Blackburn Rovers**	**Tottenham Hotspur**
Caps at start of tournament	24	8	2
Minutes played	510	-	-
Saves	11	-	-
Saves%	78.6	-	-
Catches	8	-	-
Passes	90	-	-
Passing accuracy	50	-	-

Player	Stuart Pearce	Gary Neville	Tony Adams
Club team	Nottingham Forest	Manchester United	Arsenal
Caps at start of tournament	65	10	40
Minutes played	465	390	510
Shots, total (incl. blocks)	4	2	1
Chances created (incl. assists)	5	4	1
Passes	206	163	226
Passing accuracy	72	84	89
Dribbles completed	0	0	0
Tackles	9	8	14
Aerial won	2	4	17

Player	Sol Campbell	Steve Howey	Phil Neville
Club team	Tottenham	Newcastle United	Manchester United
Caps at start of tournament	1	4	1
Minutes played	5	-	-
Shots, total (incl. blocks)	0	-	-
Chances created (incl. assists)	0	-	-
Passes	1	-	-
Passing accuracy	100	-	-
Dribbles completed	0	-	-
Tackles	0	-	-
Aerial won	0	-	-

Player	Darren Anderton	Paul Gascoigne	Steve McManaman
Club team	Tottenham	Rangers	Liverpool
Caps at start of tournament	11	38	10
Minutes played	499	497	479
Shots, total (incl. blocks)	10	10	7
Chances created (incl. assists)	13	10	7
Passes	175	295	199
Passing accuracy	78	85	80
Dribbles completed	6	13	14
Tackles	8	15	8
Aerial Won	0	2	1

Player	Paul Ince	David Platt	Steve Stone
Club team	Internazionale	Arsenal	Nottingham Forest
Caps at start of tournament	19	58	6
Minutes played	358	275	41
Shots, total (incl. Blocks)	5	2	0
Chances created (incl. assists)	3	1	1
Passes	134	97	15
Passing accuracy	87	87	80
Dribbles completed	4	0	0
Tackles	10	6	1
Aerial won	2	1	0

Player	Jamie Redknapp	Alan Shearer	Teddy Sheringham
Club team	Liverpool	Blackburn Rovers	Tottenham
Caps at start of tournament	4	23	15
Minutes played	40	496	465
Shots, total (incl. blocks)	0	17	17
Chances created (incl. assists)	0	5	4
Passes	14	136	206
Passing accuracy	93	71	80
Dribbles completed	0	1	0
Tackles	1	2	4
Aerial won	0	17	17

Player	Nick Barmby	Robbie Fowler	Les Ferdinand
Club team	Middlesbrough	Liverpool	Newcastle United
Caps at start of tournament	6	3	10
Minutes played	45	25	-
Shots, total (incl. blocks)	0	1	-
Chances created (incl. assists)	0	0	-
Passes	12	10	-
Passing accuracy	100	80	-
Dribbles completed	0	0	-
Tackles	0	0	-
Aerial won	0	1	-

Player	Gareth Southgate
Club team	**Aston Villa**
Caps at start of tournament	4
Minutes played	510
Shots, total (incl. blocks)	1
Chances created (incl. assists)	1
Passes	193
Passing accuracy	83
Dribbles completed	2
Tackles	13
Aerial won	12

No Qualify, No Quality

Hosting an international tournament may require significant investment but the one gold-plated guarantee you get in return is a place in the jamboree. Living in an era where England (Euro 2008 apart) have invariably cruised through the qualification process it is easy to forget that the 1990s were filled with failures and near misses. Graham Taylor's England scraped through to Euro 92 ahead of Ireland and Poland, winning only three of their six games, while the qualifiers for USA 94 saw England slump to comedic lows under Taylor. Events such as conceding a goal to San Marino in less than ten seconds, captured starkly in ITV's ill-judged, but endlessly entertaining documentary, *The Impossible Job*, live long in the memory. That World Cup in America remains the last edition that England failed to reach, suggesting, in fact, that the job is reasonably possible. As the table below shows, only on two occasions since the 1990 World Cup have England failed to reach an international tournament, and both times with an English manager. The experimentation with foreign coaches in the form of Sven-Göran Eriksson and Fabio Capello may have ended in tournament failure but both men guided the team to two tournaments with consummate ease.

1. England Qualifying record since 1990

England Qualifying Record Since the 1990s

Competition	Win%	Outcome	Manager
Euro 92	50	Qualified	Taylor
World Cup 94	**50**	**Failed**	**Taylor**
Euro 96	-	Hosts	Venables
World Cup 98	75	Qualified	Hoddle
Euro 2000	40	Qualified (play-off)	Hoddle/Keegan
World Cup 02	63	Qualified	Keegan/Wilkinson/ Eriksson
Euro 2004	75	Qualified	Eriksson
World Cup 06	80	Qualified	Eriksson
Euro 2008	**58**	**Failed**	**McClaren**
World Cup 2010	90	Qualified	Capello
Euro 2012	63	Qualified	Capello
World Cup 2014	60	Qualified	Hodgson
Euro 2016	100	Qualified	Hodgson

After such a dismal first half of the nineties, the fact that England would not have to enter the next round of qualifiers was definitely a relief. Graham Taylor had resigned shortly after the failure to reach the 1994 World Cup and had been replaced by Terry Venables. In an era when top football managers were paid little more than their equivalents in more prosaic professions (compared to the enormous £6 million annual salary paid to Fabio Capello or Roy Hodgson's slightly more reasonable £3.5 million), Venables wasn't alone in having numerous business interests outside the game,* ranging from board games to women's wigs, nightclubs to property and,

---

* *This is something that is not completely alien to the modern England manager. Fabio Capello launched the Capello Index in 2010, a player performance ranking system, but it had to be delayed until after the World Cup due to fears it would rank his own players badly.*

more recently, boutique hotels. He was even engaged in a long legal battle with Tottenham owner Alan Sugar over the terms of their initial partnership at Tottenham (one that ended when Sugar fired Venables as chief executive) when he took charge of England. It was an unusual move by the usually ultra-cautious FA but after the dismal on-pitch performance under Graham Taylor, off-pitch matters seemed less important. Hosting an event, be it a football tournament or an Olympics, sharpens national attention considerably. Knowing that the world will be looking on is a handy catalyst for short periods of competency.

Nevertheless, the malaise that had set in under Taylor didn't just vanish under Venables, as popularly assumed. An early thumping of World Cup-bound Greece hinted at better times but England soon settled into a pattern of dreary home games at Wembley, with ten of Venables' first 12 games as manager taking place at the fading Empire Stadium (the one trip abroad ending in abandonment in Dublin after Combat 18-led rioting by the England fans, plus a 3-3 draw with Sweden at Elland Road). The six games after the Irish fiasco saw just one win, a narrow victory against Japan in the Umbro Cup, while Brazil, also in the Umbro Cup, inflicted Venables' only official defeat in friendlies. The overall feeling was that while England were a solid enough unit under the new manager and his 4-3-2-1 Christmas tree formation, they were struggling to find a cutting edge, despite being able to call on the services of an Alan Shearer in his prime. The formation, now a historical curiosity seen only occasionally in the current game, was all the rage in the mid-1990s. It's easy to forget how much England's approach had changed in a short period. After years of stolid 4-4-2, the 1990 World Cup had seen Bobby Robson dabble with a sweeper system, something that Graham Taylor continued to use (usually when desperate). Venables' use of a solid midfield three with two creative players behind a lone powerful frontman made sense. England could boast strikers such as Shearer and Les Ferdinand, and the creative players such as

2. England friendlies under Terry Venables, 1994–96

Date	Opponents	For	Against	Scorers (mins)	Venue	Result
09/03/94	Denmark	1	0	Platt 16	Home	W
17/05/94	Greece	5	0	Anderton 23 Beardsley 37 Platt 44 (pen), 54 Shearer 65	Home	W
22/05/94	Norway	0	0		Home	D
07/09/94	USA	2	0	Shearer 33, 39	Home	W
12/10/94	Romania	1	1	Lee 44	Home	D
16/11/94	Nigeria	1	0	Platt 41	Home	W
15/02/95	Republic of Ireland (ab)	0	1		Away	ab
29/03/95	Uruguay	0	0		Home	D
03/06/95	Japan	2	1	Anderton 48 Platt 88 (pen)	Home	W
08/06/95	Sweden	3	3	Sheringham 44 Platt 88 Anderton 89	Home	D
11/06/95	Brazil	1	3	Le Saux 39	Home	L
06/09/95	Colombia	0	0		Home	D
11/10/95	Norway	0	0		Away	D
15/11/95	Switzerland	3	1	Pearce 44 Sheringham 56 Stone 78	Home	W
12/12/95	Portugal	1	1	Stone 44	Home	D
27/03/96	Bulgaria	1	0	L Ferdinand 6	Home	W
24/04/96	Croatia	0	0		Home	D
18/05/96	Hungary	3	0	Anderton 38, 52 Platt 62	Home	W
23/05/96	China	3	0	Barmby 30, 53 Gascoigne 63	Away	W

Steve McManaman and Darren Anderton were able to drift and create as they pleased. Theoretically, it worked.

Indeed, Shearer's lengthy goal drought for England ahead of the tournament was in direct contrast to his performance in the Premier League, where he scored 34 goals (and secured the league title for Blackburn) in 1994–95 and another 31 in the following season. Modern fans who know Shearer only as a pundit should not be in any doubt: England had one of the most effective and impressive strikers in world football in the early 1990s. Their failure to capitalise on this remains a great shame.

Overall, Venables won only 47% of the friendly games he contested as England manager, above only Kevin Keegan and Steve McClaren – surely the two most underwhelming national bosses in the post-Italia 90 era? But this didn't really matter because England were in the finals whatever happened. (In a related point, England slipped to their lowest ever position in the FIFA rankings in February 1996 – 27th.) It should be mentioned that they headed into the tournament not as a happy band of adventurers (on the field, at least) but instead as a work in progress that was still looking for a spark. (It's worth noting that forthcoming hosts not shining in international friendlies is not massively unusual. France's win percentage in the two years before World Cup 98 was 56% while Germany's before World Cup 2006 was 55% but, crucially, what matters is performance in these games where the result is relatively unimportant. And that's where Venables' England struggled.)

3. England managers in friendlies – Taylor–Hodgson

Manager	Games	Wins	Win%
Fabio Capello	20	13	65.0
Glenn Hoddle	13	8	61.5
Graham Taylor	19	10	52.6
Roy Hodgson	18	9	50.0

(continued)

Manager	Games	Wins	Win%
Sven-Göran Eriksson	29	14	48.3
Terry Venables	**19**	**9**	**47.4**
Kevin Keegan	7	3	42.9
Steve McClaren	6	2	33.3

The First Two Games

The draw for the group stage in December 1995 placed England in Group A alongside tournament debutants Switzerland, Euro 88 winners Holland and Scotland. England had not faced the Scots since 1989, having played each other in every single year since the resumption of football after the Second World War. So this game, scheduled as the second match, was eagerly awaited in both nations. Switzerland, who had reached World Cup 94 under Roy Hodgson, were judged a safe start for the hosts while there was an opportunity for revenge against a Netherlands team which had famously prevented England from playing in the American World Cup two years earlier.

Ahead of the tournament the tabloids grumbled at England's style and play being equivalent to having a tooth pulled. This intensified substantially after the players were pictured in a dentist's chair (converted for rapid and ostentatious alcohol consumption) in Hong Kong on a pre-event tour. Gascoigne, in particular, was attacked by the tabloids for a lack of professionalism that may have contained a kernel of truth. A reasonably sized kernel.

Either way, as England's opening game unfolded in a now familiar Venables draw, the sense of frustration grew. Alan Shearer at last ended his barren run but his three other shots went wide, while the disappointing Steve McManaman was tackled seven times by an energetic Swiss team. The team's most creative player was Stuart Pearce (the left-back creating a satisfactory but not breathtaking three chances). This was a Christmas tree with a distinct lack of baubles. England's pass completion rate of 75% would have ranked 17th in the 2014–15 Premier League, while the combined total of 674 passes in the game was surpassed by Spain on their own in five of their six games at Euro 2012. Put simply, it wasn't a classic. Only two games in the whole tournament had a lower pass completion than this game, with special mention for the deeply agricultural nature of the France v Spain match. Elland Road, on that day, did not witness a tiki-taka exhibition.

Game	Overall pass completion
Spain v Bulgaria	73.84
Romania v France	73.05
Romania v Spain	72.89
England v Switzerland	**72.06**
Czech Republic v Italy	71.85
France v Spain	64.60

Scotland had also drawn their opening game but the fact that it had come against the Netherlands placed it firmly into the brave rather than shameful category. They faced England on a Saturday afternoon at Wembley in confident mood, forcing David Seaman into four saves in the match. The most crucial of the quartet was from Gary McAllister's penalty in the closing stages. Leading 1-0 after another solid opener from Alan Shearer, it looked like the Scots would match the Swiss by pegging England back. Instead, McAllister, a precise user of the ball throughout his career, inexplicably chose to smash the kick down the middle of the goal. Seaman, diving to his right, saw the ball rebound off his elbow and fly 20 metres in the air and to safety. Minutes later England had doubled their advantage thanks to Gascoigne's timeless goal, flicking the ball over the head of Colin Hendry with his left foot and slotting it home with his right.

Aside from a brace of goals against qualification minnows Moldova, the Scotland strike was Gascoigne's last for his nation. The most talented player of his and arguably any generation of English players played in only two tournaments, but reached the semi-finals in both, and never suffered a defeat in normal time. The evolution from a precocious 23-year-old in 1990 to a ravaged but effective 29-year-old in Euro 96 is hinted at in the data below. The kid ghosting past the opposition (his total of 56 dribbles at World Cup 1990 was 20 more than any other player in the tournament) had been replaced by a more measured passer, still as capable of creating goalscoring chances for his team-mates as he had been in his youth. Gascoigne's relationship with the art of tackling was inconsistent at best (his terrible attempt in the World Cup semi-final the cause of *that* yellow card, and he should have conceded a penalty in the Euro 96 game against Spain with another mistimed effort). But his total of 15 tackles in 1996 was more than any other England player in the competition. For all of his baggage, Gascoigne remained one of his nation's most effective and talismanic performers. The sheer sense of national shock two years later when he wasn't selected by Glenn Hoddle for the 1998 World Cup was proof of that.

Paul Gascoigne	Euro 96	Italia 90
Appearances	5	6
Minutes on pitch	497	630
Goals	1	0
Shots on target	4	4
Shots off target	3	1
Goal assists	1	2
Chances created	10	12
Total passes	295	237
Pass % opp. half	80%	71.34%
Total crosses	13	32
Dribbles	22	56
Tackles made	15	10

Player	Team	Chances created (incl. assists)
Darren Anderton	England	13
Youri Djorkaeff	France	13
Rui Costa	Portugal	11
Karel Poborský	Czech Republic	11
Ronald de Boer	Netherlands	11
Thomas Häßler	Germany	11
Paul Gascoigne	**England**	10
Aljoša Asanović	Croatia	10
Dennis Bergkamp	Netherlands	10
Patrik Berger	Czech Republic	10
Gheorghe Hagi	Romania	10

Player	Team	Successful passes opp half
Paul Gascoigne	**England**	164
Zinedine Zidane	France	133
Rui Costa	Portugal	130
Luís Figo	Portugal	126
Fernando Hierro	Spain	122
Matthias Sammer	Germany	120
Paulo Sousa	Portugal	118
Youri Djorkaeff	France	113
Steve McManaman	England	111
Teddy Sheringham	England	106
Ronald de Boer	Netherlands	106

Gascoigne's goal took England from potential disaster to national acclaim in a matter of seconds, and they saw out the remaining few minutes with no further scares. Jamie Redknapp had been brought on at half-time as Venables took off Stuart Pearce and switched to three at the back, with Redknapp slotting into midfield to try and control a game in which the Scots had matched their old rivals in the first half. Received wisdom, both in 1996 and now, is that Redknapp did indeed change the game, and it is true that England were more impressive after the interval, but the Liverpool man made only 13 passes (the same number as Pearce had at left-back in the first half) before the sub was subbed off with five minutes remaining. The more significant change was Venables' willingness to abandon his Christmas tree formation and switch to a 3-5-2. It was a momentary throwback to Italia 90, where Bobby Robson's periodic adoption of the sweeper system guided England to their best ever performance on foreign soil.

The Glorious Revolution?

Rivalries in international football can be weakened by the passing of time. Put simply, teams can go years without facing each other, and the enmity fades imperceptibly in that vacuum. On the other hand, a spell of frequent, and crucial, clashes between teams can see new ones emerge. And that was something that applied to England and the Netherlands in the late 1980s and early 1990s. After being outclassed in Euro 88, England gained some revenge at the World Cup two years later. A 0-0 draw in Sardinia wasn't a win but it did announce that the Three Lions could compete with the inventors of Total Football in the style stakes. This progress was then thrown away in two USA 94 qualifying games against the Dutch. A 2-0 lead at Wembley ended in a 2-2 draw and Graham Taylor's reign all but ended in Rotterdam in 1993 as the home team prevented the English reaching a World Cup for the first time since the 1970s.

All of which meant that by the time Euro 96 was underway, games against the Dutch had a grudging quality, a temporary rival to be savoured, that is if they could be beaten for once. And, unlike three years previously, this time it was the Netherlands who were in apparent disarray. A split between the young Ajax quintet of Edgar Davids, Clarence Seedorf, Patrick Kluivert, Michael Reiziger and Winston Bogarde and the rest of the squad ensured that the Dutch unity of 1988 was gone. Even so, Guus Huddink's men had started with a draw and a win, matching England, so the match between them was a group decider and everyone knew who came out on top when Holland went head to head with the English (hint: tulips).

Heading into the game, the Netherlands had mustered the most shots in the tournament (41), the joint most shots on target (13, level with England) and the highest average possession figure (60%). This wasn't a particularly harmonious Dutch team but neither were they on the ragged edge. And, despite what people remember, or think they remember, Holland were not outclassed in this game. Sometimes performances shape a game, sometimes scorelines do, and this victory for England was definitely in the latter category. The match stats below hint at what was a much closer game than either side is ever given credit for. The Dutch had 20 shots, eight more than England. Furthermore, Venables' team hit an unusually high proportion on target. Yes, that's the point of the game but even with Shearer and Teddy Sheringham finally combining effectively, this was an unsustainable performance with an unrealistic scoreline.

The Netherlands' total of nine shots off target included some glaring misses that on another day would have been rifled into England's net to bring about the usual ennui. David Seaman's save from Bergkamp before half-time surely prevented the teams going in at 1-1, the pegged-back scoreline that caused so many issues for Venables during his short reign. Instead, England enjoyed a narrow advantage at half-time and then ended the contest early in the second half with three more goals in the opening 17 minutes. These are the minutes that make up Euro 96 for most nowadays. The five minutes between Shearer's second and Sheringham's second are the golden summer for English football, a glorious throwback to a time before foreign teams deigned to catch up with the home nations, a testament to the spirit and hard work of the Three Lions and a warning to the rest of the nations in the tournament that the hosts were ready to bring glory back to the home of football.

The truth is that the Dutch continued to have the better chances in the closing third of the game, and then scored the ultimate in consolation goals via Patrick Kluivert. A 4-0 defeat would have seen Scotland through to the quarter-finals, but instead Holland scraped through by the narrowest of margins. This only added an extra sheen of happiness for many England fans, but really it should have been a warning sign that this delicate glasshouse was on the verge of being shattered by the Spanish.

Match	Total shots
Turkey v Denmark	36
England v Spain	**36**
Denmark v Portugal	33
England v Netherlands	**32**
Scotland v Switzerland	32
Russia v Germany	32

Match	Passing accuracy
Russia v Germany	83.33
Denmark v Portugal	83.28
England v Netherlands	**81.27**
Croatia v Denmark	80.97
Croatia v Portugal	80.85

Pain for Spain

Back in the 1990s Spain were England's brothers-in-arms when it came to long-term suffering at international tournaments. Like the English, they had only a single victory to their name, and it had also come in the mid-1960s (Euro 64). Spain's national league also contained some of the most famous clubs in the world game, and like England they had been left on the sidelines as Germany and Italy hoovered up the game's biggest trophies.

Spain's berth in the quarter-finals in 1996 had been a grind rather than a gallop. An opener against World Cup 94 darlings Bulgaria had been drawn 1-1 after a late goal from Alfonso, while the second match against eventual group winners France saw them equalise with only five minutes remaining. It was another late goal that saw them beat Romania 2-1 in the final group game to leapfrog the Bulgarians and ensure a knockout game against the hosts.

Understandably, England's apparent destruction of the Netherlands had ramped up national expectation ahead of the quarter-final. A nation which had dared to dream in 1990 before being served a large helping of turnip-infused gruel under Graham Taylor, and then a tedious phony war under Terry Venables, was ready to explode with pride once more, helped along its way by the tabloid press. Spain were written off as a functional team which, if the Dutch could be thumped, was ripe for another Wembley takedown.

But Spain started like a team relishing the chance to take on the hosts at the Empire Stadium and even the most ardent England fan would have been surprised to see their team still on level terms at half-time. A pair of disallowed goals (one of which was completely, absolutely onside) and a series of squandered shots should have seen the Spanish set fair. England came back into things in the second half but even so referee Marc Batta inexplicably booked Alfonso for diving when replays clearly showed the forward had been brought down by a lunging Paul Gascoigne (who, geographically, was very near the spot of his knee-rupturing tackle on Gary Charles in the 1991 FA Cup final). Kiko then blazed wide when almost alone in front of Seaman's goal, although this was countered by an astounding miss from Alan Shearer from about one yard.

Extra-time took on a slightly different flavour: Euro 96 was the first major tournament to include the Golden Goal rule (the first team to score in extra-time would end the contest there and then). Both teams traded three shots in the first half of the additional time, but the second period saw Spain attempt four to England's zero. To the modern mind, the idea of England closing down a game to reach penalties seems insane, but at this point England had experienced (and lost) only one shoot-out. The stigma that has grown inexorably was barely a mild neurosis in 1996.

We'll look more closely at the mechanics of the penalty shootout later in the chapter, but the fact that England took the first penalty kick against the Spanish gave them an immediate advantage. The most memorable aspect of the penalties was Stuart Pearce's redemptive face when he struck England's third past Andoni Zubizarreta. What is truly noteworthy when you watch the four England kicks now is how confident and well executed they are. Shearer, David Platt, Pearce and Gascoigne all tuck their efforts away; there is no fear, no hex running through their minds. When ITV co-commentator Ron Atkinson makes the statistically incoherent statement 'David Seaman is surely gonna stop one isn't he. He always stops at least one', the goalkeeper goes and does just that to seal the victory. In a tournament where everything seemed to be falling for England, this was the high point.

Game Analysis

Paul Gascoigne was the only player to hit more than one shot on target in the game, although the leading shot maker in the match overall was Fernando Hierro with six. Hierro, a defender for much of his career but playing in midfield in Spain's Euro 96 team, actually ended the tournament with 23 shots, four more than any other player in any team. A look at Spain's shot locations from the game shows, perhaps, why Hierro was their most frequent threat. The majority came

Spain 0-0 England – Euro 1996

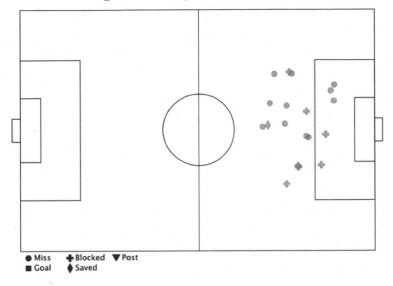

● Miss   ✚ Blocked   ▼ Post
■ Goal   ◆ Saved

from outside the penalty area and the shots off target are plentiful. A plucky, unlucky Spain team forced to shoot from range? The road to 2008 was a long one from here.

Gascoigne also led England's chance creation in this game, setting up four chances for his team-mates. But it was Spain who had the most creative player in Guillermo Amor, who ended the game with five key passes.

Always Germany

So, six years after the World Cup semi-final, England once again faced Germany in the last four. The Germans' progress to this point had been relatively serene, their group stage enlivened mainly by the surprise exit of World Cup 94 finalists Italy, and their quarter-final was a 2-1 victory over a Croatia team at their first major tournament. The fevered atmosphere surrounding the competition in England now spilled over into ill-planned jingoism epitomised by the *Daily Mirror*'s decision to declare 'football war on Germany'. England had luck on their side and a catchy song, while their opponents had been humbled by Bulgaria in the 1994 World Cup and lacked the stars who had guided them to victory in 1990.

Confidence grew as England took the lead after only three minutes, Tony Adams nodding on Gascoigne's corner for Shearer to head into a crowded goal. For Adams, one of the scapegoats for England's dire showing in Euro 88, it was a sliver of redemption.

Whenever a team scores early in a game and doesn't prevail, you'll invariably hear someone say 'they scored too early', as if opposition teams can only truly gather themselves if they have at least 80 minutes to make amends. It is, of course, not true. Just looking at the tiny sample of Euro 96 itself you'll see that four of the five instances of a goal scored in the opening ten minutes saw that very team go on to win the game. The other game was a pulsating 3-3 draw between Russia and the Czech Republic. The Czechs not only took the lead after a mere five minutes but also equalised with two minutes to go. What does it all mean? Not much.

That said, England's early goal was a positive as it meant they had taken the lead in an international semi-final for the first time since 1966. Unlike that game against Portugal 30 years earlier, they were soon pegged back, with Germany equalising after 15 minutes via Stefan Kuntz. Even so, unlike the Spain game and vast swathes of the match with the Dutch, England were clearly the better team for most of the semi-final. Darren Anderton was particularly impressive; his total of six chances created remains the highest by an England player in a single European Championships game before Euro 2016.

It wasn't just Anderton, though. The whole team exerted a level of control that has now been retrofitted to the tournament as a whole. Play well in your final proper game and the memories will remain golden for ever more (shades of 1990 here, too). Venables' team enjoyed a possession figure of 56% in the semi-final (the highest they recorded in the tournament), ten percentage points higher than they did against the

Netherlands (which was their lowest). Gascoigne was on a good day, too, making 17 successful passes in the final third, more than any other player in the match. Perhaps the only players not to shine were the two who stole the plaudits in the Netherlands game, Shearer and Sheringham. One shot on target apiece means that Shearer didn't force Andreas Köpke into a save in the whole game or hit the target after the second minute in a match that lasted over two hours.

Unlike the extra-time in the game against Spain, where England settled for penalties in the face of a superior opponent, in the semi-final they tried to finish off the Germans, perhaps knowing, deep down, that their old rivals are almost undefeatable when it comes to a shootout. Anderton hit the post and Gascoigne's lunge at a tempting cross saw him come only inches from handing England a second goal that would surely have been decisive. Gascoigne and that end of Wembley really didn't have a good history together.

In the end it was penalties again. We all know how it ends but it's easy to forget how it started. Once again England had the benefit of taking the first penalty and they stuck with the same players and same order that had served them so well in the quarter-final against Spain. So, Shearer, Platt, Pearce and Gascoigne all stepped up and all scored with surgical precision. The only difference was that Germany's penalty takers were just as impressive and David Seaman didn't really come close to saving one. So much for Ron Atkinson's theory. Seriously, though, add in the fifth penalty takers for each team, Sheringham and Kuntz, and you will struggle to find ten better penalties, particularly given the context of the game. England would spend the following decades crashing out on penalties thanks to some awful attempts but the chosen five in 1996 did all they were asked to. The problem was what came next.

Curiously, for a match that went the full distance, Venables didn't make any substitutions. Of the six players who could have taken the sixth penalty for England, Darren Anderton was surely the best candidate (ending his career with five goals from eight penalties taken in the Premier League). Instead, central defender Gareth Southgate stepped up with the result that everyone already knows and probably already knew before he stepped up. Let us not forget that Venables had Robbie Fowler on the bench, someone who took 23 penalties in the Premier League in his career (17 scored). In a world where we've seen managers change their goalkeepers in extra-time to prepare for a penalty shootout, the idea of Fowler coming on with a minute or two to go seems a no-brainer.

Southgate bumbled the spot-kick straight into Köpke's arms and it was left to human peacock Andreas Möller to take Germany through to another final. It's worth noting that studies of penalty shootouts at World Cups have shown that there is a 71% conversion rate in them, down from 80% for penalties in normal play. Interestingly, a penalty taken to stay in the game sees the success rate fall to a dismal 44%, a clear indication of the pressure on the players involved. Conversely, penalties taken to win the shootout have a success rate of 93%, far above the average. Möller was never going to miss. England were never going to make the final.

England Penalty Shootout History

Tournament	Opponent	Score	Result
World Cup 90	West Germany	3-4	Lost
Euro 96	Spain	4-2	**Won**
Euro 96	Germany	5-6	Lost
King Hassan II Cup (1998)	Belgium	3-4	Lost
World Cup 98	Argentina	3-4	Lost
Euro 04	Portugal	5-6	Lost
World Cup 06	Portugal	1-3	Lost
Euro 2012	Italy	2-4	Lost

Looking at the sorry history of England and penalty shootouts, it's worth stating that England's defeat to Germany in Euro 96 was due to a lack of quality not psychological weakness. England's initial five penalties were scored expertly; it was only when the inexperienced and clearly nervous Gareth Southgate stepped up that defeat was imminent. This contrasts with the more recent shootouts where the weight of England's terrible history with the format has weighed heavily. The contest with Portugal in 2006 was a nadir, with one successful spot-kick (in almost 600 penalty shootouts involving English sides, a team has successfully converted only one spot-kick on 71 occasions) and the feeling that once the game had ended level after 120 minutes, there was only one outcome in store. Six years later, in 2012, the penalties against Italy felt like a farcical re-enactment of a heritage activity. New players by and large, but the outcome was the same.

Final Thoughts

International tournaments are rare pearls in the world of football, and good ones are even rarer. For fans of a few select countries (Brazil, Germany, Italy, and Spain in recent years) there is a reasonable chance of enjoyment, but England have experienced such a dismal run of finals that it is no surprise that the handful of decent tournament displays are excessively lauded, Euro 96 being chief among them. When you actually look at what happened, you realise that it was a wasted chance. From the moribund build-up to the tournament to the unusual decision not to utilise substitutes in the semi-final, Terry Venables failed to make the most of a squad that contained some of the best England players in the past 25 years. As the data has hinted, Gascoigne, despite his baggage, was operating at a level comparable with his breakthrough tournament in 1990 and was arguably England's most effective player. Yet even he couldn't inspire the team to more than about a game and a half of dominant play. This was a team that should have stamped their authority on a tournament staged on their home turf. Instead, they succumbed to many of the flaws that characterised Graham Taylor's spell in charge. But while Taylor is lamented to this day, the Venables era inexplicably lives on as a brief Camelot.

II

Euro 2016

'Put your feet up and enjoy it'

England manager Graham Taylor, shortly before Euro 1992

Summer 2016 was a period when unreliable nostalgia clashed with reality in many guises. To people whose first tournament memories came in the late 1980s or early 1990s, the European Championships expanding to twenty-four teams (divided into six groups) brought back joyful glimpses of Mexico 86, Italia 90 and USA 94. But so often we forget the things that annoyed us about the past. We forget the things that persuaded people from long ago to change the system in the first place. When the World Cup was expanded to thirty-two teams in 1998 it resulted in one of the most universally revered tournaments of all time. Eighteen years later, France hosted another soccer jamboree and, like then, reached the final, but it is unlikely to be remembered with such fondness. Even so, there were moments of giddiness and greatness floating among the jetsam, so let's try and find them.

The Group Stage

Day One
(France 2-1 Romania)

The tournament began with an underwhelming opening ceremony and it looked like the hosts were following suit after a tentative start against Romania. It took until the 52nd minute for France to hit a shot on target, before Olivier Giroud, a man criticised by a fairly significant section of the French support before the tournament, opened the scoring. It was his eighth goal in his last six starts for the national side, almost enough to stem the criticism for a moment or two. But the Arsenal man was not the key London-based Premier League player in this game. West Ham's Dimitri Payet took that crown. After creating the first goal he lashed home the winner (after Romania had equalised from the penalty spot) with his left foot. Not only did Payet become the first Frenchman to score and assist in the same game at the Euros since Thierry Henry in 2000, but it was an unusual way to score for a man who had only hit four left-footed shots in the Premier League all season. Payet's swinger had got the party off with a swing.

(Tournament goals per game: 3.00)

Day Two
(Albania 0-1 Switzerland, Wales 2-1 Slovenia, England 1-1 Russia)

The second day began with Albania's debut at a major tournament and, just like previous teams making their Euros bow (Latvia in 2004, Poland and Austria in 2008), they lost. It was a day that promised so much but delivered so little, as they also became the fourth team to pick up a red card in their first Euros match.

It was a far better competition debut for the Welsh, who scored, thanks to their iconic leader Gareth Bale, with their first ever shot on target. Bale's strike was also, surprisingly, the first time any of the UK sides had scored a direct free-kick at the Euros. Even more surprisingly, Wales became the first UK team to win their opening match at the Euros. Surely England would follow suit a few hours later?

The Three Lions' match against Russia began with the team's second youngest starting XI in their major tournament history, a youthful 25 years and 206 days (beaten only by Sven-Göran Eriksson's first go at handling the 'Golden Generation' in 2002). What followed was a game that was strangely dominated by set-piece allocation. The use of centre-forward Harry Kane to take corners seemed to enrage sections of the fanbase and media, with his total of six for the game representing 5% of England's total in the competition's history. While there is no reason why a striker shouldn't take a corner (Kane is hardly noted as a danger in the penalty area when corners are being swung in), he compounded his provocation of *real* football men by not making a single touch in the opposition penalty area all game. England's eventual goal, meanwhile, came from a direct free-kick taken by Eric Dier, a player who had featured in sixty-five Premier League games without ever shooting from a dead ball. Ultimately, what looked like it would end as a baffling night ended as a frustrating one, with Russia's equaliser on 91:15, being their latest ever (normal-time) goal at a Euros game. In the end, England had cornered themselves.

(Tournament goals per game: 2.25)

Day Three
(Turkey 0-1 Croatia, Poland 1-0 Northern Ireland,
Germany 2-0 Ukraine)

Turkeys wouldn't vote for Christmas and Turkey wouldn't vote for MD1. Their defeat to Croatia was the fourth time they've lost their opening game at the Euros, in their fourth tournament appearance. It wasn't all bad, though, as Emre Mor (18 years and 323 days) became the youngest Turkish player at a major tournament. There's definitely Mor to come from the Dortmund youngster. Mor. More. Enough.

Northern Ireland's first appearance in a major tournament since 1986 seemed to get the better of them, with the smallest nation to win a game at a World Cup finals managing only two shots of any kind against Poland, a joint low in any European Championship game between 1980 and 2016.

Germany, meanwhile, went into the tournament with the youngest squad at an average age of 25 years and 296 days (but only because they had to replace Antonio Rüdiger with Jonathan Tah shortly before the tournament). Before that, England had the youngest squad. But, as usual, they were bested by the Germans, who can seemingly master the birth canal like they can penalty shootouts.

(Tournament goals per game: 1.86)

Day Four
(Spain 1-0 Czech Republic, Ireland 1-1 Sweden, Belgium 0-2 Italy)

Just a quarter of the way into the day's early game, Tomáš Rosický had already played for longer at the Euros than he had for Arsenal in the entire 2015–16 season. Rosický remains the youngest player to feature for the Czechs at the Euros (back in Euro 2000) and sixteen years later, he became the oldest. Reigning champions Spain could only score once, but they did force Petr Cech into making more passes than any of his outfield colleagues. The Arsenal keeper is a master with his gloves but he is most definitely not a playmaker.

When the Republic of Ireland took the lead against Sweden, they dreamt big. Their introduction to the Euros back in 1988 couldn't have started better, with a 1-0 win against old pals England, but since then they had failed to win another game or keep a clean sheet. Could their match against the Swedes in Paris be a new dawn? Sadly not. Despite failing to hit a single shot on target in the whole game, Sweden equalised via an own goal from Ciaran Clark, who found innovative new ways to experience despair after a season playing for Aston Villa.

Belgium, the eternal dark horses, fell at the first hurdle with a 2-0 reverse against Italy. In a move seemingly designed to annoy England, the *Azzurri* appeared to have been coached to be more than a sum of their parts. Goals from players with experience of playing for Premier League teams who wear red and white stripes (Emanuele Giaccherini and Graziano Pellè) meant that the Italians have lost only one of their last eleven opening games at a major tournament, keeping their 17th clean sheet at the Euros. As will be said forever, until the end of time: 'you can't rule out the Italians'. And you can't.

(Tournament goals per game: 1.80)

Day Five
(Austria 0-2 Hungary, Portugal 1-1 Iceland)

Mysterious Group F began on day five. Cristiano Ronaldo's Portugal (their official moniker) were joined by the Habsburg duo of Austria and Hungary as well as tournament debutants Iceland (the only team representing a country using Greenwich Mean Time during the tournament).

Austria, having been tipped by some as potential dark horses, promptly lost to Hungary, whose goalkeeper, former Crystal Palace player and tracksuit bottom loyalist Gábor Király, became the first man in his forties to appear at the European Championships. Should men in their forties really be wearing tracksuit bottoms? That's not really an answer I feel qualified to give.

In the other game, group favourites Portugal were held by Iceland who, despite allowing the Iberians twenty-six shots, only conceded once. Ronaldo had ten of the efforts (although only one was on target), meaning that by the end of the first round of games, the Real Madrid man had hit more shots than nine of the twenty-four countries taking part. Was this the start of a theme? Yes, yes it was.

(Tournament goals per game: 1.83)

Day Six
(Russia 1-2 Slovakia, Romania 1-1 Switzerland, France 2-0 Albania)

England's failure to beat Russia was put into context in the day's first game. Slovakia eased past the wounded Bear with only their second ever tournament win. Of course, with the new tournament format in place, even Russia's dismal performance in their first two games still left them with an excellent chance of reaching the second round (should they beat Wales). But anyone who had watched their 180 minutes thus far would have been under few illusions that they could actually do it.

Group A restarted with a 1-1 draw between Romania and Switzerland. Even though the Swiss mustered nineteen shots, it's a game that has already faded from consciousness. More memorable was hosts France's second game, a 2-0 win against Albania that may have looked comfortable on paper but required two late goals from Antoine Griezmann (89:10) and Dimitri Payet (95:02). It left the home fans cock-a-hoop, but those two goals were the only shots on target of the *entire game* and meant that three of France's four goals at this point had come in or after the 89th minute. In a tournament where goals were at a premium, France's 100% record after two games was coated with only the thinnest of wallpapers.

(Tournament goals per game: 1.93)

Day Seven
(England 2-1 Wales, Ukraine 0-2 Northern Ireland,
Germany 0-0 Poland)

June 16 was local derby day, with England v Wales in the early afternoon and Germany against Poland in the evening. Sandwiched in-between was Ukraine v Northern Ireland, a fixture that most definitely doesn't have a history of border disputes. (Not between the two nations in question, anyway.)

Although England's clash with the Welsh seemed like the start of something better at the time, it was in fact the high (but really quite low) water mark of the tournament for Roy Hodgson's team. After falling behind to Gareth Bale's free-kick goal (the Welshman becoming the first player to score twice via this method in the same Euros since Thomas Hässler in 1992), the English laboured to come back. At half-time Hodgson utilised the large number of forwards he had selected for the squad by replacing Raheem Sterling and Harry Kane with Jamie Vardy and Daniel Sturridge, and it was the replacements who scored the two goals that ensured England won a tournament game after having trailed at the break for the first time. Sturridge's late, late winner was timed at 91:00 and assured that England went into the third round of matches top of their group. Nothing could go wrong now.

Northern Ireland's win against Ukraine also saw a late goal. A very late goal. Niall McGinn's goal after 95:52 is in fact the latest ever scored in regulation time at the Euros and although it looked like just an embellishment to the scoreline, the two-goal margin was in fact crucial in guaranteeing the Northern Irish reached the second round as one of the best third-placed teams. For Ukraine it was another dismal display and marked the two-thirds mark in their goalless odyssey of atrociousness.

The final match of the day saw Poland hold Germany, their illustrious neighbours and reigning world champions, to a goalless draw. Like the France game the previous evening, the game was light on action and heavy on ennui. Poland did not hit a single shot on target in the entire game, while Germany failed to register one in the first half of a Euros game since 1988. It was also the first 0-0 in a group stage game since France v Romania in the 2008 tournament. Across the continent, people were starting to wonder when the promised entertainment was due to begin.

(Tournament goals per game: 1.89)

Day Eight
(Italy 1-0 Sweden, Czech Republic 2-2 Croatia, Spain 3-0 Turkey)

'Ambassador, with these goals you are really spoiling us.' Finally, like an Icelandic trawler returning with its catch, we were treated to some rippling nets. Not immediately, though, as Italy eased past Sweden 1-0. The Swedes became the first team in Euros history to fail to hit a shot on target in either of their first two group games. The game itself had only twelve shots, the lowest ever seen in a European Championships game (later equalled by the similarly rustic Wales v Northern Ireland match in the second round), with Italy's 88th-minute winner (oh hello, late goals theme) was the first shot on target of the entire second half.

But, just as people started to weep with confusion at the dire fare they were being offered, joy arrived in the form of the Czech Republic's 2-2 draw with Croatia. It was the first game of the tournament to contain more than three goals. Despite the Croats clearly being the better team, the Czechs came back with two late goals to leave everyone smiling. Except Croatians.

Later that evening the Spanish indicated that they might be in the mood as they became the first team to score three times in one game at Euro 2016. They also extended their run without conceding in the competition to 690 minutes. The third goal, in particular, was a thing of beauty. Gerard Piqué was the only Spanish outfielder not to touch the ball in the build-up and the move of twenty-one passes preceding the goal the longest of the tournament at that point.

(Tournament goals per game: 2.00)

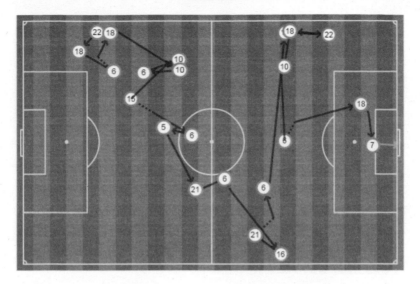

Third Spanish goal v Turkey – 17 June

Day Nine
(Belgium 3-0 Republic of Ireland, Iceland 1-1 Hungary,
Portugal 0-0 Austria)

Belgium's opening-match defeat to Italy was avenged in style against Ireland, who slumped to a 3-0 defeat in which, joining in with the general theme of Euro 2016, they didn't register a shot on target. For the Belgians, it was their joint biggest win in a tournament game (matching the result they recorded against El Salvador in the 1970 World Cup, and a margin they later surpassed by beating Hungary 4-0 in the second round).

The Group F games produced two draws, with Iceland's Birkir Már Sævarsson scoring a late own goal that denied his team a famous win. That Hungary equaliser took the running total of goals scored in the 87th minute or later to thirteen which, at the time, represented more than a quarter (28%) of all goals in the tournament. This was proving useful to no one except highlights compilers, who could feel safe in fast-forwarding to the last ten minutes to pan for gold.

The other match was a case of Cristiano Ronaldo v Austria, and no one came out of it with much credit. The Real Madrid man once again unleashed a wild array of shots including a missed penalty, without scoring. His attempts from direct free-kicks at major international tournaments also rose to thirty-six taken/zero scored. His views on Gareth Bale's success from dead balls elsewhere in the tournament remain unknown.

(Tournament goals per game: 1.96)

Day Ten
(Switzerland 0-0 France, Romania 0-1 Albania)

Group A concluded with two games that produced a total of one goal. Switzerland and France knew that a draw would see both teams through to the next round and the game played out in a manner familiar to that scenario. The first half was an open contest with fifteen shots, while the second was a more measured affair (indicated by a total of only five efforts at goal). This wasn't quite West Germany v Austria in the *Disgrace of Gijon* (look it up) in 1982, but it wasn't swashbuckling football either.

There was more romance in the other match, where Albania scored their first ever goal, via Armando Sadiku and secured their first ever win, climbing above Romania into third place in Group A. Their goal difference of −2, though, was always likely to count against them in the race to be one of the fourth best third-placed teams, and so it proved over subsequent days.

(Tournament goals per game: 1.85)

Day Eleven
(Russia 0-3 Wales, Slovakia 0-0 England)

Group B concluded as expected, with Wales, England and Slovakia all progressing to the next stage, but perhaps not in the expected order. The Welsh romped past the sorry Russians, thanks to goals from Aaron Ramsey, Neil Taylor and Gareth Bale. Taylor's goal was his first in any game since scoring for fifth-tier Wrexham at Grays in April 2010 (2,263 days prior). Bale, meanwhile, became the first player to score in all three group games at the Euros since Milan Baroš and Ruud van Nistelrooy in 2004. Wales also became the first competition debutants to top their group since Sweden in 1992. For Russia, it was their third tournament in a row where they had failed to qualify from the group stage. With their own World Cup now less than two years away, you'd imagine some urgent planning is required.

Wales's win wouldn't have been enough to win the group had England managed to defeat Slovakia. But despite setting up camp in their opponents' half for almost the entire match, England failed to do so. Hodgson's team had twenty-nine shots in the game but only five of them forced Matúš Kozáčik into a save and, as the game progressed, it became clear that despite bringing five centre-forwards to the tournament, England had left their cutting edge behind at Luton airport. The Three Lions had forty-six shots more than Slovakia in the group stage, yet scored just one more goal. As the team management bemoaned other nations that sat back and soaked up pressure (all but eliminating the threat from players such as Jamie Vardy on the counter-attack), advancement to the knockout stages went from expected progression to protracted depression.

(Tournament goals per game: 1.82)

Day Twelve
(Northern Ireland 0-1 Germany, Ukraine 0-1 Poland,
Czech Republic 0-2 Turkey, Croatia 2-1 Spain)

The upside of sixteen teams progressing from six groups of four is that it is hard to find dead rubbers. The downside is that it can lead to some unsettling 'impure' game scenarios – as seen in Northern Ireland's defeat to Germany. Michael O'Neill's team knew they were probably going to lose to the Germans but because of the goal difference of third-place teams in other groups (particularly Albania in Group A), a narrow defeat would not be a disastrous result for them. So fans were treated to Northern Ireland all but defending their 1-0 deficit in their final game and celebrating wholeheartedly when they 'held out'. A stark illustration of the one-sidedness of the game was the fact that Northern Ireland completed only 110 passes in the whole game, eleven fewer than Germany's Toni Kroos managed on his own.

In the other Group C match Ukraine unlocked the 'no goals scored' achievement in the tournament, while Poland progressed to the knockout stages without conceding but having scored just twice in 270 minutes. Bayern hit man deluxe Robert Lewandowski, meanwhile, failed to hit a shot on target in any of the games. How very Euro 2016.

Later that day, Group D concluded with a shock. Croatia inflicting Spain's first ever defeat at the Euros in a game in which they had led and ensuring that the reigning champions would end the group in second place. In the other game, a win for the Czechs would have taken them to the next round ahead of Northern Ireland but instead they lost 2-0 to Turkey. Veteran goalkeeper Petr Cech, for whom this was probably his final European Championship, has conceded twenty-one goals in the competition, more than any other goalkeeper in the tournament's history. One more than another Premier League icon, Denmark's Peter Schmeichel.

(Tournament goals per game: 1.81)

Day Thirteen (Iceland 2-1 Austria, Hungary 3-3 Portugal,
Italy 0-1 Republic of Ireland, Sweden 0-1 Belgium)

The final day of the group stages produced arguably the game of the tournament when Hungary and Portugal shared six goals in Lyon. With 6% of the goals in the entire tournament coming in this one game, it was quite literally the 'Lyon's share'. It also saw Ronaldo finally get on the scoresheet (twice, in fact, taking him to eight goals and just one behind record holder Michel Platini). What decline? Ronaldo also became the first player to score in four different European Championships (2004, 2008, 2012 and 2016). To put it into context, the last Euros that didn't see a Ronaldo goal did see Dennis Wise turn out for England. Horses for courses, you take your pick. Hungary played their part, too, scoring all three goals from outside the box for an extra aesthetic bonus and becoming the first team to do so in a Euro finals game (1980 onwards). They also managed to win the group in their first tournament appearance since the 1986 World Cup, which looked delightful until they realised they'd have to face Belgium in the second round.

It looked like England, due to face the second-placed team in Group F in the Last 16, would once again be paired with Portugal. Instead, to the short-term joy of many, a last-minute winner for the Icelanders from Arnór Ingvi Traustason pushed the plucky islanders into second place and a clash with their old enemies from the Cod Wars. Portugal came third, and qualified for the next round having not won a single game, a vagary of the 24-team structure and one on which they would go on to capitalise considerably.

That evening, Group E concluded with Sweden's damp squib of a summer ending with a 1-0 defeat to the Belgians. The Swedes hit just four shots on target in three games and, along with fellow yellow-shirted strugglers Ukraine, did little to suggest they deserved to be there.

Elsewhere, Ireland secured a famous win against Italy to sneak through as the second-best third-placed team. Italy and future Chelsea manager Antonio Conte did, however, rest most of his players with the *Azzurri* already through to the next round as group winners. Is beating essentially a reserve team something to celebrate? Probably not. Is getting through to the knockout stages something to cherish? Almost certainly.

(Tournament goals per game: 1.92)

Conclusion

Ultimately the group stage was blighted by defensive, unimaginative play, with teams knowing that invariably not losing was more important than winning. As the graph below shows, by the third day of the tournament the goals per game rate was pretty consistent for the remainder of the section, with only occasional forays (hello Portugal v Hungary) into the world of entertainment. In the two-day break between the end of the group stage and the start of the knockout round, many people theorised that now the phony war was over the fireworks would begin. We were about to find out.

Group stage goals/game by game – Euro 2016 and Euro 2012

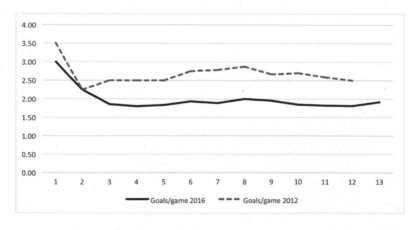

The Knockout Stages
The Defenestration of England

'I think it's bad news for the English game'

Alan Hansen

'We're not creative enough, we're not positive enough'

Trevor Brooking

'We'll go on getting bad results'

Jimmy Hill

The pundits have changed in twenty years, but the message is the same. England's biennial departure from major tournaments is usually accompanied by howls of outrage, buckets of blame and bouts of introspection. All of which gradually fade to a whisper during a competent qualifying campaign (before beginning once again sometime in the summer of years that end with an even number).

There seem to be two broad schools of thought when it comes to England's persistent failure at tournaments. The long-term-decline camp sees structural issues at the heart of the game, encapsulated by the great (but not as in good) discussion of the number of overseas players in English league football that erupts every few years. The alternative is a simpler one: England suffer from a mixture of poor management and bad luck. The truth is, unsurprisingly, probably somewhere in the middle. But it seems that the long-term issues, the coaching and all of that, get more focus than the simple things that other, often smaller, nations seem to be able to do without any major issues.

The truth is that England, whatever the state of coaching in the country, had one of the strongest squads at Euro 2016, and that under an alternative regime they would surely have prospered. That they didn't was down to a lack of invention when faced with a packed defence, a corollary of the opposition being rightly apprehensive about facing the relative might of the Three Lions (and it wasn't something that was new to 2016).

Roy Hodgson largely got away with a substandard World Cup in 2014, the fans, along with the media, seemingly letting him off with their worst ever points haul (1) and a first group stage elimination since 1958. Failure in Brazil came two years after Hodgson's England had lost a Euros quarter-final to Italy – one of the most one-sided games in recent knockout memory, a game in which the entire England team made just fifteen passes in the second period of extra-time (fewer than Andrea Pirlo managed on his own). A free pass was handed out here, too, with Hodgson escaping censure as he only had control of the team shortly before the tournament, after the protracted departure of overseas villain Fabio Capello.

The first real signs of the England manager being questioned about his team not being able to break the opposition down came after a friendly against Norway at Wembley in September 2014. England's only goal came from a Wayne Rooney penalty won by Raheem Sterling (sound familiar?). In the 90 minutes against a limited team ranked 53rd in the world, England, including their captain's spot-kick, could only manage two shots on target. When questioned about this after the match, an agitated Hodgson said, 'don't hit me with statistics' before describing the shots figures as 'absolute fucking bollocks'. Overall in that game against Norway, England had fourteen shots with only two on target, which actually compares quite well with their efforts at Euro 2016 (see diagram that follows).

England at Euro 2016	Possession	Goals	Shots on target	Total shots
Iceland	67.99	1	4	18
Slovakia	60.61	0	5	29
Wales	69.67	2	5	20
Russia	52.31	1	5	15

A monster haul of eighty-two shots in four games at Euro 2016 looks good, until you see that it led to only four goals. Eighty-two shots, but only five big chances (an opportunity defined by Opta as one where you'd reasonably expect the player to score). To put that into context, Spain's Alvaro Morata had five big chances by himself at the tournament, despite playing for a team which also disappointed and exited at the Last 16 stage. If England were the wolf that planned to terrorise and/or eat the three pigs, they would have struggled to blow down even the house made of straw.

Hodgson was rightfully delighted with his team's injury-time win against Wales, noting, 'we played so well against Russia and conceded in the 93rd minute, and today we worked so hard in the second half and pushed and pushed and then scored in the 92nd minute. I suppose it shows things do even out but it is rare to see them even out in the space of two games', missing the point that the two games were very similar. You could replay both in the same manner and England might defeat Russia and draw with Wales, or draw both, or, heavens above, win both, but it doesn't justify an approach that results in sterile dominance.

Even so, the expected goals numbers for England's games show that their results 'should' have been a 1-0 win against Russia, 2-0 v Wales, 2-1 v Slovakia and 2-1 v Iceland. Had the games panned out like that (and remember that the very point of xG is to suggest the most likely outcome, not necessarily the one that transpired), then the reception the team would have received would have been very different. In 38-game seasons, shock draws and defeats are evened out and brushed under the carpet by the sheer length of the competition, but in international tournaments they are magnified considerably. England didn't create great opportunities in their four-game adventure, but they still should have done better than they did.

Helpfully for our purposes, England-stiflers Slovakia and Iceland went on to face Germany and France respectively, and neither team suffered the same fate as the Three Lions, creating better chances which they also had the wherewithal to take.

Team	Opponent	Shots, on target	Possession	Goals	Big chance total
France	Iceland	8	60.71	5	3
Germany	Slovakia	7	60.84	3	4
England	Iceland	4	67.99	1	1
England	Slovakia	5	60.61	0	2

Now you might argue that, in the case of Iceland, France did not have to face a team sitting back on a lead as England did, and instead had racked up a comfortable four-goal lead by half-time. And yet, England managed to take the lead after three minutes and fifty-four seconds, but were level within seconds and trailing fifteen minutes later thanks to basic defensive errors. Hodgson's England had a fundamental problem with cutting loose and it's notable that in his spell as manager the team scored more than four in a game on only five occasions, and four of those instances were against semi-professional whipping boys San Marino.

In the all-too-short exultant aftermath of the Wales game, Hodgson said, 'I am not a great statistics person and I don't even trust them' but there are a few cast-iron ones he cannot escape. Three wins in eleven tournament games as England manager is below par at the very least, coming against Ukraine and Sweden in 2012 (arguably two of the worst sides in the competition four years later) and Wales. All of which means that since winning the World Cup on home soil in 1966, England have a dire record in knockout games.

You can just about make an argument they have 'won' six knockout games at tournaments since lifting the ultimate prize in 1966. A third-place play-off with the USSR in 1968, a pair of extra-time wins in 1990, a win in a penalty shootout after a drawn match in 1996 (which really isn't a win) and a pair of World Cup wins (both in 90 minutes!) under Sven-Göran Eriksson, one in 2002, one in 2006. That is an awful record given that in the same period Germany have won six tournaments. Football's coming home? I'm not sure it was ever really here in the first place.

Even the customary scapegoating of England players went badly awry. The chosen media target this time round seemed to be Raheem Sterling, conveniently ignoring the fact that his incisive run into the box against Iceland, and subsequent penalty won, was the high point of a sorry evening's work. No England player came away from the tournament with much credit but to single out Sterling seemed mistaken at the very least. Meanwhile, goalkeeper Joe Hart has made a total of nine saves over the past two international tournaments, while letting in eight goals. It's not Hart's fault that England have struggled in the past two years but he has still largely escaped censure in the media despite obvious errors such as Gareth Bale's goal for Wales.

Ultimately, while this tournament was more of the same for England, there was a crucial difference, namely the presence of Wales and Northern Ireland. The successful campaigns by two other UK teams, filled mostly with players who are fundamentally less talented than most of those in the England squad, was a kind of blind test as to how England could do if they were more organised, or set up in a coherent system.

Hodgson chose to play a 4-3-3 despite selecting only one true wide midfielder in the squad (Andros Townsend, left at home, could actually have been effective shooting from distance in the Slovakia and Iceland games). Like Marc Wilmots' Belgium, Hodgson presided over a collection of talented players who were never really turned into a team. Hal Robson-Kanu, released by second-tier Reading shortly before Euro 2016, was a much more effective forward than Premier League Golden Boot winner Harry Kane. That isn't misfortune, that's bad management.

Quiz Question: Name the last time England won a tournament game by two clear goals.*

The Irish Question

While England's exit at the Last 16 stage was a fully-fledged outrage, both Northern Ireland and the Republic of Ireland were broadly satisfied with reaching that juncture. It is fair to say that Northern Ireland were the most 'functional' (for which read agricultural) team at the tournament, making fewer successful passes than any other side (despite reaching the knockout stages). Their pass completion, meanwhile, saw almost two of every five they made go astray, 62.5% putting them slightly below the most inaccurate team in the Championship in 2015–16 (Rotherham United).

Essentially – and it isn't a surprise given they had players from clubs such as Doncaster, Notts County and Millwall – Michael O'Neill's team played to their limits and played like a team from the English lower leagues, failing to score in three of their four games. If they live on in the memories of people outside the UK it will be for the Will Grigg song which echoed across France. Time spent playing at Euro 2016 by Will Grigg: zero minutes.

* Answer: v Trinidad & Tobago in 2006. Raheem Sterling was eleven years old.

Lowest in tournament

Successful passes	Northern Ireland	640
Pass completion	Northern Ireland	62.5%
Pass completion final third	Northern Ireland	47.1%
% passes short	Northern Ireland	72.1%

The Republic, meanwhile, veered from good to bad and sort of back again. A promising start against Sweden ended with an own goal, a thumping at the hands of an unusually on-song Belgium before the famous victory against Italy that saw them through to the knockout stages, albeit with the tough assignment against hosts France.

It was fitting that Robbie Brady scored the Irish goal against France (the earliest ever goal from the penalty spot at a European Championships), as the Norwich man had been one of the most impressive performers for Martin O'Neill's side. He ended the tournament with as many goals as Romelu Lukaku, while creating seven goalscoring chances, one more than England's hot prospect Dele Alli.

Even so, by losing at the Last 16 stage, the Republic ultimately reached the same point they had four years earlier, albeit with much more enjoyment for the fans along the way. And that, really, is the aim of the game.

Retirement Village

One of the biggest flaws in international tournaments is the sudden death of enticing narratives. Just as you think that a certain player is going to play so well that all future mentions of that year's event will forever be associated with him (see also: 1986 and Maradona), he is dumped unceremoniously from it by the cruel vagaries of knockout football.

Perhaps the best example of this in Euro 2016 was Andrés Iniesta. The balding Spanish schemer was finally, after the retirement of Xavi, the key creative fulcrum in the 2008 and 2012 European Championship winners' midfield and he started this year's tournament as if he was enjoying that increase in responsibility.

As the table below shows, he was creating an additional chance from open play per game at the Euros as well as being three times more likely to hit a shot from outside the box. When you have Messi, Neymar and Suarez ahead of you, shooting from distance is probably a bit rude, but when on holiday in France . . .

	Andrés Iniesta	
Competition	Open play chances created/90	Long range shots/90
Euro 2016	2.25	1.5
La Liga 2015–16	1.24	0.6

But as we know, the Iniesta Finals never really went anywhere. Spain won their first two games of the tournament to ignite hopes of a third successive continental title but then lost their final game, and top spot in the group, to Croatia, dumping them into a second-round game with old rivals Italy, who, as so often in the past (but not much recently), bested their Mediterranean pals. It was the first time Spain had lost a European Championship finals game by two goals since Euro 88, a few weeks before Sergio Busquets was born.

But there were eleven players older than Busquets in the Spanish squad and between them they played more than 2,500 minutes at Euro 2016. The only Spanish outfielder born in the 1990s to get more than half an hour of action was Alvaro Morata. In fact, long-serving manager Vicente del Bosque remained deeply loyal to his long-serving players, naming the same starting XI in all four games. Koke, who amassed fourteen assists for Atlético Madrid in La Liga in 2015–16 was given only nineteen minutes in France. Not quite zero, but not enough Koke to add some sparkle to the team.

So, like England, Spain have exited the last two tournaments at the group stage (World Cup) and the second round (Euros). Although, quite rightly, Del Bosque leaves his post with far, far more credit than any England manager has ever amassed. The only person to coach teams to the Champions League, the World Cup and the European Championships, Del Bosque won more than three-quarters (87 of 114) of his games in charge of Spain. He may have been lucky enough to manage the country's golden generation but he did so with aplomb. Just not this year.

Paying the Penalty

While they don't possess a record quite as bad as England's, Italy's experience of penalty shootouts is not hugely joyous, with the exit against Germany in the quarter-final their sixth from nine. They did force/trick/play no part in the Germans missing three penalties in a marathon version of the popular drawn-game deciding device. Before this match, Germany had only ever failed to score with two penalties in their entire tournament shootout history, and it was faintly amusing that two of the three Germans to err were Premier League players (Özil and Schweinsteiger), both of whom have clearly been infected with Mad Pen Disease in their spell away from the continental mainland.

Italy tournament shootouts	Opponents	Pens scored	Pens conceded	Result
E1980	Czechoslovakia	8	9	L
WC1990	Argentina	3	4	L
WC1994	Brazil	2	3	L
WC1998	France	3	4	L
E2000	Netherlands	3	1	W
WC2006	France	5	3	W
E2008	Spain	2	4	L
E2012	England	4	2	W
E2016	Germany	5	6	L

In what seemed like a penalty shootout designed specifically for the Twitter generation, where attempted jokes were hitting their mark and stuttering like Simone Zaza in equal measure, as fast as the scenario unfolded, a total of seven spurned spot-kicks was a new record in a World Cup or European Championships. This was two more than a host of other memorable shootouts, including England's against Portugal in 2006, which featured Jamie Carragher scoring, and then missing once the referee had cruelly ordered a re-take. Statistically, the World Cup/Euros shootout with the highest percentage of missed kicks was the famously dire clash between Switzerland and Ukraine in 2006. After 120 minutes of bleak play, only three of the seven penalties were scored, with Ukraine recording a rare clean sheet in a shootout.

Year	Competition	Team 1	Team 2	Total pens missed
2016	Euros	Italy	Germany	7
1990	WC	Argentina	Yugoslavia	5
2002	WC	Spain	Rep. of Ireland	5
2014	WC	Brazil	Chile	5
2006	WC	Portugal	England	5

One final, seemingly pedantic but actually necessary, point about penalty shootouts is that they are simply a mechanism to decide who progresses from a drawn game. Much was made before this quarter-final of Italy's unbeaten record against Germany in competitive games, and that remains the case even after the events in Bordeaux. The match ended as a draw but, with no provision for a replay, the tie-breaker in this instance was a penalty shootout. Had a coin toss or a leg-wrestling match between the managers been used instead, you'd hope more people would grasp the difference between the game of football and the method used to decide who progresses. As it stands, for at least two more years Germany await their first ever competitive win against Italy.

Pole Fault

Poland's exit from the quarter-final stage after *kicks taken from the penalty mark* (see Paying the Penalty) ensured that they would leave the competition without having trailed at any point. Not once did Adam Nawałka's team trail and yet they were, departing at the same stage as minnows Iceland.

As the table below shows, it's neither rare nor common for this to happen in an international tournament. Perhaps somewhat predictably, England turn out to be the masters of losing while never losing, having done so at the 1982 and 2006 World Cups as well as hosts of Euro 96.

**Teams not to trail at a European Championships/
World Cup and not win the trophy**

Year	Team	Competition	Games won	Games drawn	Stage reached
1982	England	World Cup	3	2	2nd group
1986	Brazil	World Cup	4	1	Quarter-final
1986	Mexico	World Cup	3	2	Quarter-final
1990	Italy	World Cup	6	1	Semi-final
1996	England	European Championships	2	3	Semi-final
1996	France	European Championships	2	3	Semi-final
1998	Belgium	World Cup	0	3	Group stage
2006	England	World Cup	3	2	Quarter-final
2006	Switzerland	World Cup	2	2	Last 16
2008	Croatia	European Championships	3	1	Quarter-final
2016	Poland	European Championships	2	3	Last 16

Italy in 1990 are perhaps the unluckiest team in this list, having won all three of their group games, the second round and quarter-final matches before drawing with Argentina and losing a penalty shootout. A sixth win of the tournament in a third-place play-off against an England team increasingly hampered by a madcap Peter Shilton was scant consolation.

The Tour of Flounders

While Belgium's underperformance was not quite at England's level, losing to Wales in the quarter-finals was not what the country's golden generation had planned. A country that can function without a government for 589 days knows how to muddle through but the fact remains that Belgium have failed to progress past the quarter-finals of a tournament since 1986. The good news, though, is that there should be future opportunities for the gang to shine (given the sheer youth of the team that faced the Welsh at the Stade Pierre-Mauroy). The starting XI had an average age of 24 years and 242 days, the youngest in a Euro finals game since Yugoslavia's fledglings against Italy in 1968 (23 years and 170 days). When Eden Hazard is among the veterans in your team, you know you have time on your side.

Belgium team v Wales	Age
Jason Denayer	21y 3d
Jordan Lukaku	21y 341d
Yannick Carrasco	22y 300d
Romelu Lukaku	23y 49d
Thibaut Courtois	24y 51d
Thomas Meunier	24y 293d
Kevin De Bruyne	25y 3d
Eden Hazard	25y 175d
Toby Alderweireld	27y 121d
Axel Witsel	27y 170d
Radja Nainggolan	28y 58d

The oldest player in the team, Radja Nainggolan, born a day before the singer Adele in May 1988, scored Belgium's goal. It was his second from outside the box in the tournament from open play, something achieved previously by Michel Platini in 1984 and Wayne Rooney in 2004. By the time the 2018 World Cup kicks off, Nainggolan will be in his thirties, an object of curiosity in a Belgian generation that still – maybe – has a bright future.

Saved by the Wales

With England stinking up another tournament, Northern Ireland hitting their ceiling in the second round and Scotland, well, let's not go there, it was left to Wales to represent the United Kingdom at the business end of the Euros.

1. Wales top their group ahead of England: good story
2. Wales edge past Northern Ireland via an own goal: reasonable
3. Wales outplay and defeat Belgium in the quarter-finals: now we're talking.

Before we start, it should be noted that Chris Coleman's team didn't sneak their way into the semi-finals. In getting there, Wales outplayed one of the most promising group of players in the competition. By doing so, they became the first British team to reach a semi-final since England back in 1996 (and, as we've seen earlier in the book, England's progression past Spain in 1996 was hardly impressive).

Ahead of the tournament, the focus was understandably on Gareth Bale. In the end, it was a group effort with six players (including Bale with three) scoring for the Dragons in their six-game adventure. Of the UK teams, only England in their year of grace, 1966, have ever scored more goals at a tournament than Wales did in 2016, their haul of ten matching England's last decent tournament showing twelve years ago.

World Cup/Euro	Team	Goals
1966	England	11
2016	**Wales**	10
2004	England	10
1990	England	8
1996	England	8
1982	Scotland	8
1954	England	8
1998	England	7
1986	England	7

While Bale grabbed the attention with three goals, Hal Robson-Kanu stole hearts with his superbly off-kilter strike against Belgium and Neil Taylor ended the competition having created as many chances as Andrés Iniesta, it was Aaron Ramsey who was the fulcrum in the Welsh team. It's arguable that the crucial point of Wales's entire campaign came after seventy-four minutes and fifteen seconds of the game against Belgium, when Ramsey was shown a yellow card for what is invariably called a 'needless handball'. It was his second booking of the tournament and ruled him out of the semi-final, and almost certainly condemned his team to defeat. As someone who gave away three of the twelve Arsenal handballs in the Premier League in 2015–16, Ramsey's subconscious reactions to a ball moving past him ended with dire consequences.

Ramsey left Euro 2016 with four assists; no player in the entire tournament recorded more, two of them coming in that memorable game with Belgium. No player for a UK side (for which read England) had assisted multiple times in a tournament game since David Beckham v Portugal in 2000, but Wales had to face the Iberians without their creative force. Their record without him since the start of 2015? Drawn one, lost three.

But let's not focus on what could have been and instead look at what Wales achieved in their glorious summer. They were the first debutants to reach the semi-finals since Sweden in 1992 (the Swedes, of course, activating the cheat mode that is being the tournament hosts). Wales's appearance in the semis was only the fifth time a team from the UK has ever reached the semi-final of a major tournament (alongside England's efforts in 1966, 1968, 1990 and 1996), which for the nation(s) who codified the modern game, is fairly abject. Indeed, the only place where the UK dominates international football is its four-pronged presence on the International Football Association Board, which meets annually to discuss and determine the laws of the game. The new style kick-offs that were unveiled at Euro 2016 (whereby you no longer need to pass the ball forward with a team-mate standing next to you) are a fine contribution to the game, but you suspect British fans would prefer some trophies.

Two Years of Hurt

Gregory (Scotland Yard detective): *'Is there any other point to which you would wish to draw my attention?'*
Holmes: *'To the curious incident of the dog in the night-time.'*
Gregory: *'The dog did nothing in the night-time.'*
Holmes: *'That was the curious incident.'*

For dog, read Thomas Müller. For night-time, read Euro 2016. In fact, you can include Euro 2012 as well, for Müller's disappearing act in the continental tournament looks even odder when you add in his contributions to the national team in World Cups. With four years until the next European Championships (by which time he'll be thirty), Müller has never scored in the finals, despite playing eleven games.

Contrast this with his contribution at World Cups where he has ten goals in just thirteen appearances. To put this in perspective, he has two fewer goals than Pelé in World Cups but at the Euros he has two fewer than Nicklas Bendtner. Like Rio Ferdinand, who made ten World Cup appearances but never featured at the Euros, Müller is a victim of continental drift, and time is running out.

World Cups	Thomas Müller	Euros
13	Games played	11
1155	Minutes played	874
10	Goals	0
6	Assists	1
0.8	Games/goal	–
115.5	Mins/goal	–
85%	Games won	64%

Looking at Germany overall, their failure to negotiate a way past France in the semi-final was the fourth time in six semi-final appearances at major tournaments that they have fallen at this stage (2006, 2010, 2012 and 2016), which is contrary to the clichéd UK-centric view of the German national team as a bastion of ruthless efficiency. Maybe against England that's the case, but other nations have no such fears. At least in Germany they don't have to listen to people claiming that the lack of a winter break has harmed the national team. It's almost as if you can fail to win football tournaments despite having a surfeit of UEFA A Licensed coaches and cheap season tickets.

The Denouement

It was apt, in the end, that the tournament that never really got to grips with scoring saw the final reach the end of ninety minutes with no goals, the first time a European Championships final had ever had to go to extra-time with no strikes to show for it. Portugal, shorn of Ronaldo after just twenty-five minutes due to a knee injury (for clarity on how rare the sight of CR7 trudging, or in this case being carried, off the pitch is, he has been substituted just twenty times in his entire La Liga career), only became more committed to their defensive but controlled outlook, figuring that reducing the chances available to the tournament top scorers was the best plan of action.

And so it proved. France had ten shots in the second half to Portugal's two, but to no avail. The first Portuguese shot on target of *the entire match* came in the eightieth minute, via Ricardo Quaresma. But, more importantly, it came one minute and seven seconds after Eder was brought on. He had begun the season as a new signing at Swansea but managed just one shot on target in his ill-fated thirteen-game spell with the Welsh club, a figure he doubled in the space of five extra-time minutes against France. The second of those Eder shots on target was a fine effort from outside the box which sneaked past Hugo Lloris in the France goal. The nation which produced Victor Hugo now had a Defeated Hugo to complete the collection.

But were Portugal worthy winners of the tournament? They were only the third team ever to finish third in their group and make a tournament final (alongside Argentina in the 1990 World Cup and Italy four years later – both of whom failed to lift the trophy). A particular risk of this 24-team structure is that, as in 2016, a team can fail to win any of its group games and still lift the trophy. But the rules were the same for everyone and Portugal used them in a very marginal gains kind of way. Wales were the only team to lose to the Portuguese in the regulation ninety minutes, yet will look back on the competition with immense fondness and pride. England, like Portugal, managed one win in ninety minutes, and, like Ronaldo's men, it came against the Welsh. Yet for English football, 2016 will be another dark cloud on the most endless of rainy afternoons in international football.

The margins in short-game tournaments are so fine. The best team doesn't always win; in fact it should be as much of a surprise if they do.

France will point to the seven saves Portugal goalkeeper Rui Patrício had to make (a joint record in a European Championship final, alongside Peter Schmeichel in 1992), but the fact remains that they didn't look like the team which had outplayed and outscored so many other teams earlier in the competition. Antoine Griezmann ended the tournament with twice as many goals (six) as any other player (and as many as England and Northern Ireland combined) but also lost the Champions League final and the European Championships final in the space of forty-three days. Ronaldo, who tasted victory in both of those games, finally has an international honour (one more than Lionel Messi) and his reaction to Portugal's win, and the handing over of the trophy, suggests that he is not ruminating on his own relation to the number 43 (the number of direct free-kicks he has taken at World Cups without scoring even once).

Long-term, Euro 2016 is unlikely to live long in the memory of anyone outside Portugal, Wales and Iceland. It seemed to confirm the trend of international football being a popular but poor cousin of the club game. As you can see in the table below, it was behind the Champions League in virtually all aspects of the game (albeit from a sample size roughly half of the world's premier club competition) and was significantly behind the Premier League when it came to converting shots into goals. England's issues at Euro 2016 were actually symptomatic of a wider trend, where players not used to working with each other week in, week out were unable to create as many high-quality chances as they would for their clubs, thus allowing defensively organised teams to prosper more than they would in club football. The result was a trophy for a supremely solid Portugal team. The outcome was a gap of only three or four weeks until the new club season began. 2015–16 is over: let's welcome its successor.

	Euro 2016	2015–16 Champions League	2015–16 Premier League
Goals/game	2.12	2.78	2.70
Passes/game	906.1	974.2	874.2
Pass completion	80.83%	82.40%	78.44%
Shots/game	26.8	27.4	25.7
Conversion rate	10.48%	13.29%	14.45%

Appendix

Outfield Players to Play Every Minute of Every Game

Season	Team	Player
1992–93	Aston Villa	Earl Barrett
1992–93	Norwich City	Mark Bowen
1992–93	**Manchester United**	**Gary Pallister**
1993–94	Norwich City	Ian Culverhouse
1993–94	Wimbledon	Robbie Earle
1993–94	Leeds United	Gary Kelly
1993–94	Leeds United	Gary McAllister
1993–94	Ipswich Town	Mick Stockwell
1993–94	Swindon Town	Shaun Taylor
1993–94	Queens Park Rangers	Clive Wilson
1994–95	Manchester United	Gary Pallister
1994–95	Crystal Palace	Gareth Southgate
1995–96	Manchester City	Kit Symons
1995–96	Aston Villa	Alan Wright
1996–97	Aston Villa	Ugo Ehiogu
1996–97	Coventry City	Gary McAllister
1998–99	Middlesbrough	Dean Gordon
1998–99	Leicester City	Steve Guppy
1998–99	West Ham United	Frank Lampard
1998–99	Aston Villa	Gareth Southgate
1999–2000	Bradford City	David Wetherall
2000–01	Southampton	Wayne Bridge
2001–02	Southampton	Wayne Bridge
2001–02	Fulham	Steve Finnan
2001–02	Ipswich Town	Matt Holland

(continued)

Season	Team	Player
2001–02	Ipswich Town	Hermann Hreidarsson
2002–03	Aston Villa	Olof Mellberg
2003–04	Manchester City	Sylvain Distin
2003–04	Liverpool	Sami Hyypiä
2003–04	Aston Villa	Jlloyd Samuel
2004–05	Liverpool	Jamie Carragher
2004–05	Norwich City	Craig Fleming
2004–05	Tottenham Hotspur	Ledley King
2006–07	Manchester City	Richard Dunne
2006–07	Reading	Ivar Ingimarsson
2006–07	Sheffield United	Phil Jagielka
2006–07	Everton	Joseph Yobo
2007–08	Birmingham City	Stephen Kelly
2008–09	Portsmouth	Sylvain Distin
2008–09	Hull City	Michael Turner
2009–10	Birmingham City	Roger Johnson
2009–10	Burnley	Tyrone Mears
2010–11	Everton	Leighton Baines
2010–11	Liverpool	Martin Skrtel
2011–12	Fulham	Brede Hangeland
2011–12	Wolverhampton Wanderers	Stephen Ward
2012–13	Everton	Leighton Baines
2013–14	Cardiff City	Steven Caulker
2014–15	West Ham United	Aaron Cresswell
2014–15	**Chelsea**	**John Terry**
2015–16	Bournemouth	Andrew Surman
2015–16	**Leicester City**	**Wes Morgan**

Won PL title in same season

Premier League Appearances by Nationality

Country	Premier League Appearances
England	108,324
Republic of Ireland	14,169
France	12,505
Scotland	11,360
Wales	9,025
Netherlands	6,896
Spain	5,348
Northern Ireland	4,772
Norway	4,585
Denmark	3,295
Brazil	3,212
Australia	3,038
Argentina	2,991
Nigeria	2,989
Sweden	2,844
Jamaica	2,838
USA	2,827
Italy	2,527
Germany	2,444
Belgium	2,360
Senegal	2,147
Portugal	2,113
Côte d'Ivoire	1,913
Czech Republic	1,750
Serbia	1,512
Finland	1,503
Cameroon	1,477
Iceland	1,331
Croatia	1,318
Trinidad and Tobago	1,297
South Africa	1,084
Switzerland	936

(continued)

Country	Premier League Appearances
Bulgaria	853
Morocco	826
Turkey	821
Israel	768
Austria	740
Ghana	737
Canada	663
Russia	663
Uruguay	632
Poland	629
Colombia	625
Korea Republic	621
Greece	620
Ecuador	581
Congo DR	556
Slovakia	534
Mali	528
Romania	485
Honduras	432
Algeria	384
Chile	375
Bosnia and Herzegovina	369
NewZealand	346
Peru	346
Hungary	345
Egypt	344
Zimbabwe	339
CostaRica	313
Japan	264
Togo	258
Georgia	248
Mexico	246
Barbados	231

(continued)

Country	Premier League Appearances
Grenada	231
Montserrat	223
Ukraine	218
Gibraltar	210
Paraguay	207
Benin	201
Congo	179
Latvia	172
ChinaPR	171
Guyana	150
Curaçao	138
Estonia	138
Tunisia	136
Guinea	123
Belarus	114
Oman	111
Slovenia	95
Kenya	85
Antigua and Barbuda	80
Iran	65
Bermuda	59
Venezuela	57
Montenegro	54
Macedonia	53
Liberia	46
St. Kitts and Nevis	37
Gambia	33
Albania	31
Gabon	30
Sierra Leone	28
Zambia	23
Pakistan	21

(continued)

Country	Premier League Appearances
Bolivia	19
Angola	14
Burundi	13
BurkinaFaso	10
Cyprus	9
Malta	5
Cape Verde Islands	4
Lithuania	3
Faroe Islands	1
Guadeloupe	1
Guinea-Bissau	1
Kosovo	1
Seychelles	1

Premier League Hat-Tricks

Player	Hat-Tricks
Alan Shearer	11
Robbie Fowler	9
Michael Owen	8
Thierry Henry	8
Luis Suárez	6
Wayne Rooney	6
Andrew Cole	5
Dimitar Berbatov	5
Ian Wright	5
Sergio Agüero	5
Robin van Persie	5
Ruud van Nistelrooy	5
Les Ferdinand	4
Dwight Yorke	4
Matthew Le Tissier	4
Jimmy Floyd Hasselbaink	4
Yakubu	4
Carlos Tévez	4
Teddy Sheringham	4
Kevin Campbell	4
Fernando Torres	4
Jermain Defoe	4
Chris Sutton	4
Tony Cottee	3
Emmanuel Adebayor	3
Ole Gunnar Solskjaer	3
Dion Dublin	3
Theo Walcott	3
Nicolas Anelka	3
Didier Drogba	3
Robbie Keane	3
Frank Lampard	3

(continued)

Player	Hat-Tricks
Andy Carroll	2
Fabrizio Ravanelli	2
Sadio Mané	2
Maxi Rodríguez	2
Anthony Yeboah	2
Kevin Gallacher	2
Steven Gerrard	2
Darren Huckerby	2
Christian Benteke	2
Steffen Iversen	2
Demba Ba	2
Kevin Nolan	2
Mark Viduka	2
Benjani	2
Paul Scholes	2
Harry Kane	2
Andrei Kanchelskis	2
Kevin Phillips	2
Paul Kitson	2

All-Time Top-Flight Goals Per Game

Season	Goals/game
1888–89	4.45
1889–90	**4.63**
1890–91	4.20
1891–92	4.26
1892–93	3.90
1893–94	3.92
1894–95	3.82
1895–96	3.36
1896–97	3.13
1897–98	3.02
1898–99	2.84
1899–00	2.80
1900–01	2.80
1901–02	2.75
1902–03	2.89
1903–04	3.07
1904–05	2.95
1905–06	3.27
1906–07	3.02
1907–08	3.09
1908–09	3.12
1909–10	3.14
1910–11	2.71
1911–12	2.78
1912–13	3.03
1913–14	2.90
1914–15	3.16
1919–20	2.88
1920–21	2.76
1921–22	2.69
1922–23	2.63
1923–24	2.47

(continued)

Season	Goals/game
1924–25	2.58
1925–26	3.69
1926–27	3.61
1927–28	3.82
1928–29	3.65
1929–30	3.81
1930–31	3.95
1931–32	3.74
1932–33	3.56
1933–34	3.30
1934–35	3.63
1935–36	3.37
1936–37	3.37
1937–38	3.10
1938–39	3.07
1946–47	3.27
1947–48	2.91
1948–49	2.82
1949–50	2.70
1950–51	3.06
1951–52	3.23
1952–53	3.26
1953–54	3.52
1954–55	3.40
1955–56	3.31
1956–57	3.49
1957–58	3.73
1958–59	3.66
1959–60	3.50
1960–61	3.73
1961–62	3.42
1962–63	3.32
1963–64	3.40

(continued)

Season	Goals/game
1964–65	3.34
1965–66	3.15
1966–67	3.00
1967–68	3.03
1968–69	2.63
1969–70	2.62
1970–71	**2.36**
1971–72	2.51
1972–73	2.51
1973–74	2.40
1974–75	2.63
1975–76	2.66
1976–77	2.56
1977–78	2.66
1978–79	2.63
1979–80	2.51
1980–81	2.66
1981–82	2.54
1982–83	2.74
1983–84	2.71
1984–85	2.79
1985–86	2.79
1986–87	2.63
1987–88	2.50
1988–89	2.53
1989–90	2.59
1990–91	2.76
1991–92	2.54
1992–93	2.65
1993–94	2.59
1994–95	2.59
1995–96	2.60
1996–97	2.55

(continued)

Season	Goals/game
1997–98	2.68
1998–99	2.52
1999–00	2.79
2000–01	2.61
2001–02	2.63
2002–03	2.63
2003–04	2.66
2004–05	2.57
2005–06	2.48
2006–07	2.45
2007–08	2.64
2008–09	2.48
2009–10	2.77
2010–11	2.80
2011–12	2.81
2012–13	2.80
2013–14	2.77
2014–15	2.57
2015–16	2.70

All-Time Premier League Clean Sheets

Player	Clean Sheets
Petr Čech	178
David James	169
Mark Schwarzer	151
David Seaman	140
Nigel Martyn	137
José Reina	134
Edwin van der Sar	132
Tim Howard	132
Brad Friedel	132
Peter Schmeichel	128
Joe Hart	119
Shay Given	113
Jussi Jääskeläinen	108
Thomas Sørensen	107
Paul Robinson	86
Tim Flowers	80
Ian Walker	77
Mark Bosnich	74
Simon Mignolet	64
Carlo Cudicini	64
Neil Sullivan	64
Neville Southall	62
David de Gea	61
Shaka Hislop	58
Paul Jones	58
Ben Foster	56
Kasey Keller	55
Dean Kiely	54
Jens Lehmann	54
Steve Ogrizovic	53
Robert Green	53
John Lukic	52

(continued)

Player	Clean Sheets
Mark Crossley	52
Asmir Begović	50
Kevin Pressman	49
Jerzy Dudek	49
Wojciech Szczesny	48
Chris Kirkland	47
Maik Taylor	47
Pavel Srniček	47
Luděk Mikloško	47
Ed de Goey	46
Hugo Lloris	44
Manuel Almunia	43
Mart Poom	42
Heurelho Gomes	42
Tim Krul	41
Dmitri Kharine	37
Lukasz Fabiański	34
Antti Niemi	34

Acknowledgements

First of all, thanks to all at Penguin Random House for their help and support during the process of putting this book together, particularly editors Ben Brusey and Huw Armstrong, and copy editor Richard Collins. They are not only excellent at their job but full of genuinely good ideas when it came to mine.

It's always been a monumental team effort at Opta/Perform and I couldn't have written this book without the help and inspiration of the editorial team, particularly Rob Bateman who has had the misfortune to listen to my ideas for many, many years. Huge thanks to the heroic Matt Furniss, Alan Duffy and his all-time results, Johannes Harkins, Tom Ede, Chris Mayer, Mark Hazell, Jack Supple, Jonny Cooper, Mark Segal, Sam Green, Michiel Jongsma, Bart Frouws, Javier Moreno & Christof Greiner who all helped directly or indirectly (or both). Huge gratitude also to all the data collection folk without whom we'd have no data. Pretty much every number you see on the Premier League starts with their unique skills.

Thanks also to Simon Farrant for allowing the sacred Opta Joe brand out into a real book and Richard Ewing for sorting the contractual machinations that allowed me to plunder every aspect of Opta's vast and endless archives.

Thank you to a couple of people whose knowledge and enthusiasm about football is relentless, namely Stefano Faccendini who likes the sport more than you could ever imagine possible and Joe Thornton who remembers things that need remembering. Oh, and the many, many people whom we have interacted with on Twitter since 2009, even the ones who issue death threats if you criticise Mesut Özil's contribution.

Acknowledgements

Thanks to my amazing family, particularly my parents, for paying for the stickers, the magazines, the phone cards (misspent on 49p/min clubcall lines) that form the bedrock of my knowledge and my wife Zoe whose genuine disinterest in football is a refreshing break from 99% of my conversations most days, along with her love, support and reasonably useful advice.

Finally, thanks to Arthur and Edie; I love you billions.